the SECRET

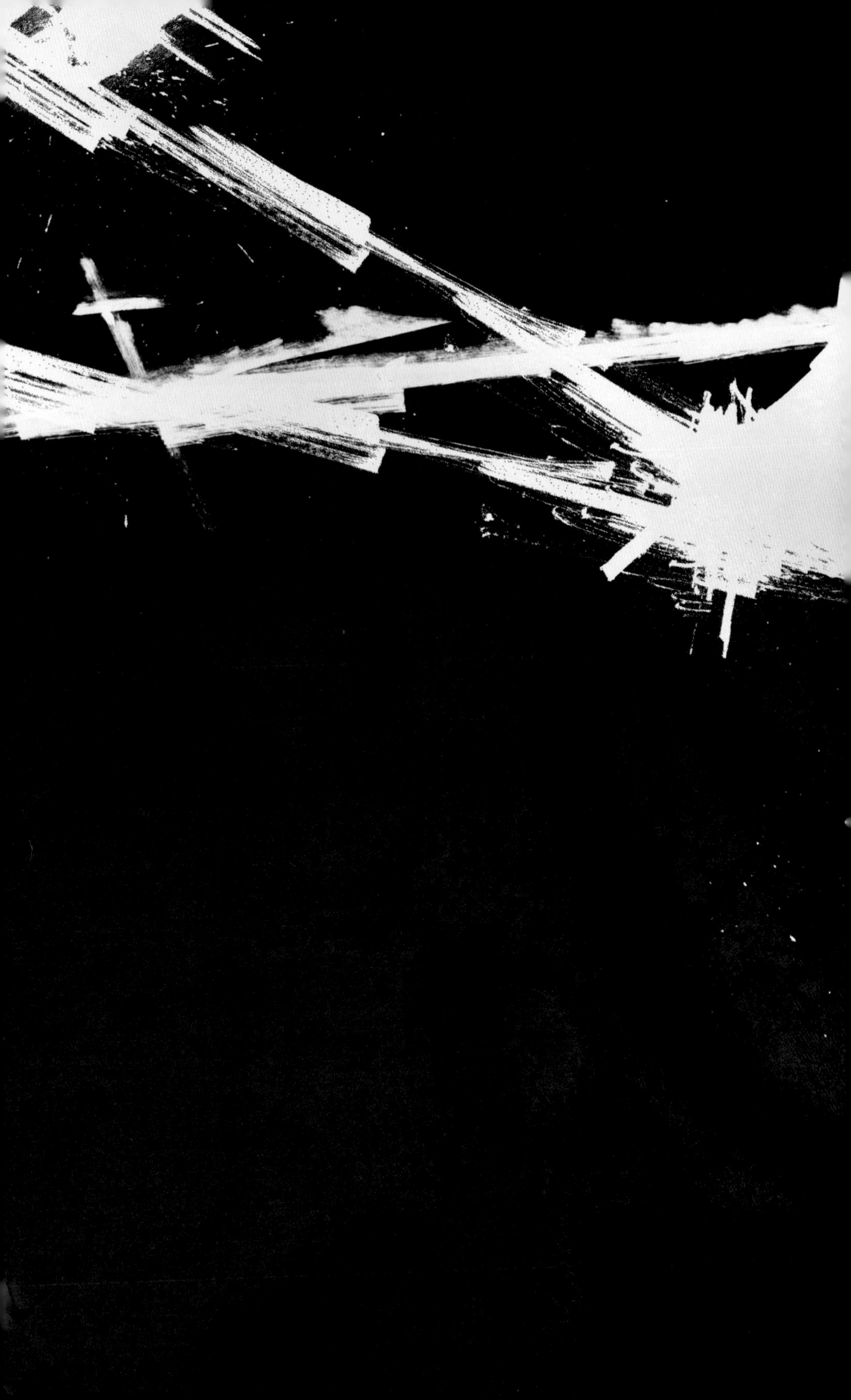

the SECRET ™

Created by
MIKE RICHARDSON

Story by
MIKE RICHARDSON

Art and Covers by
JASON SHAWN ALEXANDER

Letters by
CLEM ROBINS

Dark Horse Books®

Publisher
MIKE RICHARDSON

Editor
SCOTT ALLIE

Assistant Editor
KATIE MOODY

Collection Designer
SCOTT COOK

Art Director
LIA RIBACCHI

THE SECRET™

This book collects issues 1 through 4 of the Dark Horse comic-book series *The Secret*.

Published by
Dark Horse Books
A division of
Dark Horse Comics, Inc.
10956 SE Main Street
Milwaukie, OR 97222

darkhorse.com

To find a comics shop in your area, call the Comic Shop Locator Service toll-free at (888) 266-4226.

First edition: November 2007
ISBN-10: 1-59307-821-8
ISBN-13: 978-1-59307-821-8

10 9 8 7 6 5 4 3 2 1

Printed in China

Cover:
Cold
36x24 in.
Oil on canvas

Facing:
Stranger
36x24 in.
Oil on canvas

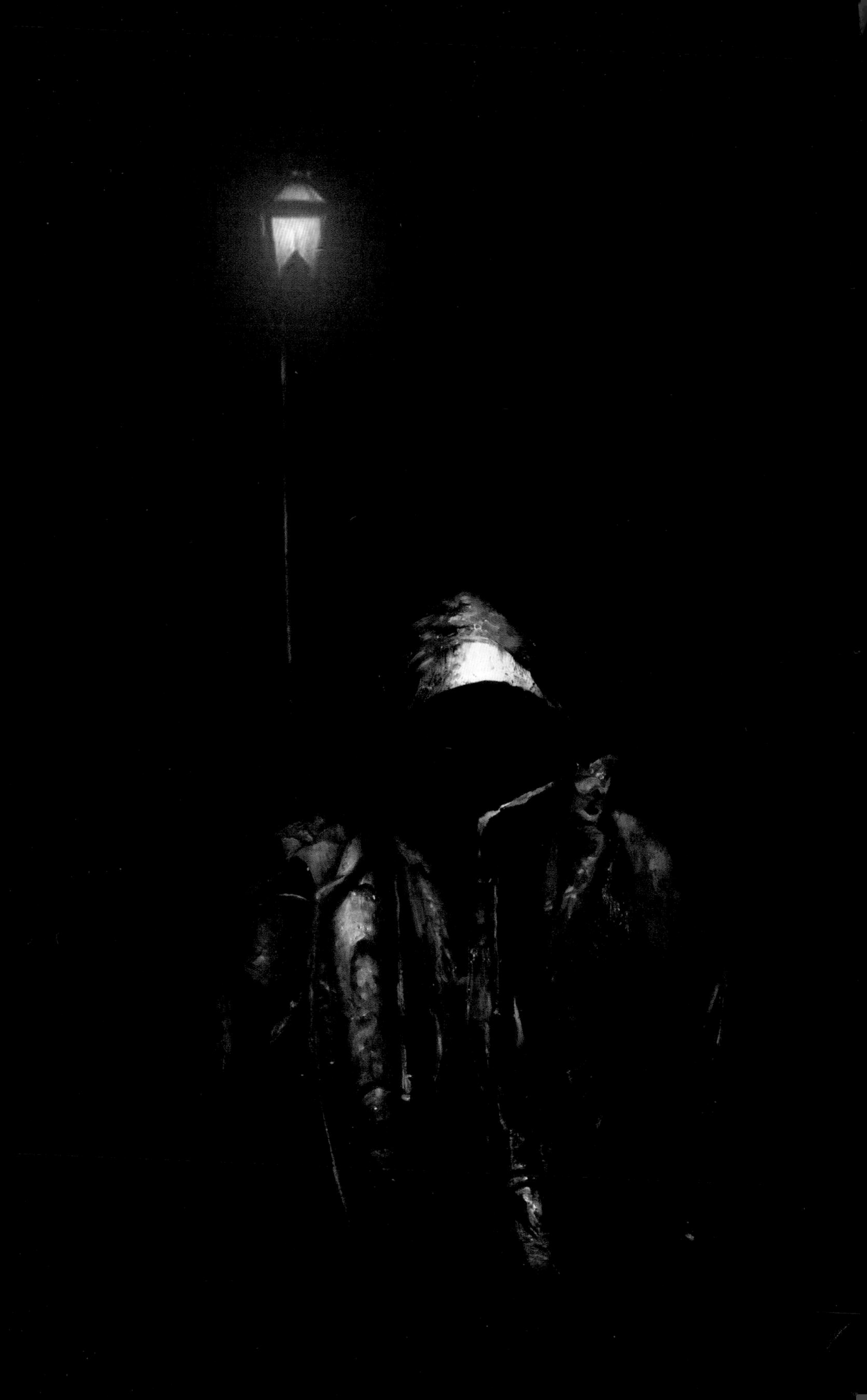

"I KNOW YOUR SECRET"

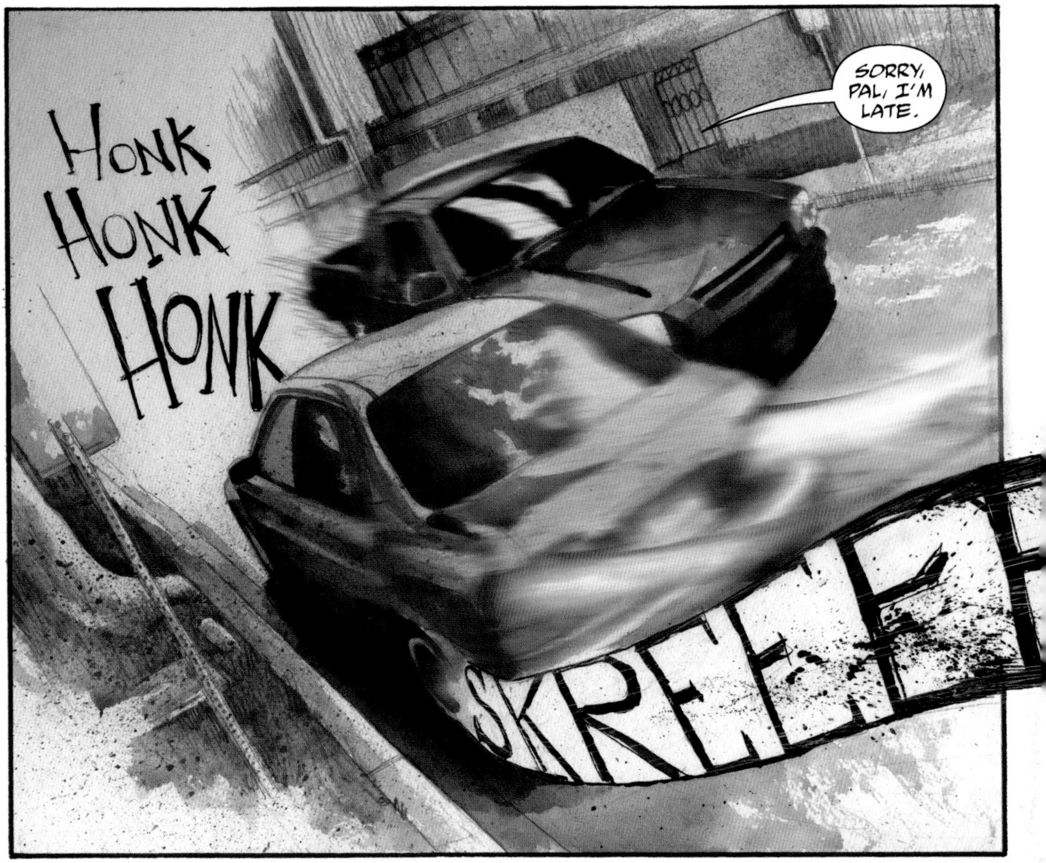
HONK
HONK
HONK
SORRY, PAL, I'M LATE.
SKREE

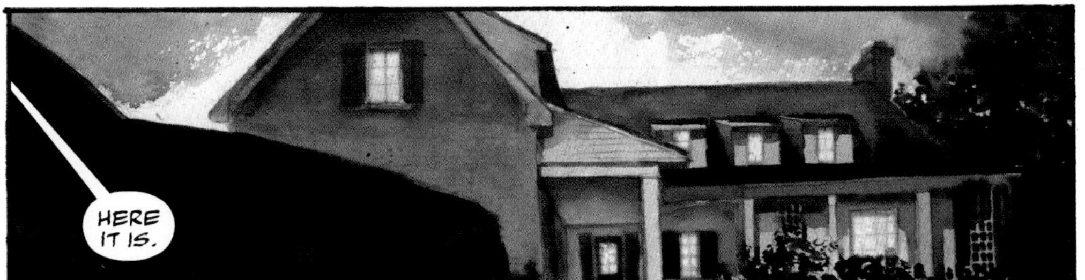
HERE IT IS.

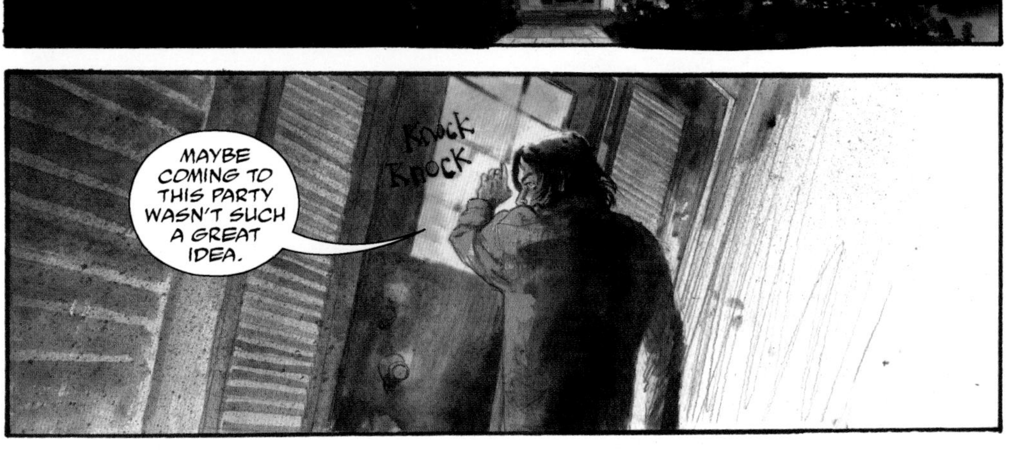
KNOCK
KNOCK
MAYBE COMING TO THIS PARTY WASN'T SUCH A GREAT IDEA.

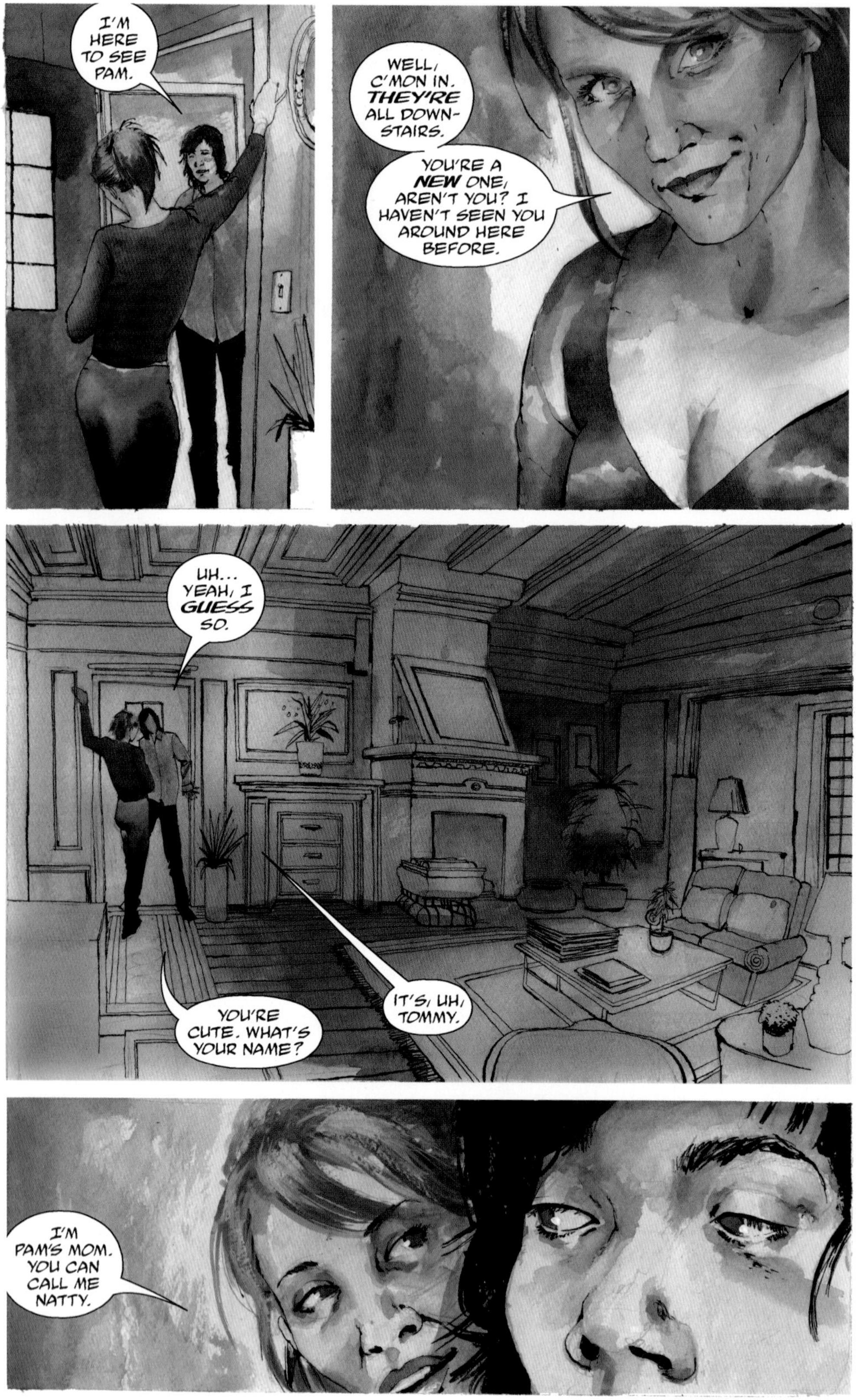
I'M HERE TO SEE PAM.
WELL, C'MON IN. **THEY'RE** ALL DOWN-STAIRS.
YOU'RE A **NEW** ONE, AREN'T YOU? I HAVEN'T SEEN YOU AROUND HERE BEFORE.
UH... YEAH, I **GUESS** SO.
YOU'RE CUTE. WHAT'S YOUR NAME?
IT'S, UH, TOMMY.
I'M PAM'S MOM. YOU CAN CALL ME NATTY.

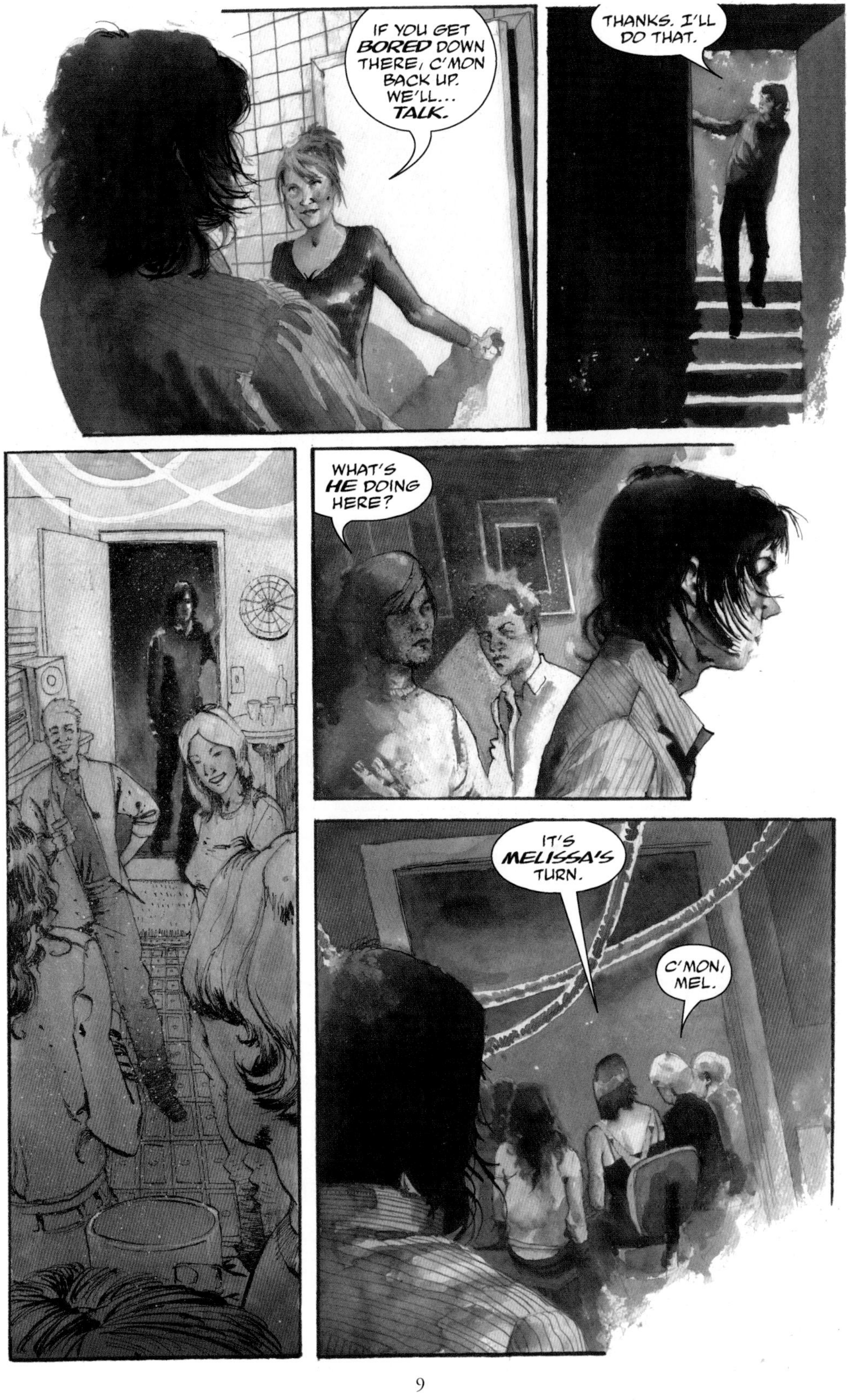
IF YOU GET BORED DOWN THERE, C'MON BACK UP. WE'LL... TALK.
THANKS. I'LL DO THAT.
WHAT'S HE DOING HERE?
IT'S MELISSA'S TURN.
C'MON, MEL.

...FOUR...
...THREE...
...SEVEN...
...TWO...
...TWO...
...ONE...
...SIX. JUST HIT SEND.
Riiing
c-click
SPEAKER MODE
11:05PM
SENDING
HELLO?
SPEAKER MODE
11:05PM
I KNOW YOUR SECRET.

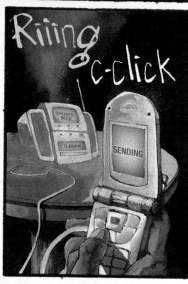

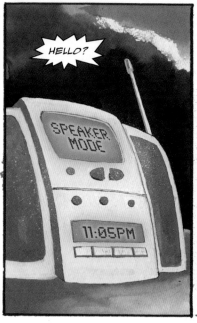

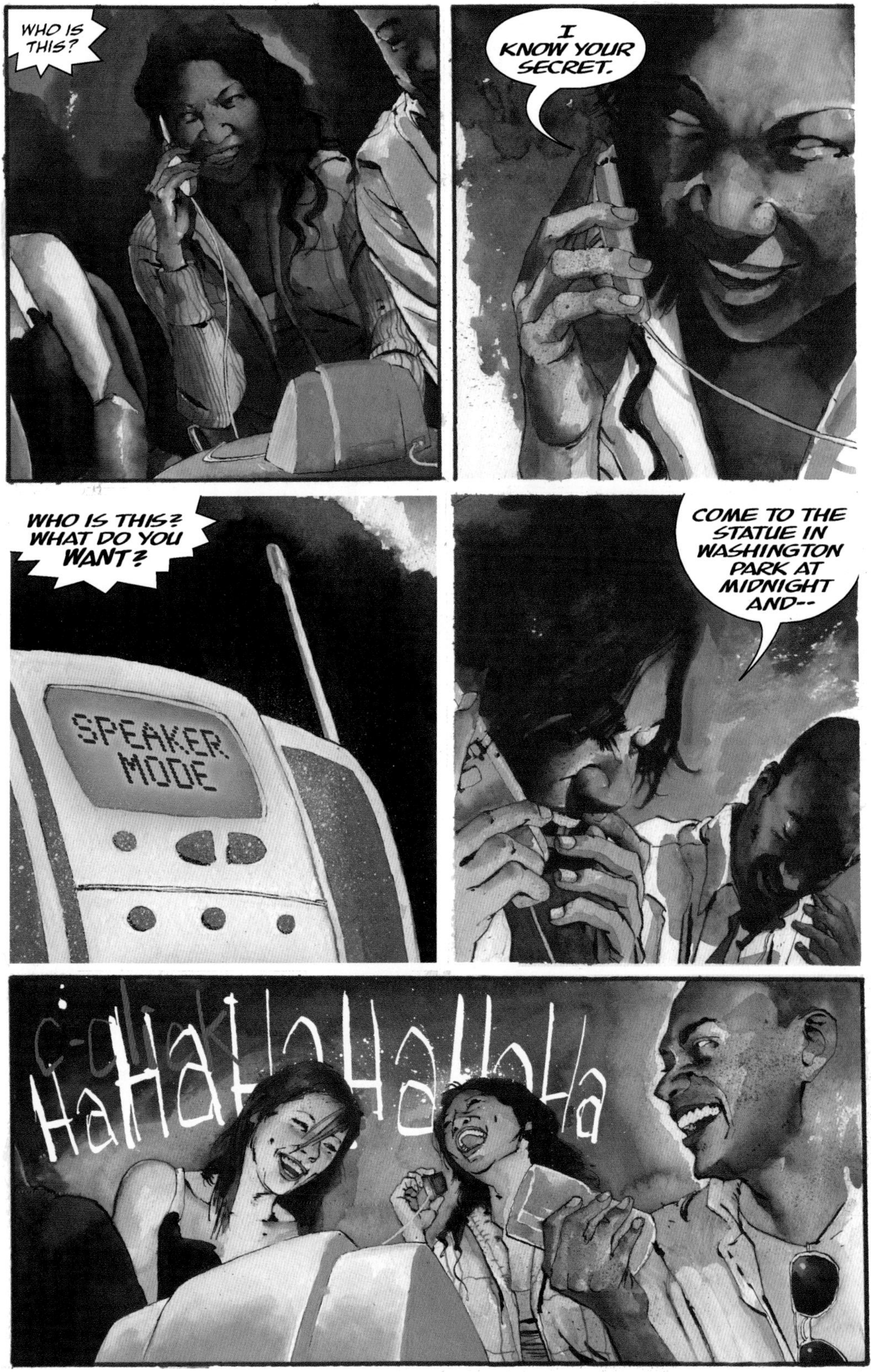
WHO IS THIS?
I KNOW YOUR SECRET.
WHO IS THIS? WHAT DO YOU WANT?
SPEAKER MODE
COME TO THE STATUE IN WASHINGTON PARK AT MIDNIGHT AND--
c-click
HaHaHaHaHaHaHa

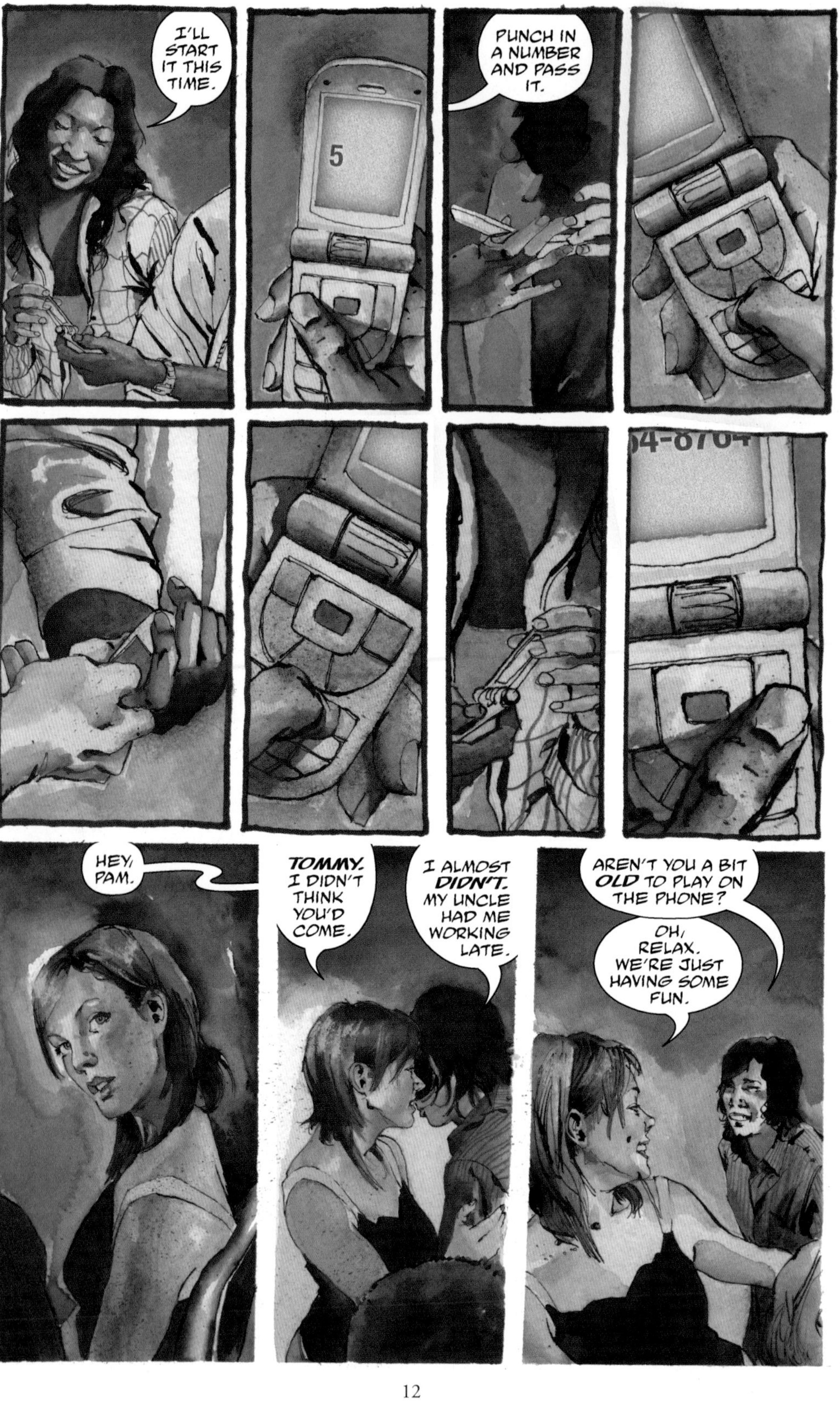
I'LL START IT THIS TIME.
5
PUNCH IN A NUMBER AND PASS IT.
HEY, PAM.
TOMMY. I DIDN'T THINK YOU'D COME.
I ALMOST DIDN'T. MY UNCLE HAD ME WORKING LATE.
AREN'T YOU A BIT OLD TO PLAY ON THE PHONE?
OH, RELAX. WE'RE JUST HAVING SOME FUN.

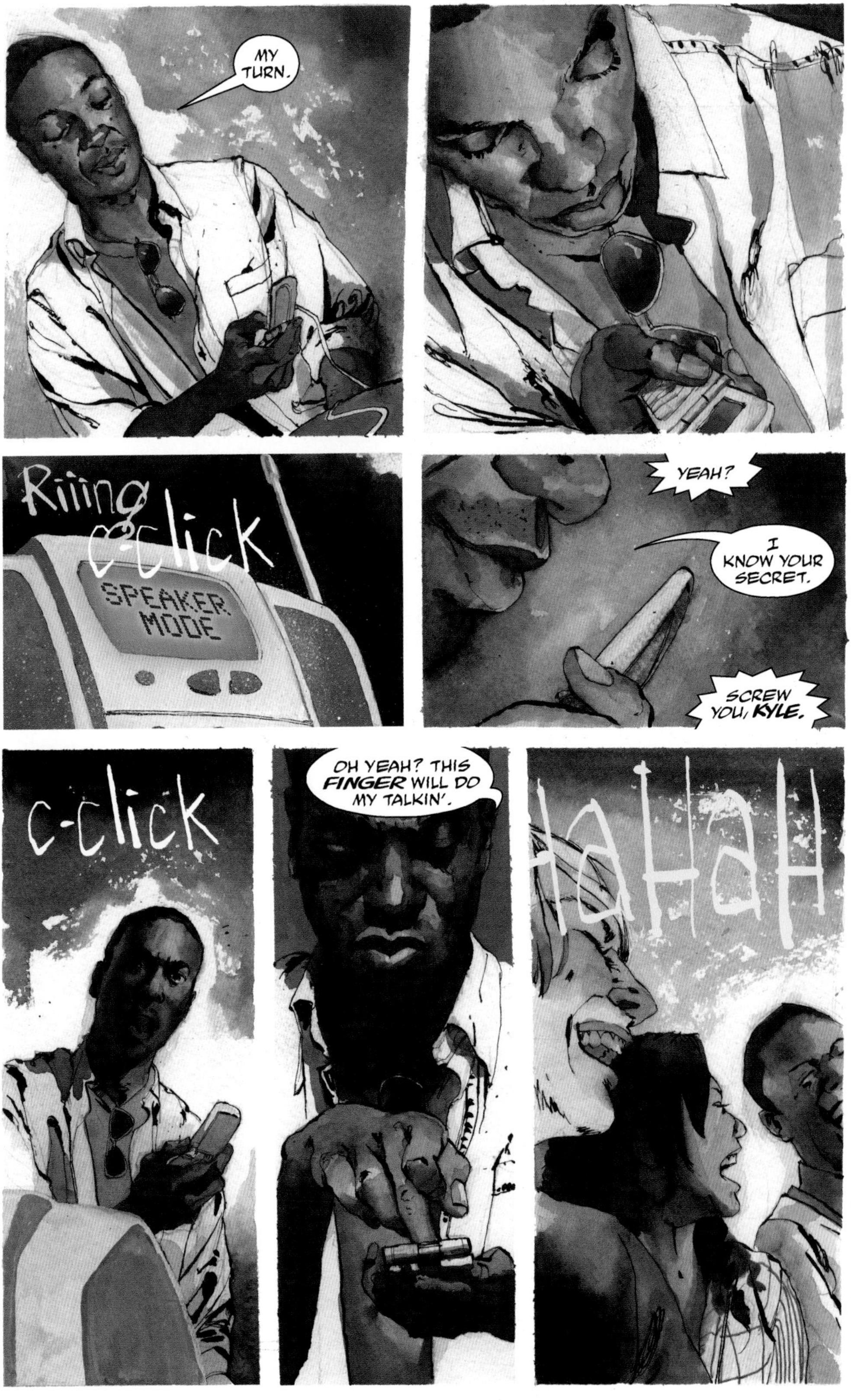
MY TURN.
Riiing
c-click
SPEAKER MODE
YEAH?
I KNOW YOUR SECRET.
SCREW YOU, **KYLE.**
c-click
OH YEAH? THIS **FINGER** WILL DO MY TALKIN'.
HaHaH

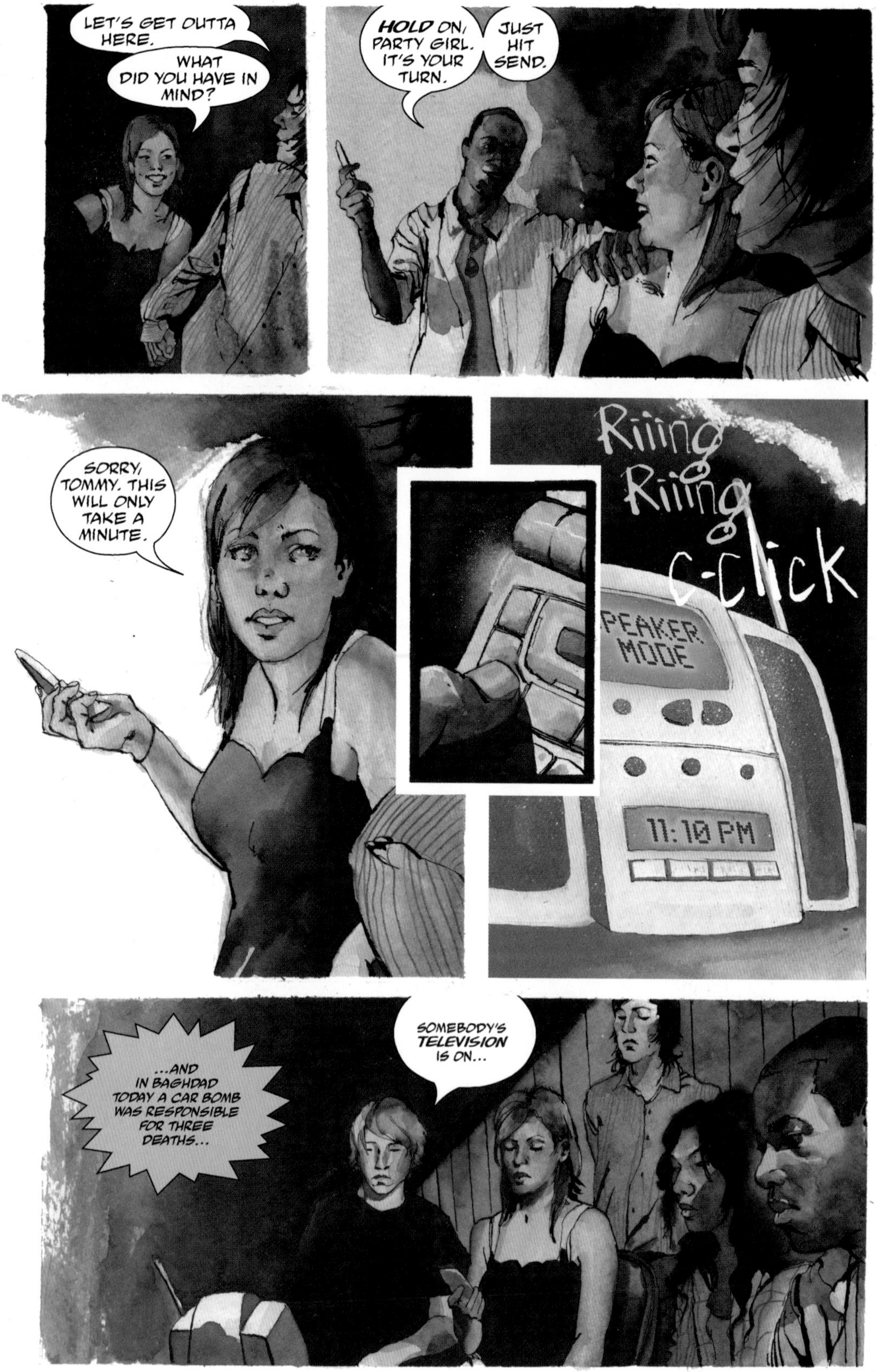
LET'S GET OUTTA HERE.
WHAT DID YOU HAVE IN MIND?
HOLD ON, PARTY GIRL. IT'S YOUR TURN.
JUST HIT SEND.
SORRY, TOMMY. THIS WILL ONLY TAKE A MINUTE.
Riiing
Riiing
C-Click
PEAKER MODE
11:10 PM
...AND IN BAGHDAD TODAY A CAR BOMB WAS RESPONSIBLE FOR THREE DEATHS...
SOMEBODY'S TELEVISION IS ON...

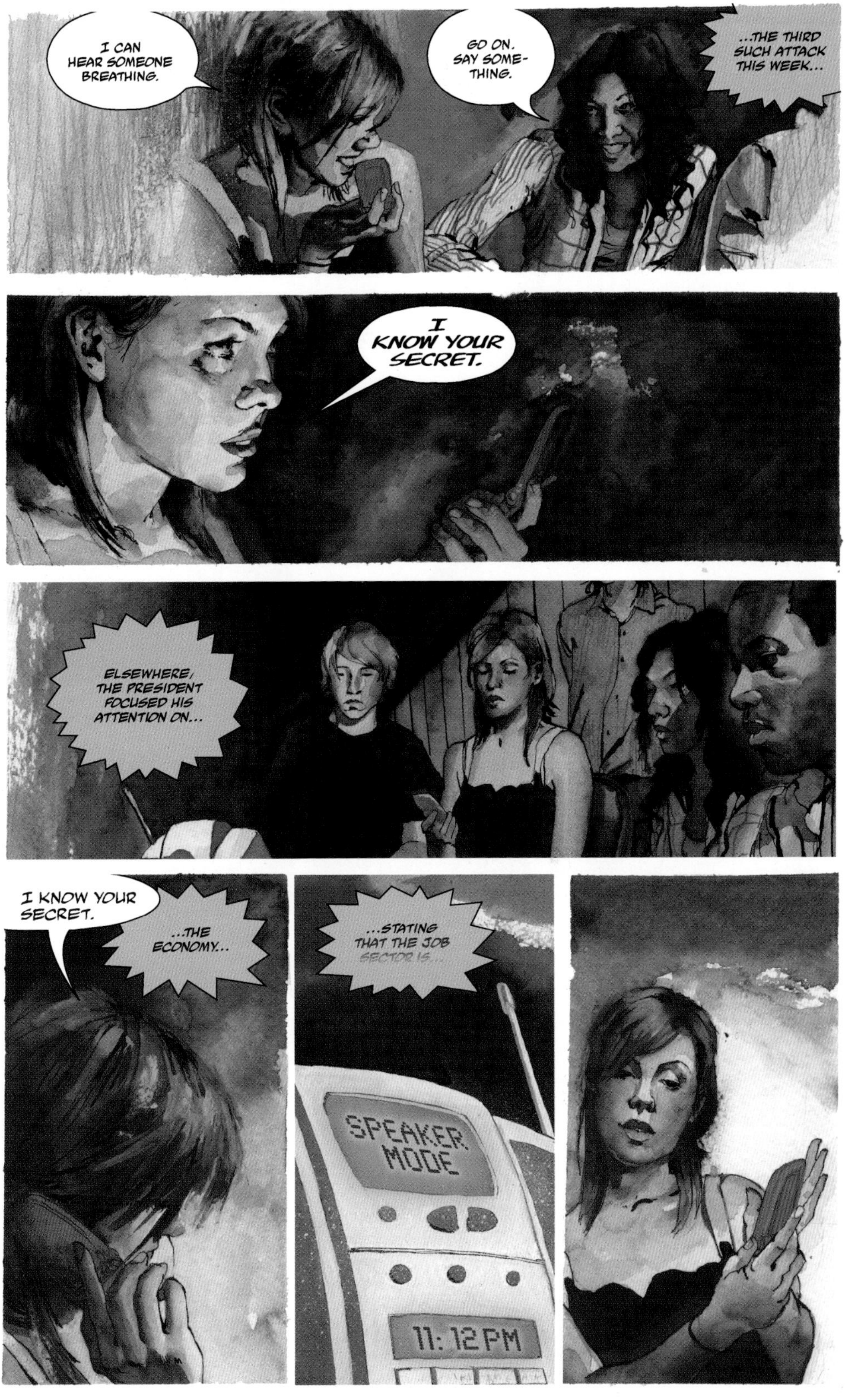

I CAN HEAR SOMEONE BREATHING.
GO ON. SAY SOME-THING.
...THE THIRD SUCH ATTACK THIS WEEK...
I KNOW YOUR SECRET.
ELSEWHERE, THE PRESIDENT FOCUSED HIS ATTENTION ON...
I KNOW YOUR SECRET.
...THE ECONOMY...
...STATING THAT THE JOB SECTOR IS...
SPEAKER MODE
11:12PM

How do you know My Secret?

HaHaHaHa

TELL HIM, PAM.

COME TO THE STATUE IN WASHINGTON PARK AT MIDNIGHT.

c-click

SPEAKER MODE

11:13PM

OKAY. THAT DOES IT. I'M OUT OF HERE.

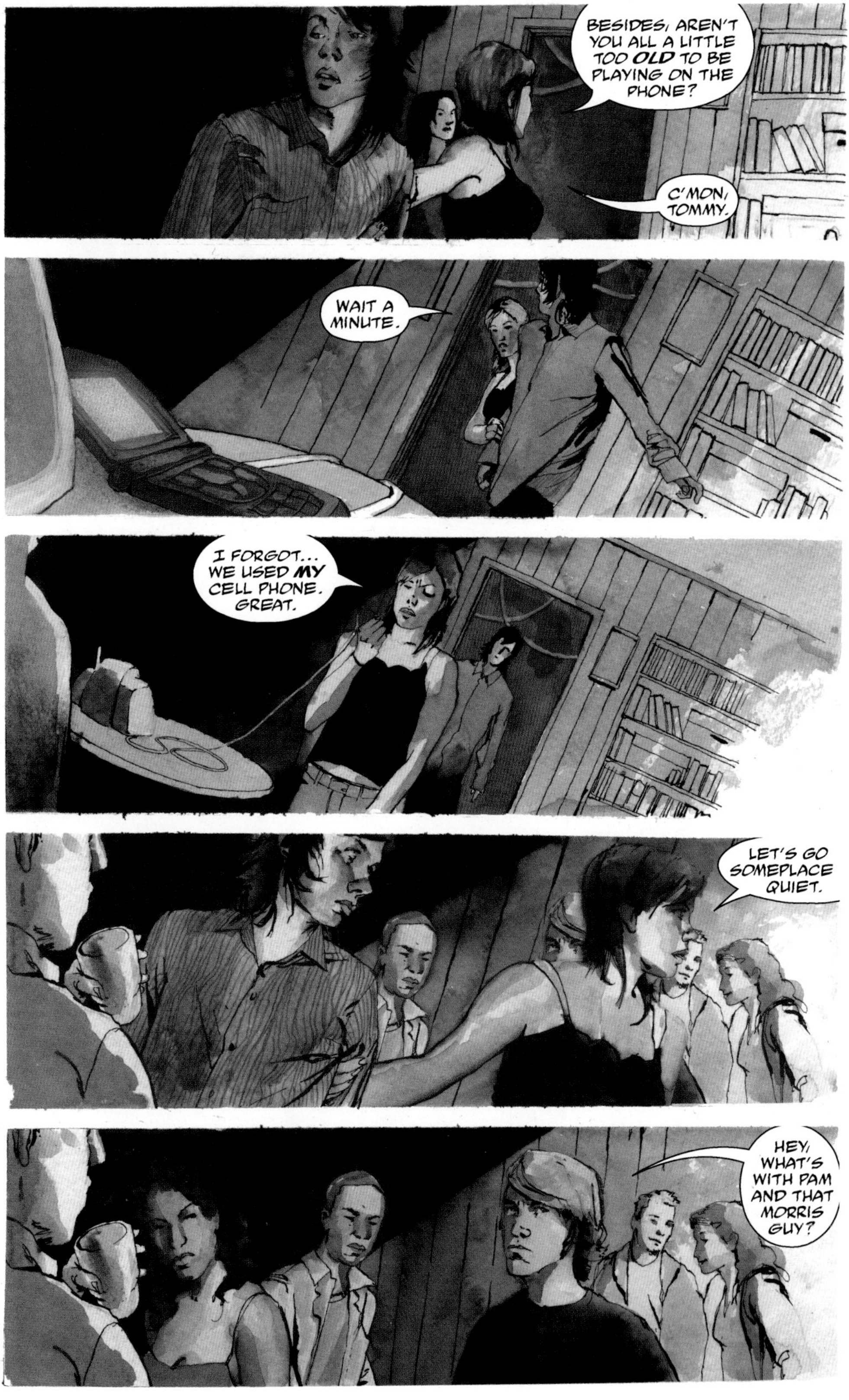
BESIDES, AREN'T YOU ALL A LITTLE TOO OLD TO BE PLAYING ON THE PHONE?
C'MON, TOMMY.
WAIT A MINUTE.
I FORGOT... WE USED MY CELL PHONE. GREAT.
LET'S GO SOMEPLACE QUIET.
HEY, WHAT'S WITH PAM AND THAT MORRIS GUY?

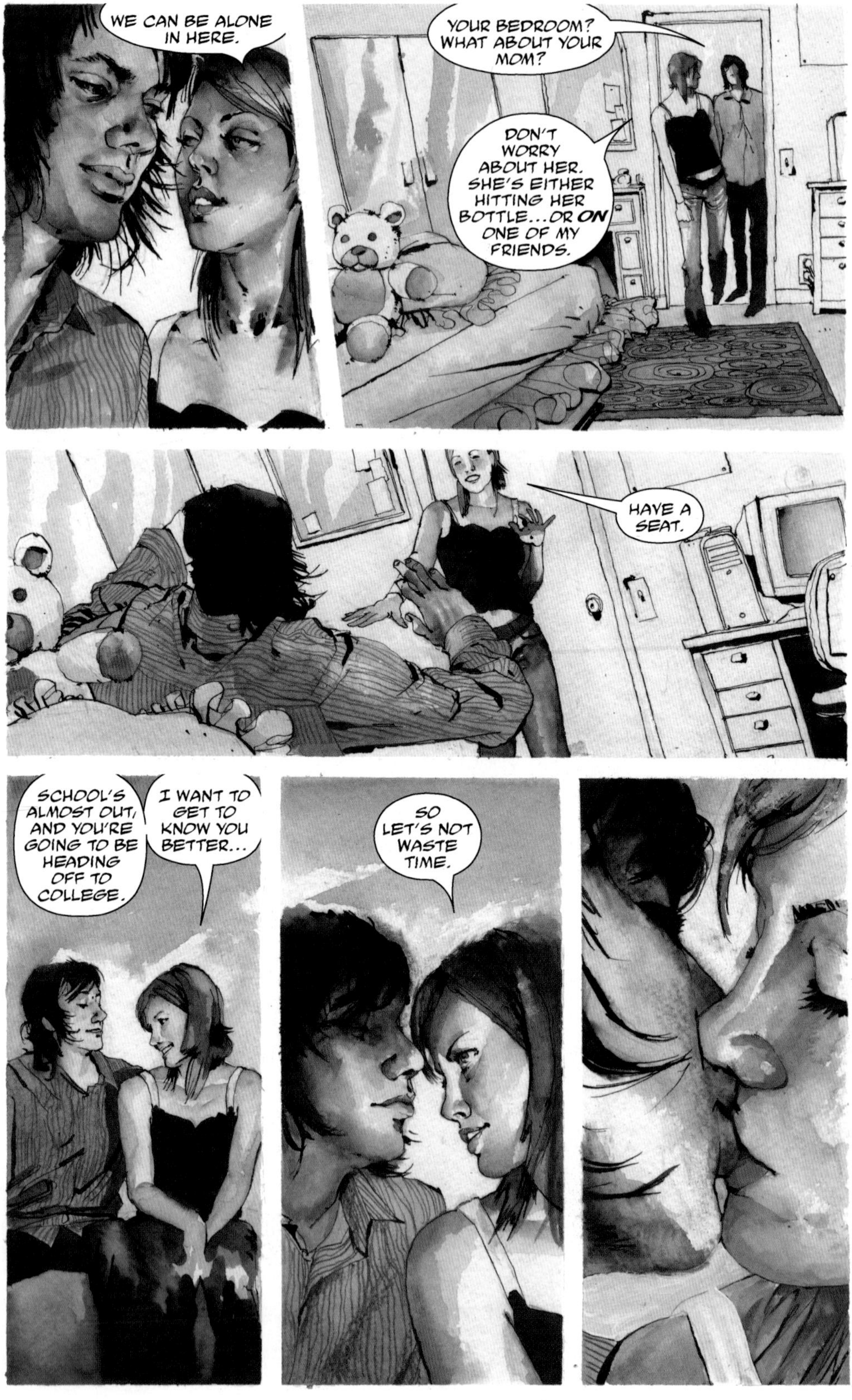
WE CAN BE ALONE IN HERE.
YOUR BEDROOM? WHAT ABOUT YOUR MOM?
DON'T WORRY ABOUT HER. SHE'S EITHER HITTING HER BOTTLE...OR **ON** ONE OF MY FRIENDS.
HAVE A SEAT.
SCHOOL'S ALMOST OUT, AND YOU'RE GOING TO BE HEADING OFF TO COLLEGE.
I WANT TO GET TO KNOW YOU BETTER...
SO LET'S NOT WASTE TIME.

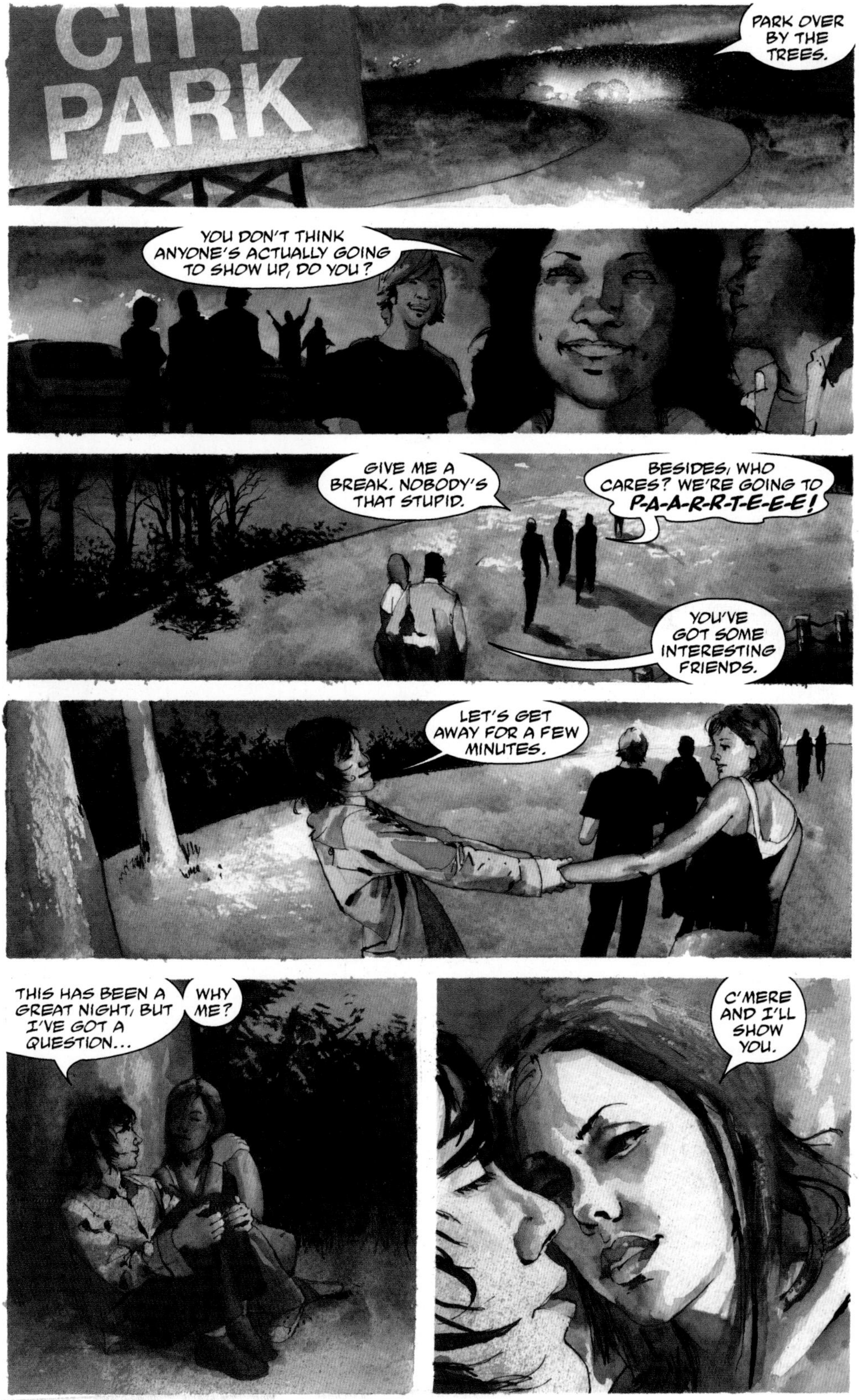
CITY PARK
PARK OVER BY THE TREES.
YOU DON'T THINK ANYONE'S ACTUALLY GOING TO SHOW UP, DO YOU?
GIVE ME A BREAK. NOBODY'S THAT STUPID.
BESIDES, WHO CARES? WE'RE GOING TO P-A-A-R-R-T-E-E-E!
YOU'VE GOT SOME INTERESTING FRIENDS.
LET'S GET AWAY FOR A FEW MINUTES.
THIS HAS BEEN A GREAT NIGHT, BUT I'VE GOT A QUESTION...
WHY ME?
C'MERE AND I'LL SHOW YOU.

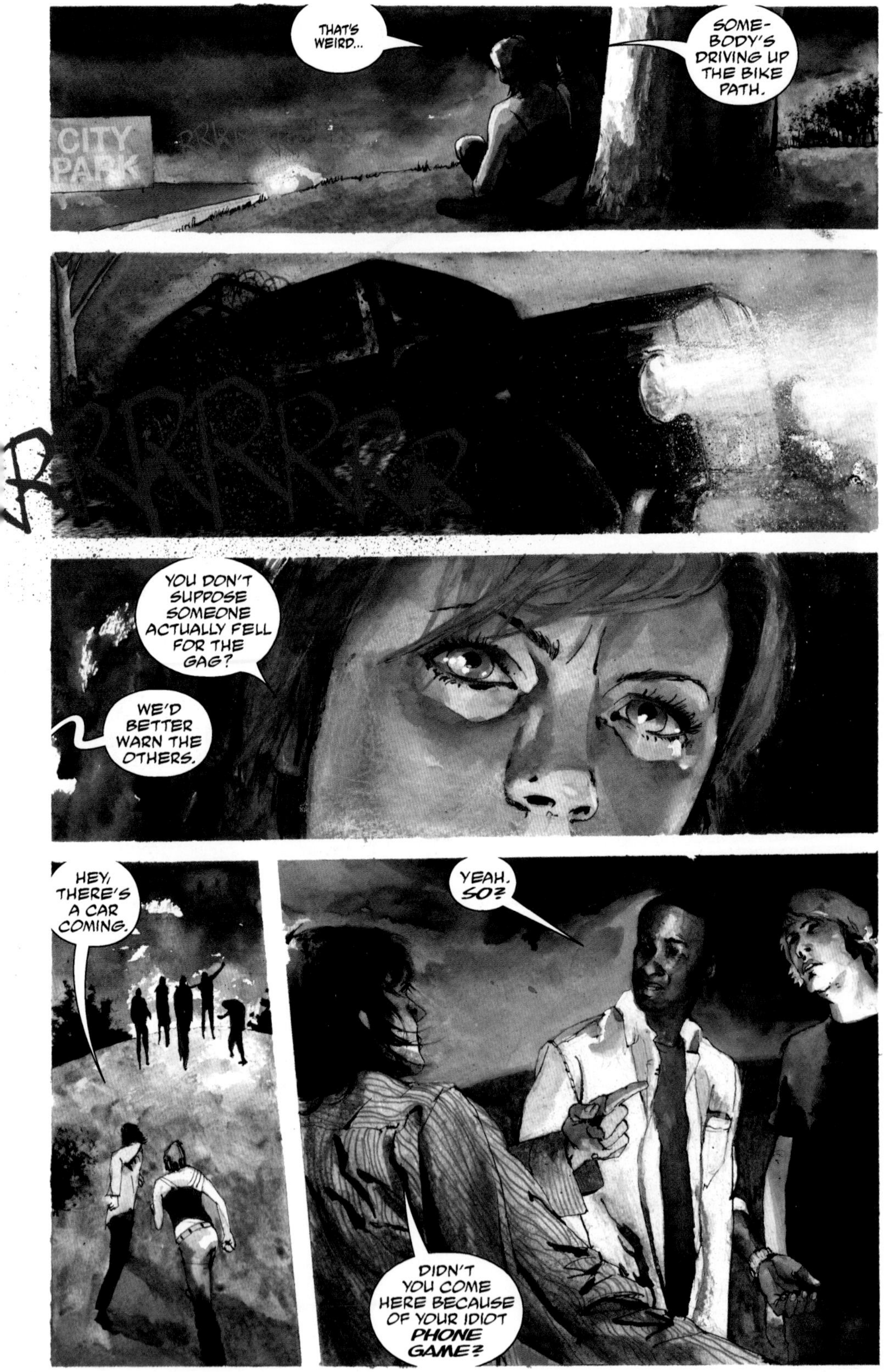
THAT'S WEIRD...
SOME-BODY'S DRIVING UP THE BIKE PATH.
CITY PARK
RRRRRRR
YOU DON'T SUPPOSE SOMEONE ACTUALLY FELL FOR THE GAG?
WE'D BETTER WARN THE OTHERS.
HEY, THERE'S A CAR COMING.
YEAH. SO?
DIDN'T YOU COME HERE BECAUSE OF YOUR IDIOT PHONE GAME?

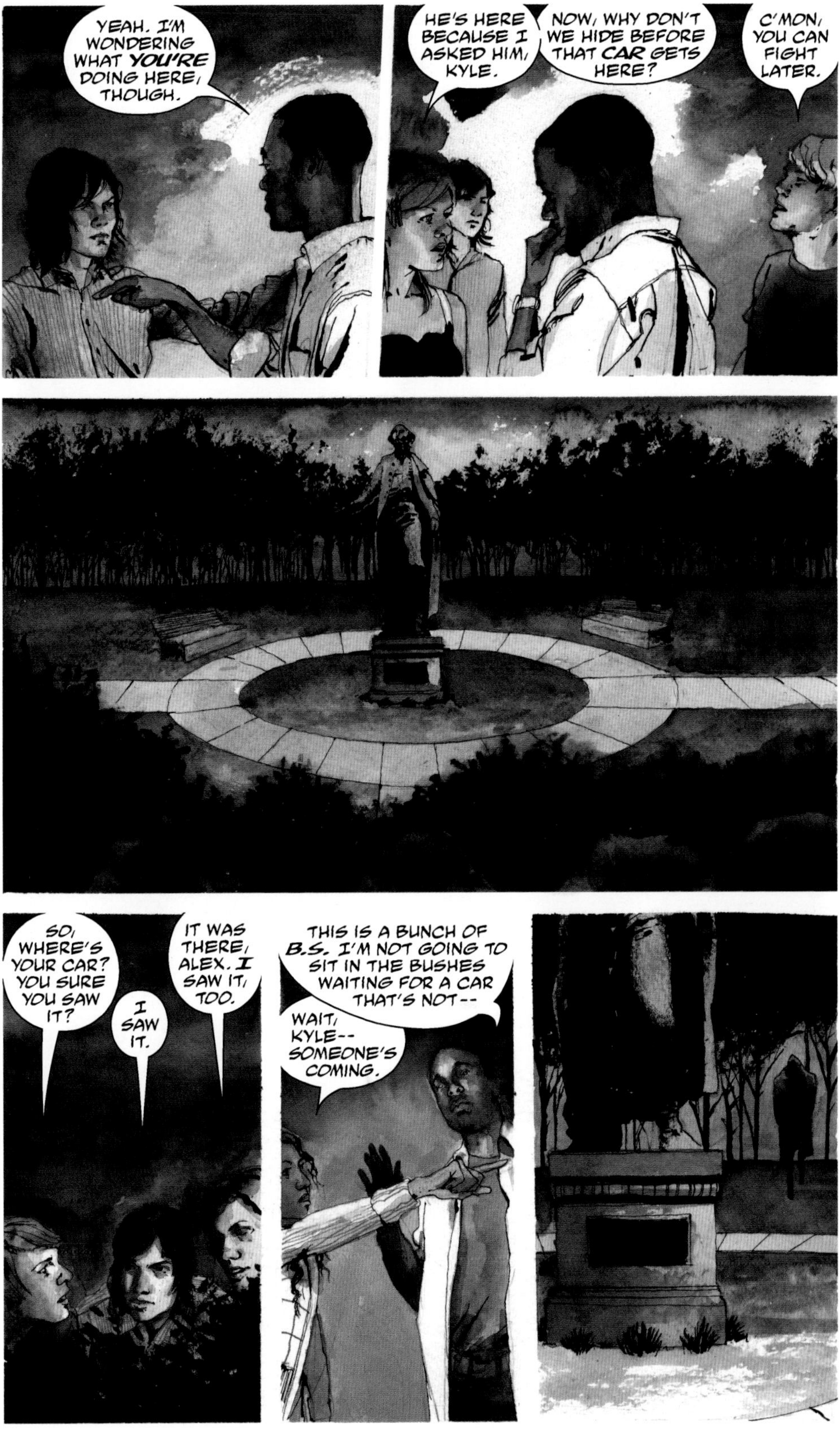
YEAH. I'M WONDERING WHAT YOU'RE DOING HERE, THOUGH.
HE'S HERE BECAUSE I ASKED HIM, KYLE.
NOW, WHY DON'T WE HIDE BEFORE THAT CAR GETS HERE?
C'MON, YOU CAN FIGHT LATER.
SO, WHERE'S YOUR CAR? YOU SURE YOU SAW IT?
I SAW IT.
IT WAS THERE, ALEX. I SAW IT, TOO.
THIS IS A BUNCH OF B.S. I'M NOT GOING TO SIT IN THE BUSHES WAITING FOR A CAR THAT'S NOT--
WAIT, KYLE-- SOMEONE'S COMING.

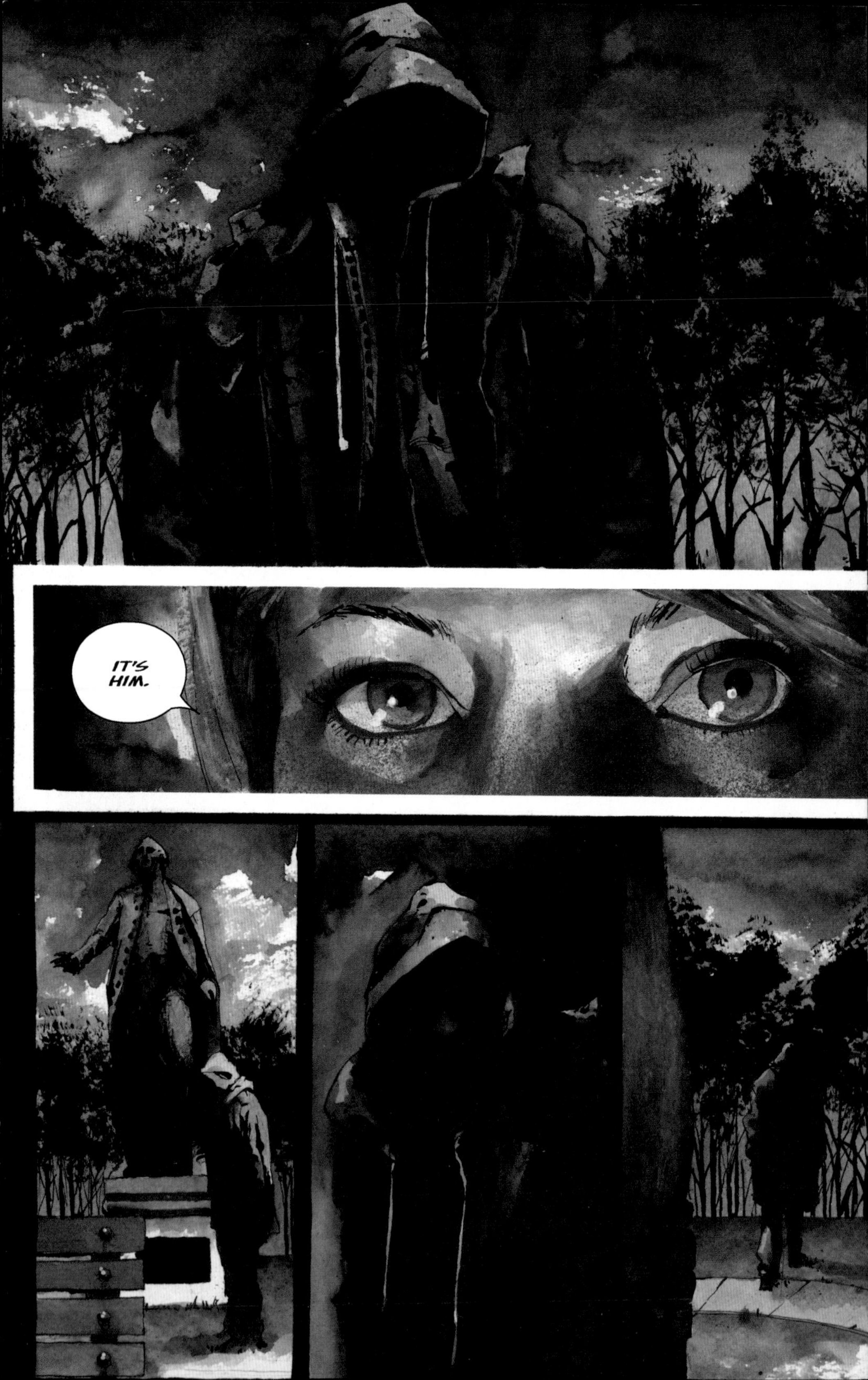
IT'S HIM.

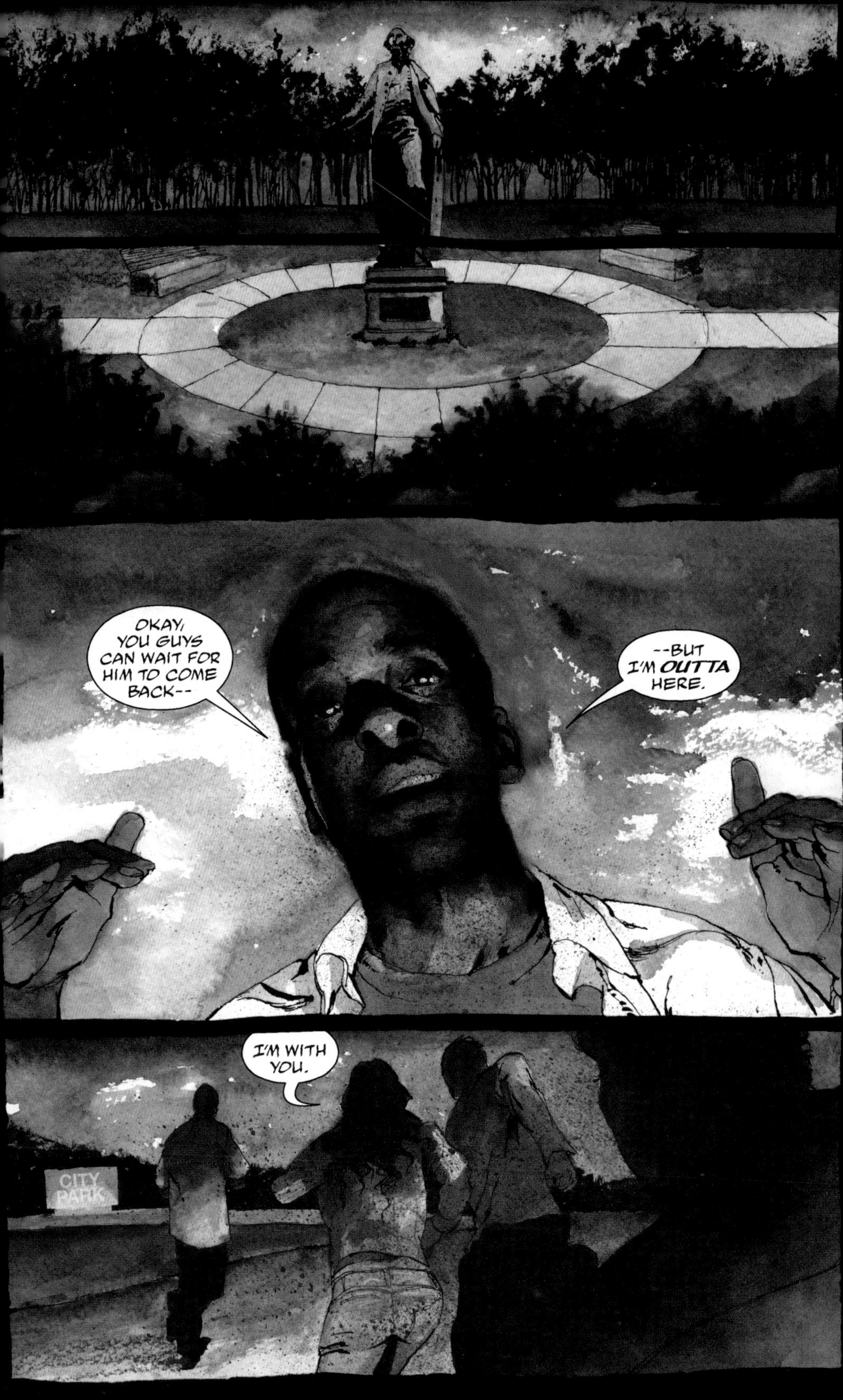
OKAY, YOU GUYS CAN WAIT FOR HIM TO COME BACK--
--BUT I'M *OUTTA* HERE.
I'M WITH YOU.
CITY PARK

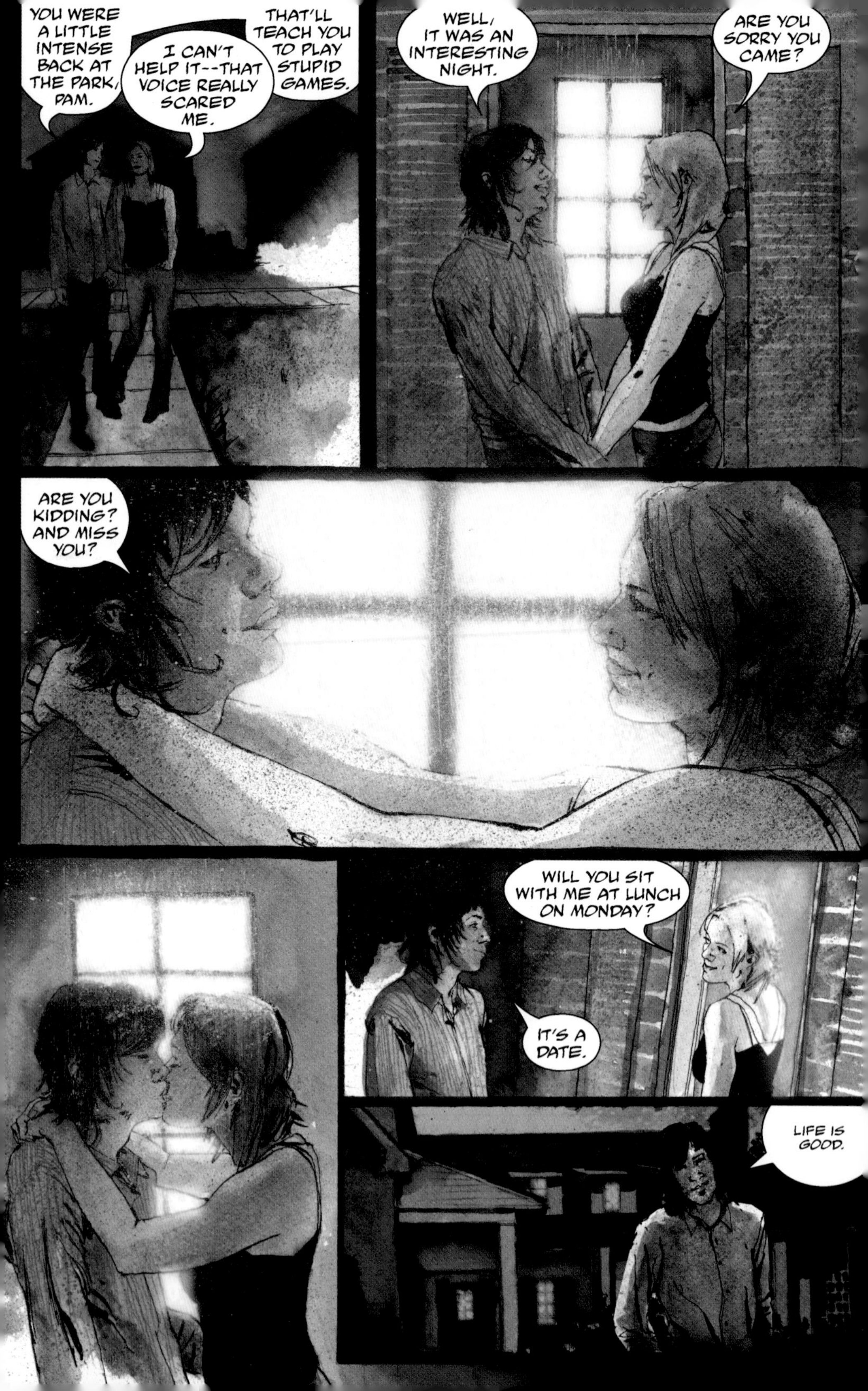
YOU WERE A LITTLE INTENSE BACK AT THE PARK, PAM.
I CAN'T HELP IT--THAT VOICE REALLY SCARED ME.
THAT'LL TEACH YOU TO PLAY STUPID GAMES.
WELL, IT WAS AN INTERESTING NIGHT.
ARE YOU SORRY YOU CAME?
ARE YOU KIDDING? AND MISS YOU?
WILL YOU SIT WITH ME AT LUNCH ON MONDAY?
IT'S A DATE.
LIFE IS GOOD.

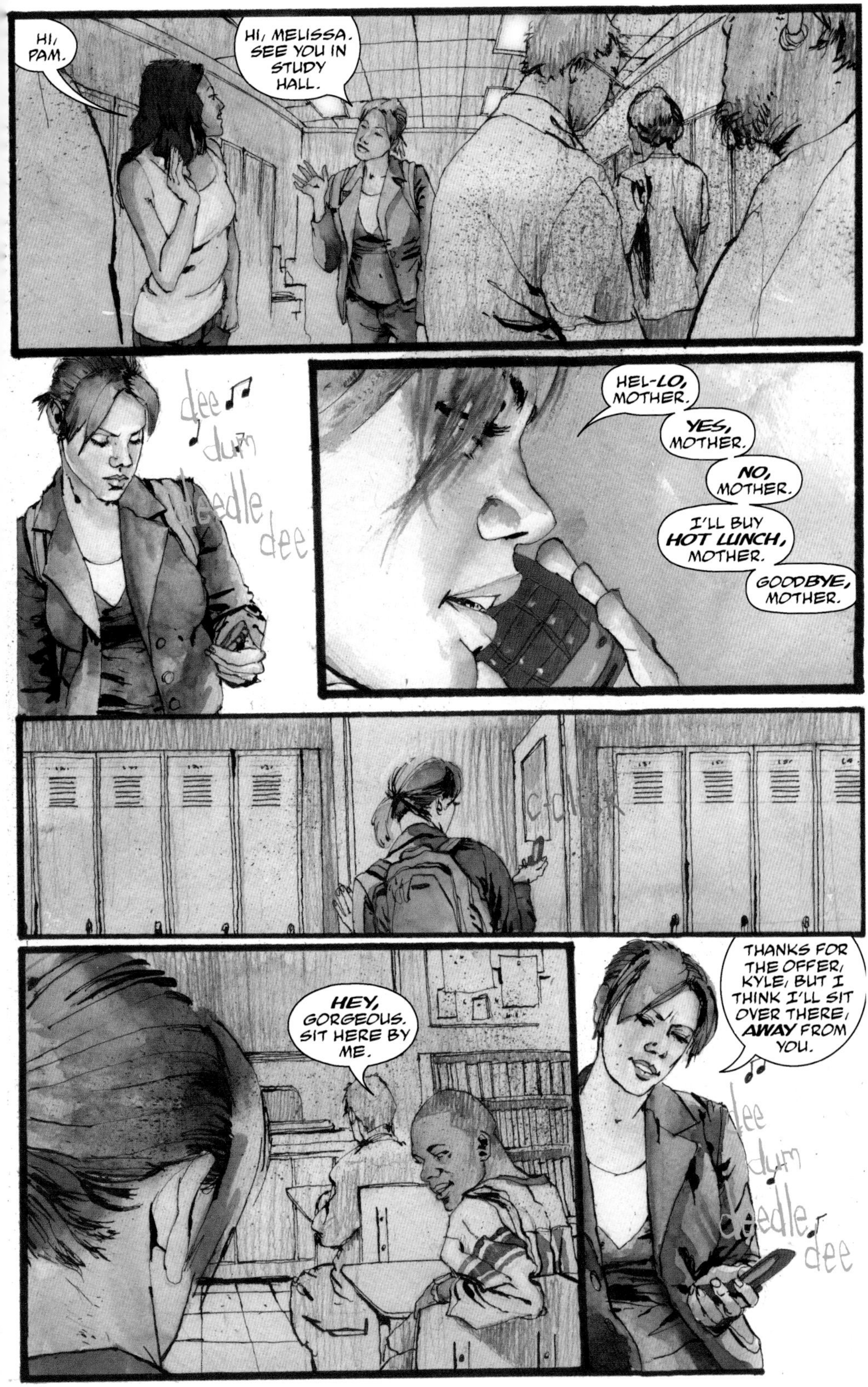
HI, PAM.
HI, MELISSA. SEE YOU IN STUDY HALL.
dee dum deedle dee
HEL-LO, MOTHER.
YES, MOTHER.
NO, MOTHER.
I'LL BUY HOT LUNCH, MOTHER.
GOODBYE, MOTHER.
HEY, GORGEOUS. SIT HERE BY ME.
THANKS FOR THE OFFER, KYLE, BUT I THINK I'LL SIT OVER THERE, AWAY FROM YOU.
dee dum deedle dee

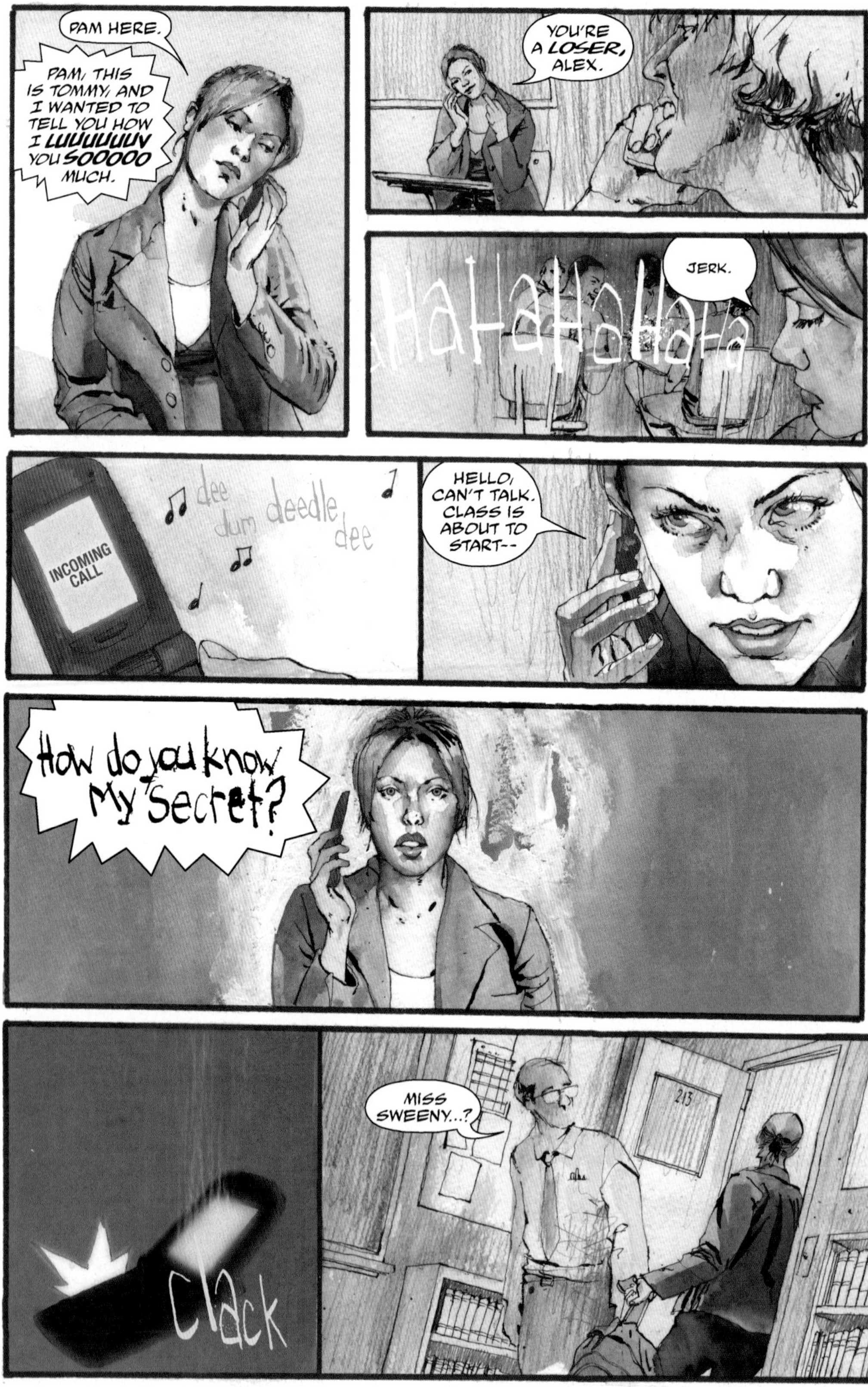
PAM HERE.
PAM, THIS IS TOMMY, AND I WANTED TO TELL YOU HOW I LUUUUUUV YOU SOOOOO MUCH.
YOU'RE A LOSER, ALEX.
HaHaHaHaHaHa
JERK.
dee dum deedle dee
INCOMING CALL
HELLO, CAN'T TALK. CLASS IS ABOUT TO START--
How do you know My Secret?
clack
MISS SWEENY...?
213

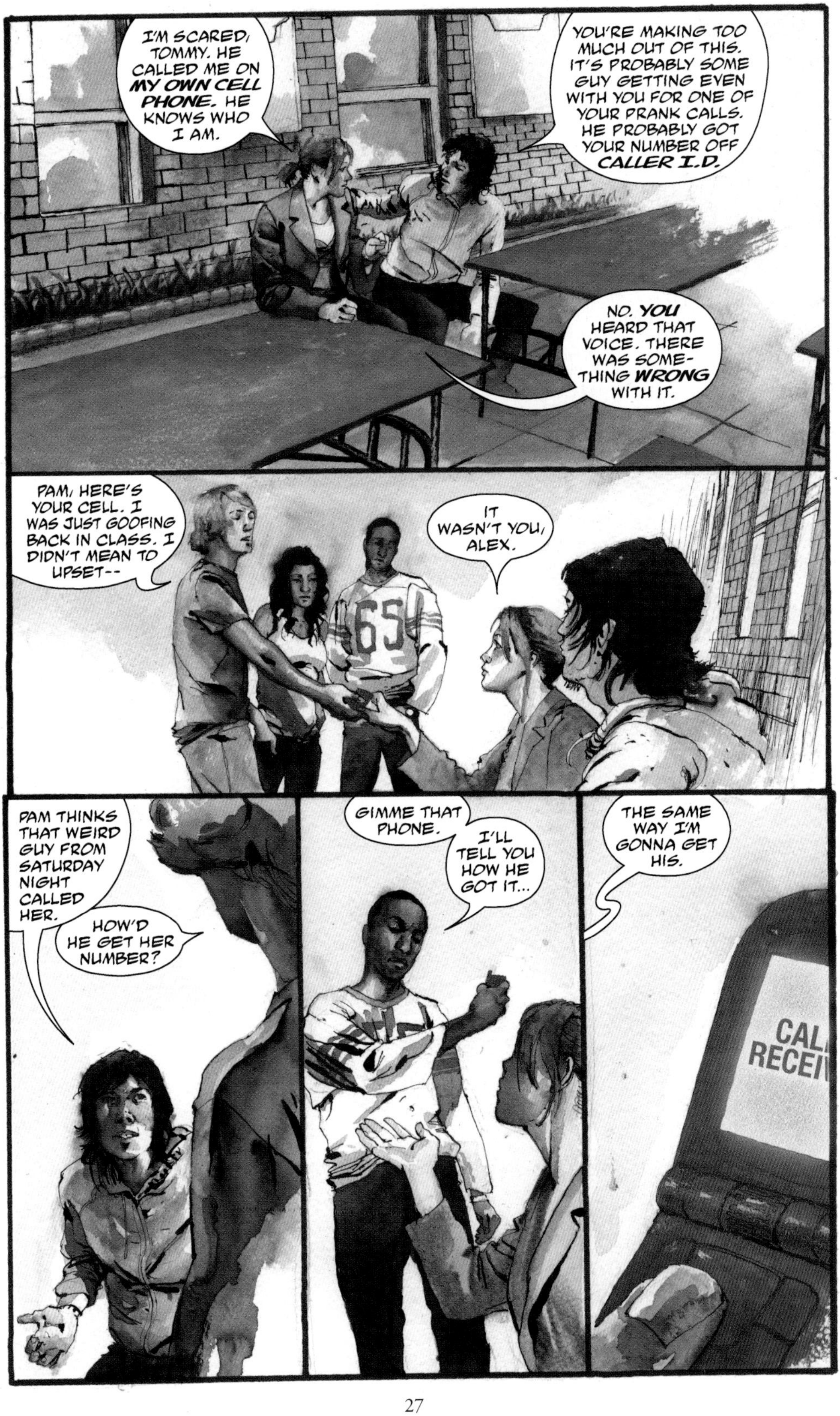
I'M SCARED, TOMMY. HE CALLED ME ON **MY OWN CELL PHONE.** HE KNOWS WHO I AM.
YOU'RE MAKING TOO MUCH OUT OF THIS. IT'S PROBABLY SOME GUY GETTING EVEN WITH YOU FOR ONE OF YOUR PRANK CALLS. HE PROBABLY GOT YOUR NUMBER OFF **CALLER I.D.**
NO. **YOU** HEARD THAT VOICE. THERE WAS SOME-THING **WRONG** WITH IT.
PAM, HERE'S YOUR CELL. I WAS JUST GOOFING BACK IN CLASS. I DIDN'T MEAN TO UPSET--
IT WASN'T YOU, ALEX.
65
PAM THINKS THAT WEIRD GUY FROM SATURDAY NIGHT CALLED HER.
HOW'D HE GET HER NUMBER?
GIMME THAT PHONE.
I'LL TELL YOU HOW HE GOT IT...
THE SAME WAY I'M GONNA GET HIS.

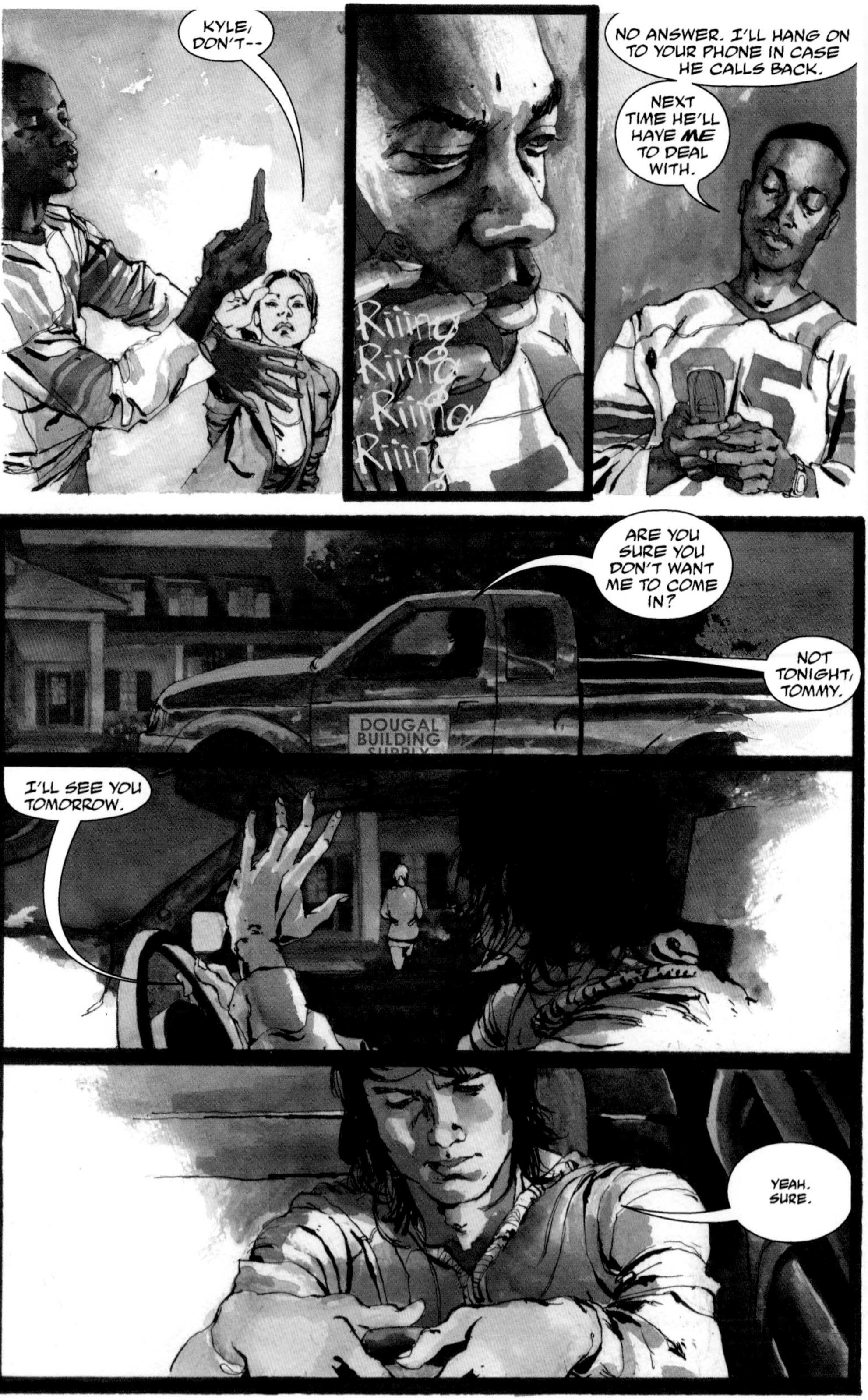
KYLE, DON'T--
Riiing
Riiing
Riiing
Riiing
NO ANSWER. I'LL HANG ON TO YOUR PHONE IN CASE HE CALLS BACK.
NEXT TIME HE'LL HAVE *ME* TO DEAL WITH.
ARE YOU SURE YOU DON'T WANT ME TO COME IN?
NOT TONIGHT, TOMMY.
DOUGAL BUILDING
I'LL SEE YOU TOMORROW.
YEAH. SURE.

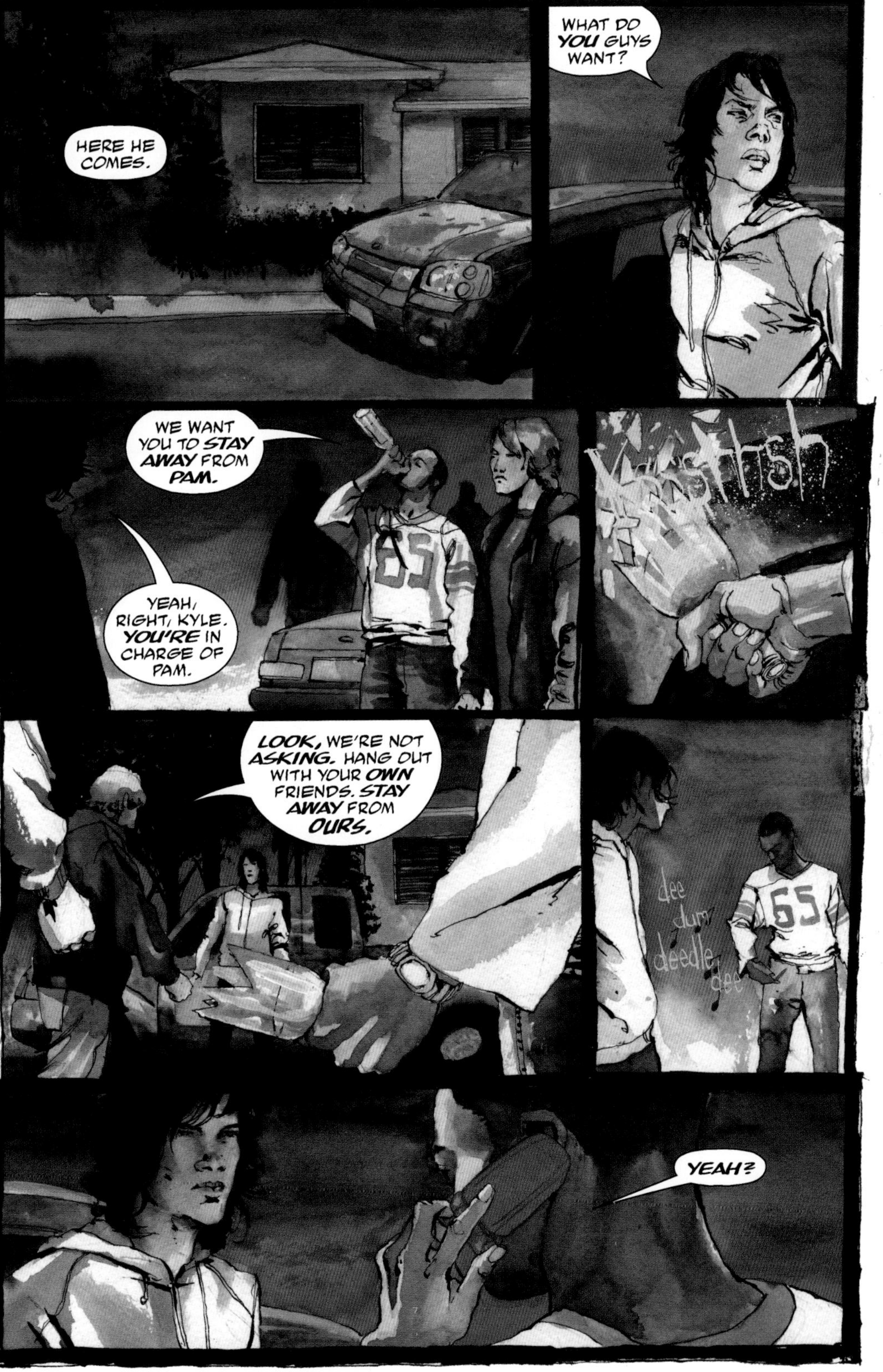

HERE HE COMES.
WHAT DO *YOU* GUYS WANT?
WE WANT YOU TO *STAY AWAY* FROM *PAM.*
YEAH, RIGHT, KYLE. *YOU'RE* IN CHARGE OF PAM.
LOOK, WE'RE NOT ASKING. HANG OUT WITH YOUR OWN FRIENDS. STAY AWAY FROM OURS.
dee dum deedle dee
YEAH?

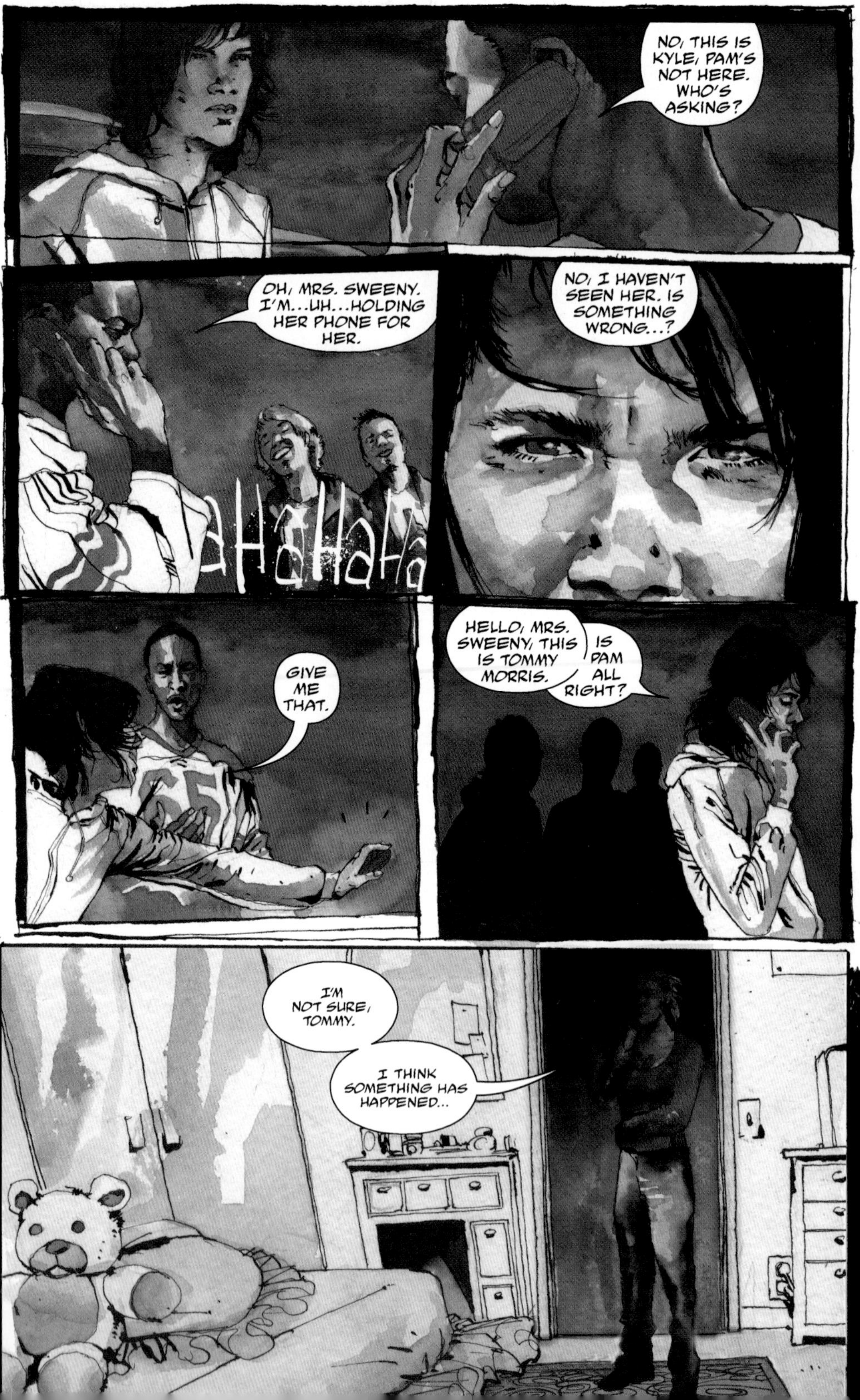
NO, THIS IS KYLE, PAM'S NOT HERE. WHO'S ASKING?
OH, MRS. SWEENY. I'M...UH...HOLDING HER PHONE FOR HER.
HAHAHAHA
NO, I HAVEN'T SEEN HER. IS SOMETHING WRONG...?
GIVE ME THAT.
HELLO, MRS. SWEENY, THIS IS TOMMY MORRIS.
IS PAM ALL RIGHT?
I'M NOT SURE, TOMMY.
I THINK SOMETHING HAS HAPPENED...

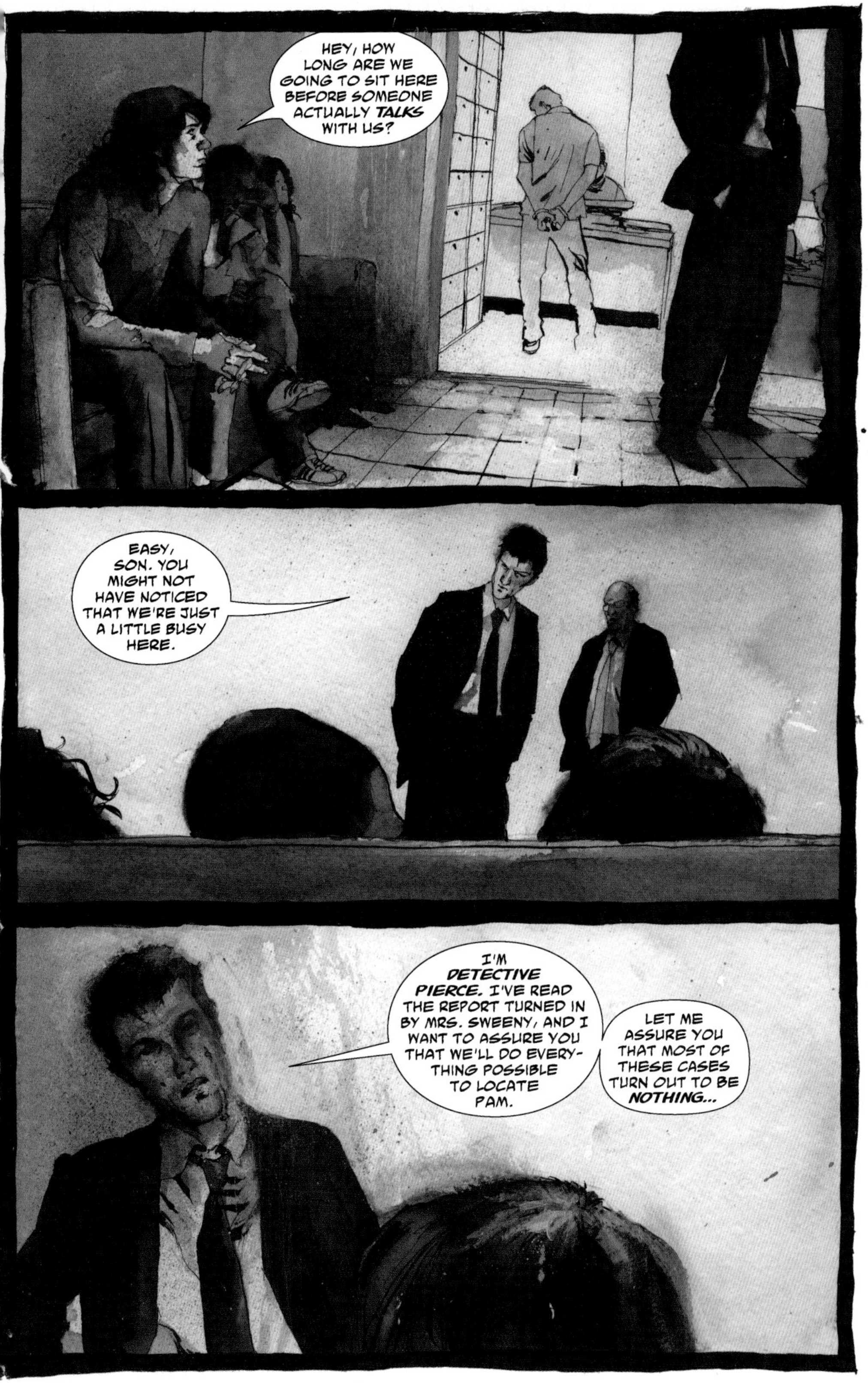
HEY, HOW LONG ARE WE GOING TO SIT HERE BEFORE SOMEONE ACTUALLY TALKS WITH US?
EASY, SON. YOU MIGHT NOT HAVE NOTICED THAT WE'RE JUST A LITTLE BUSY HERE.
I'M DETECTIVE PIERCE. I'VE READ THE REPORT TURNED IN BY MRS. SWEENY, AND I WANT TO ASSURE YOU THAT WE'LL DO EVERY-THING POSSIBLE TO LOCATE PAM.
LET ME ASSURE YOU THAT MOST OF THESE CASES TURN OUT TO BE NOTHING...

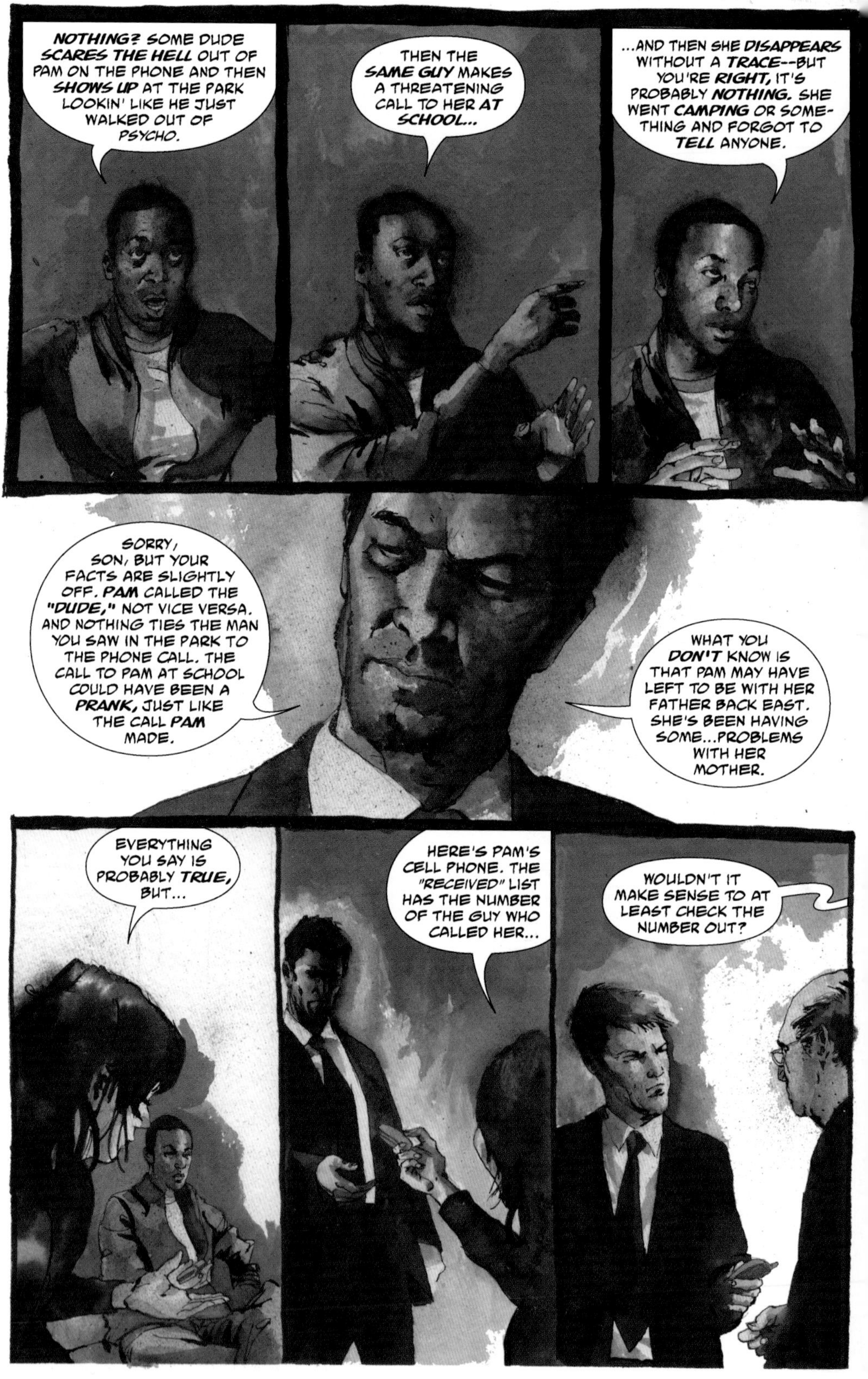
NOTHING? SOME DUDE SCARES THE HELL OUT OF PAM ON THE PHONE AND THEN SHOWS UP AT THE PARK LOOKIN' LIKE HE JUST WALKED OUT OF PSYCHO.
THEN THE SAME GUY MAKES A THREATENING CALL TO HER AT SCHOOL...
...AND THEN SHE DISAPPEARS WITHOUT A TRACE--BUT YOU'RE RIGHT, IT'S PROBABLY NOTHING. SHE WENT CAMPING OR SOMETHING AND FORGOT TO TELL ANYONE.
SORRY, SON, BUT YOUR FACTS ARE SLIGHTLY OFF. PAM CALLED THE "DUDE," NOT VICE VERSA. AND NOTHING TIES THE MAN YOU SAW IN THE PARK TO THE PHONE CALL. THE CALL TO PAM AT SCHOOL COULD HAVE BEEN A PRANK, JUST LIKE THE CALL PAM MADE.
WHAT YOU DON'T KNOW IS THAT PAM MAY HAVE LEFT TO BE WITH HER FATHER BACK EAST. SHE'S BEEN HAVING SOME...PROBLEMS WITH HER MOTHER.
EVERYTHING YOU SAY IS PROBABLY TRUE, BUT...
HERE'S PAM'S CELL PHONE. THE "RECEIVED" LIST HAS THE NUMBER OF THE GUY WHO CALLED HER...
WOULDN'T IT MAKE SENSE TO AT LEAST CHECK THE NUMBER OUT?

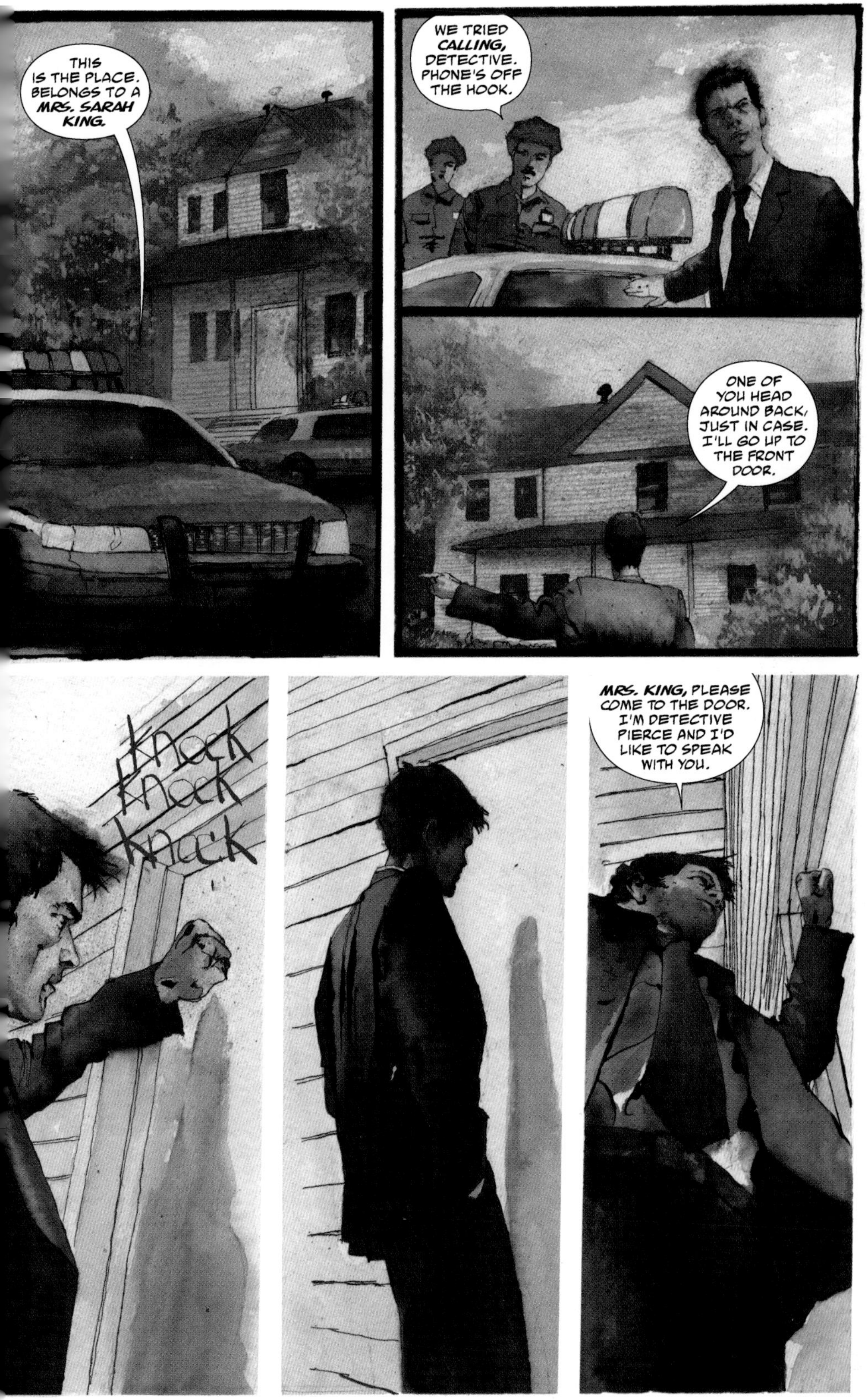
THIS IS THE PLACE. BELONGS TO A **MRS. SARAH KING.**
WE TRIED **CALLING,** DETECTIVE. PHONE'S OFF THE HOOK.
ONE OF YOU HEAD AROUND BACK, JUST IN CASE. I'LL GO UP TO THE FRONT DOOR.
Knock Knock Knock
MRS. KING, PLEASE COME TO THE DOOR. I'M DETECTIVE PIERCE AND I'D LIKE TO SPEAK WITH YOU.

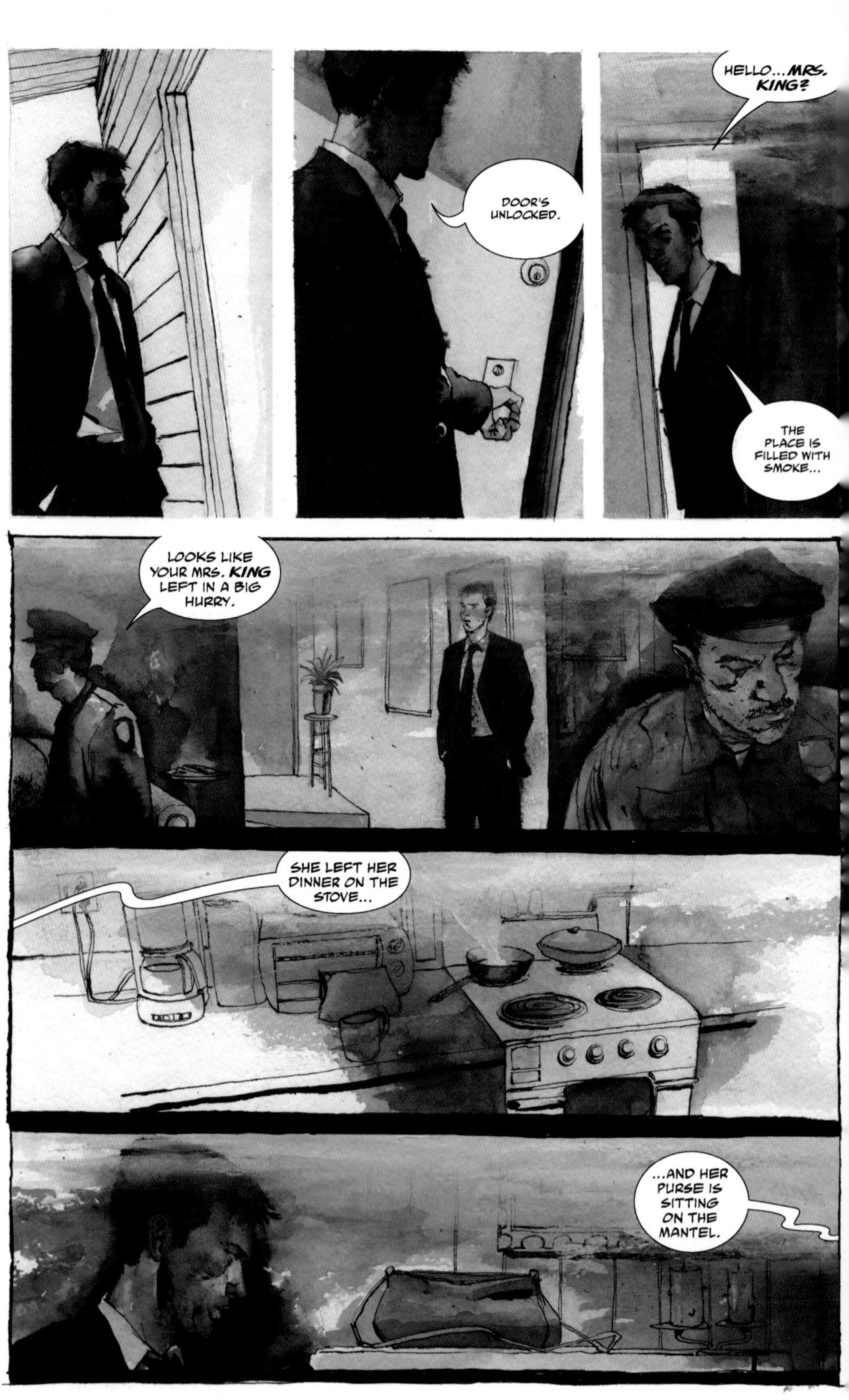
DOOR'S UNLOCKED.
HELLO... MRS. KING?
THE PLACE IS FILLED WITH SMOKE...
LOOKS LIKE YOUR MRS. KING LEFT IN A BIG HURRY.
SHE LEFT HER DINNER ON THE STOVE...
...AND HER PURSE IS SITTING ON THE MANTEL.

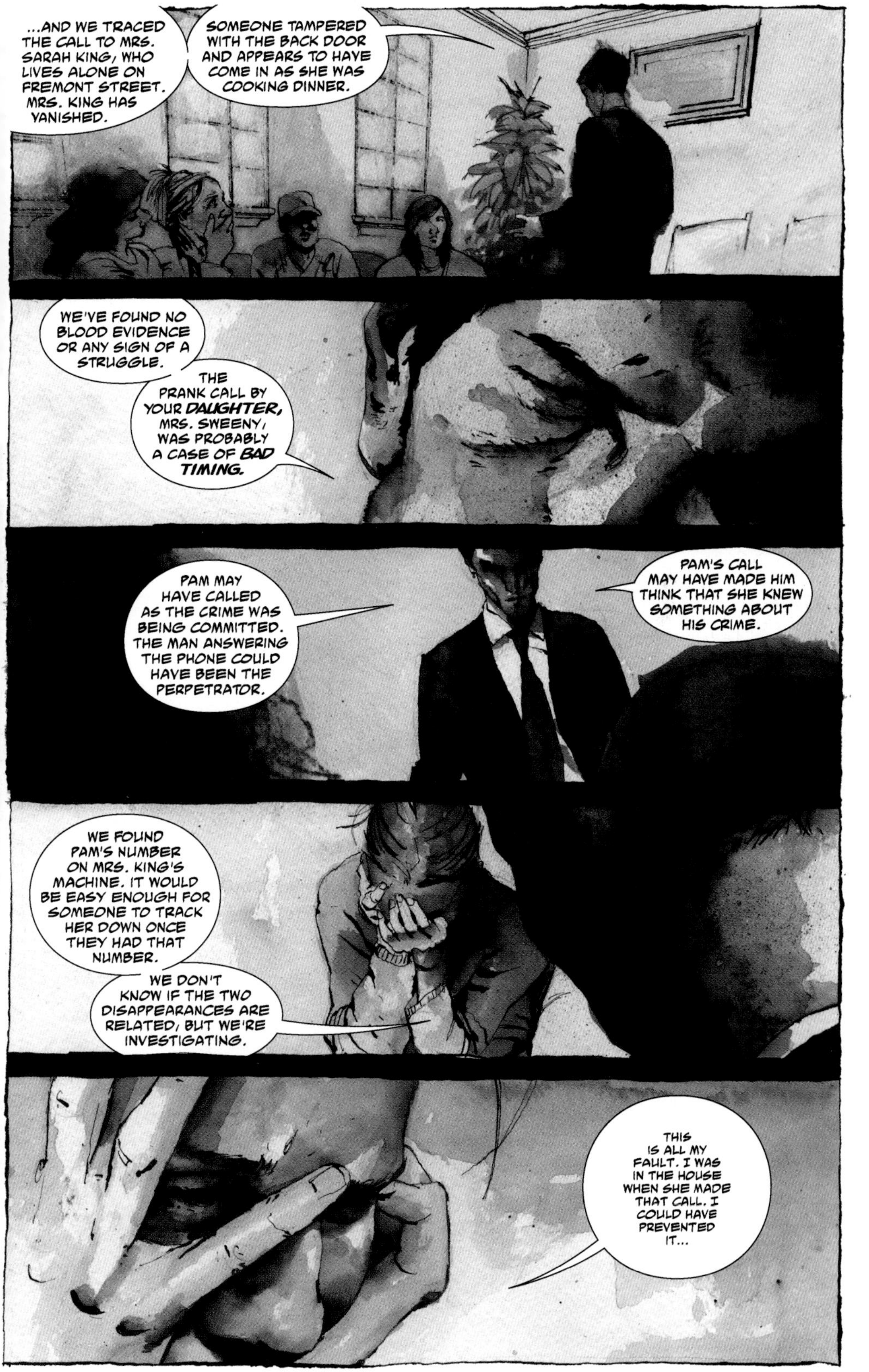
...AND WE TRACED THE CALL TO MRS. SARAH KING, WHO LIVES ALONE ON FREMONT STREET. MRS. KING HAS VANISHED.
SOMEONE TAMPERED WITH THE BACK DOOR AND APPEARS TO HAVE COME IN AS SHE WAS COOKING DINNER.
WE'VE FOUND NO BLOOD EVIDENCE OR ANY SIGN OF A STRUGGLE.
THE PRANK CALL BY YOUR DAUGHTER, MRS. SWEENY, WAS PROBABLY A CASE OF BAD TIMING.
PAM MAY HAVE CALLED AS THE CRIME WAS BEING COMMITTED. THE MAN ANSWERING THE PHONE COULD HAVE BEEN THE PERPETRATOR.
PAM'S CALL MAY HAVE MADE HIM THINK THAT SHE KNEW SOMETHING ABOUT HIS CRIME.
WE FOUND PAM'S NUMBER ON MRS. KING'S MACHINE. IT WOULD BE EASY ENOUGH FOR SOMEONE TO TRACK HER DOWN ONCE THEY HAD THAT NUMBER.
WE DON'T KNOW IF THE TWO DISAPPEARANCES ARE RELATED, BUT WE'RE INVESTIGATING.
THIS IS ALL MY FAULT. I WAS IN THE HOUSE WHEN SHE MADE THAT CALL. I COULD HAVE PREVENTED IT...

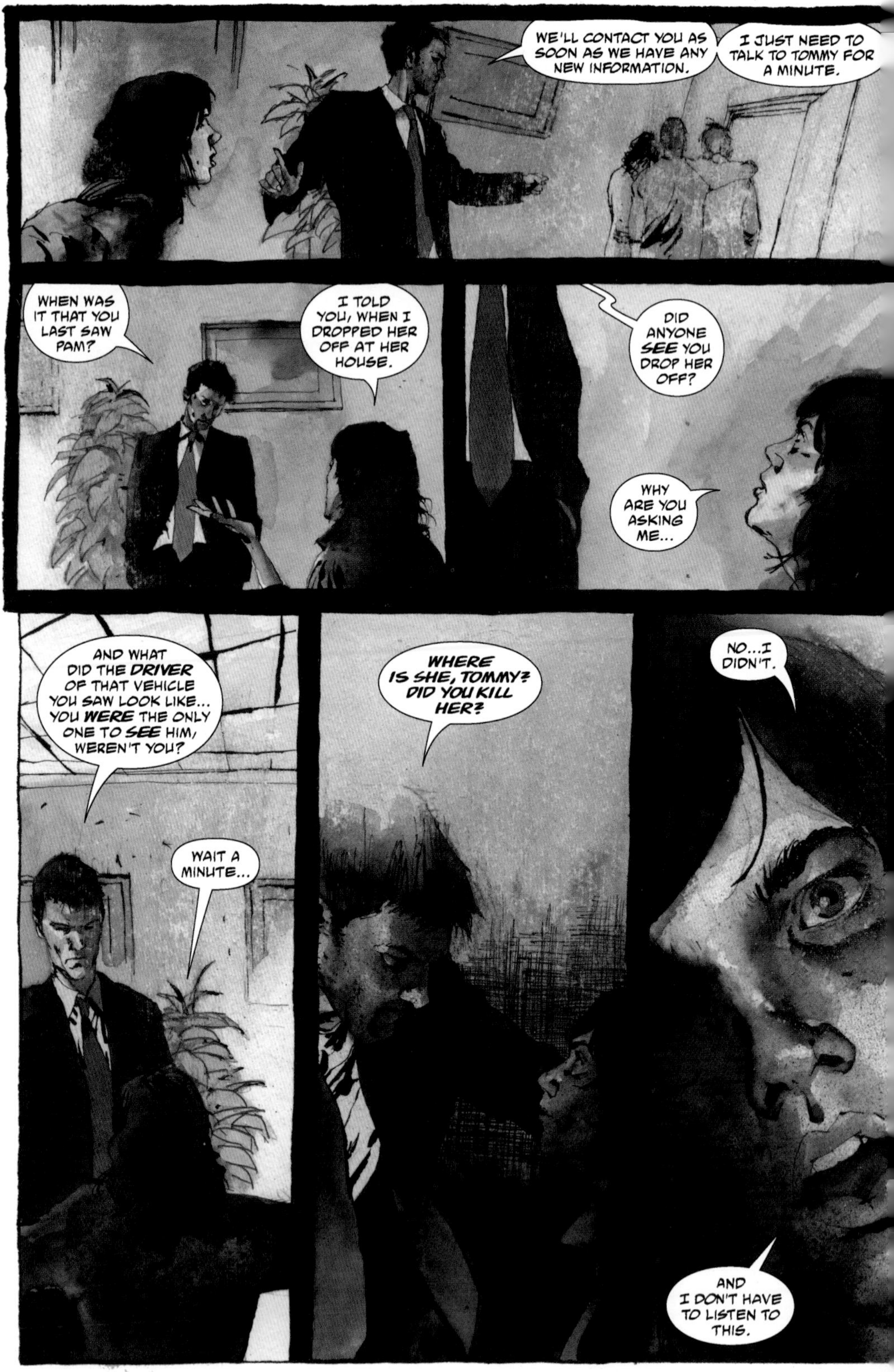
WE'LL CONTACT YOU AS SOON AS WE HAVE ANY NEW INFORMATION.
I JUST NEED TO TALK TO TOMMY FOR A MINUTE.
WHEN WAS IT THAT YOU LAST SAW PAM?
I TOLD YOU, WHEN I DROPPED HER OFF AT HER HOUSE.
DID ANYONE *SEE* YOU DROP HER OFF?
WHY ARE YOU ASKING ME...
AND WHAT DID THE *DRIVER* OF THAT VEHICLE YOU SAW LOOK LIKE... YOU *WERE* THE ONLY ONE TO *SEE* HIM, WEREN'T YOU?
WAIT A MINUTE...
WHERE IS SHE, TOMMY? DID YOU KILL HER?
NO...I DIDN'T.
AND I DON'T HAVE TO LISTEN TO THIS.

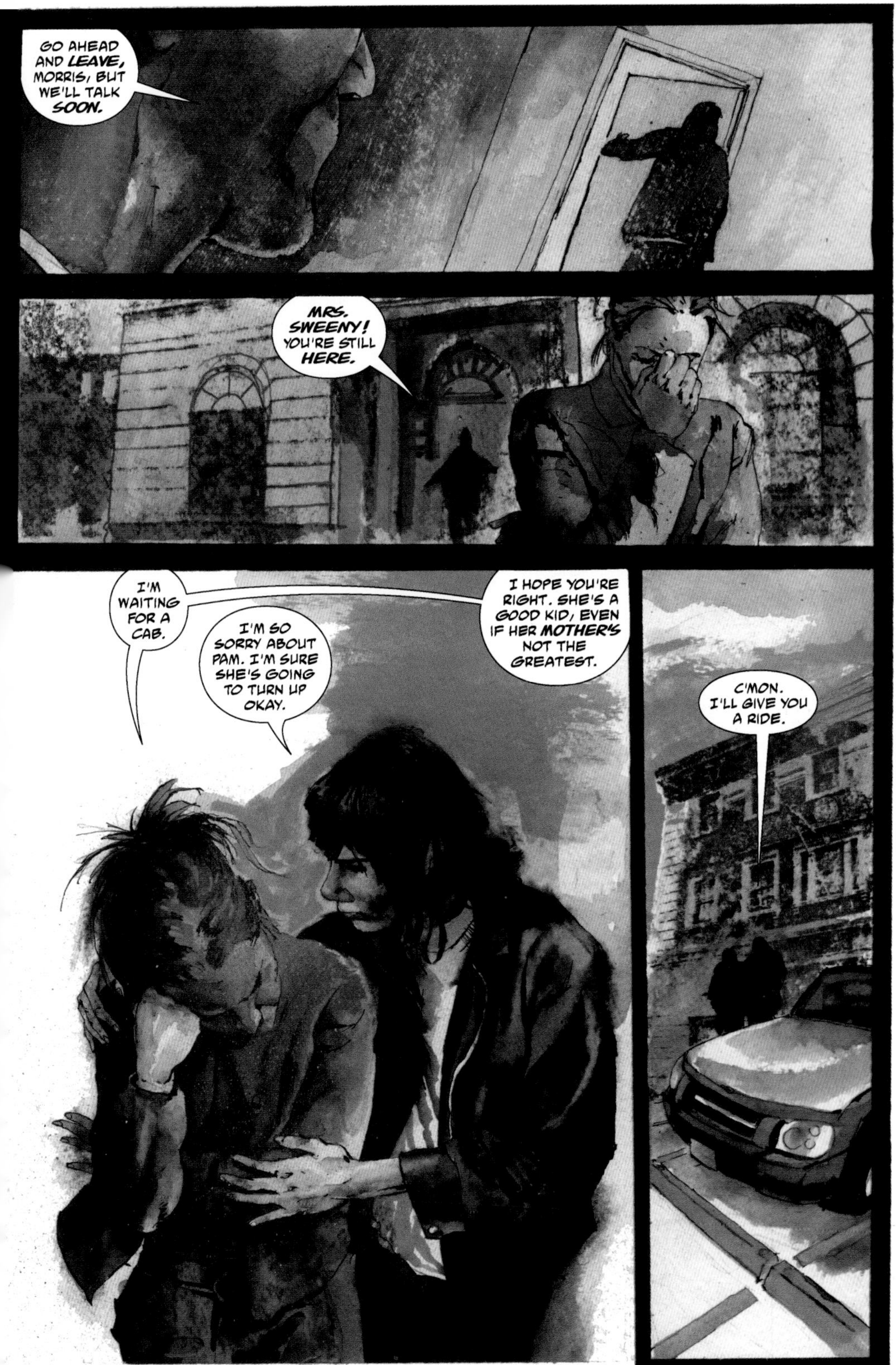
GO AHEAD AND LEAVE, MORRIS, BUT WE'LL TALK SOON.
MRS. SWEENY! YOU'RE STILL HERE.
I'M WAITING FOR A CAB.
I'M SO SORRY ABOUT PAM. I'M SURE SHE'S GOING TO TURN UP OKAY.
I HOPE YOU'RE RIGHT. SHE'S A GOOD KID, EVEN IF HER MOTHER'S NOT THE GREATEST.
C'MON. I'LL GIVE YOU A RIDE.

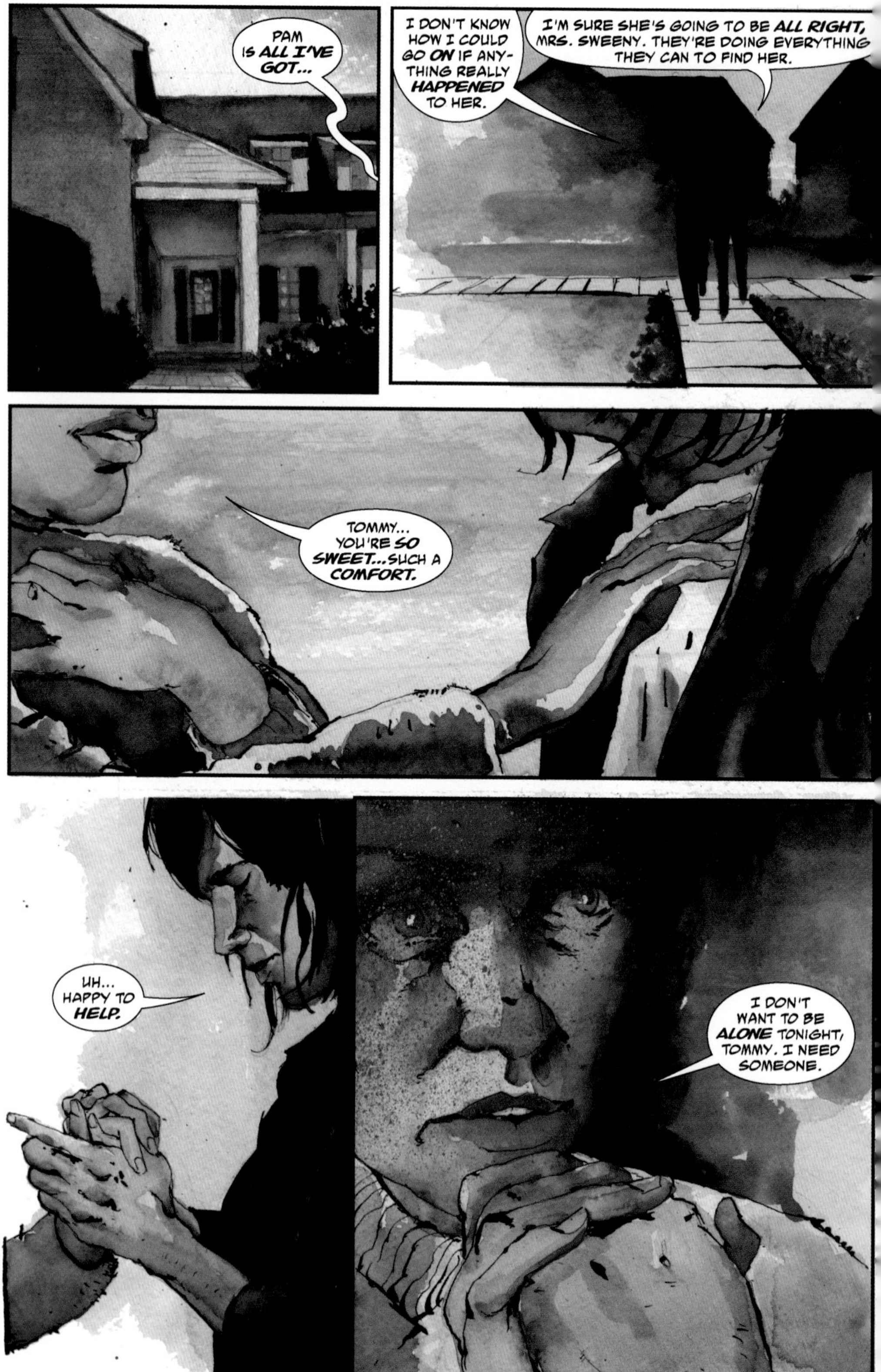
PAM IS ALL I'VE GOT...
I DON'T KNOW HOW I COULD GO ON IF ANYTHING REALLY HAPPENED TO HER.
I'M SURE SHE'S GOING TO BE ALL RIGHT, MRS. SWEENY. THEY'RE DOING EVERYTHING THEY CAN TO FIND HER.
TOMMY... YOU'RE SO SWEET...SUCH A COMFORT.
UH... HAPPY TO HELP.
I DON'T WANT TO BE ALONE TONIGHT, TOMMY. I NEED SOMEONE.

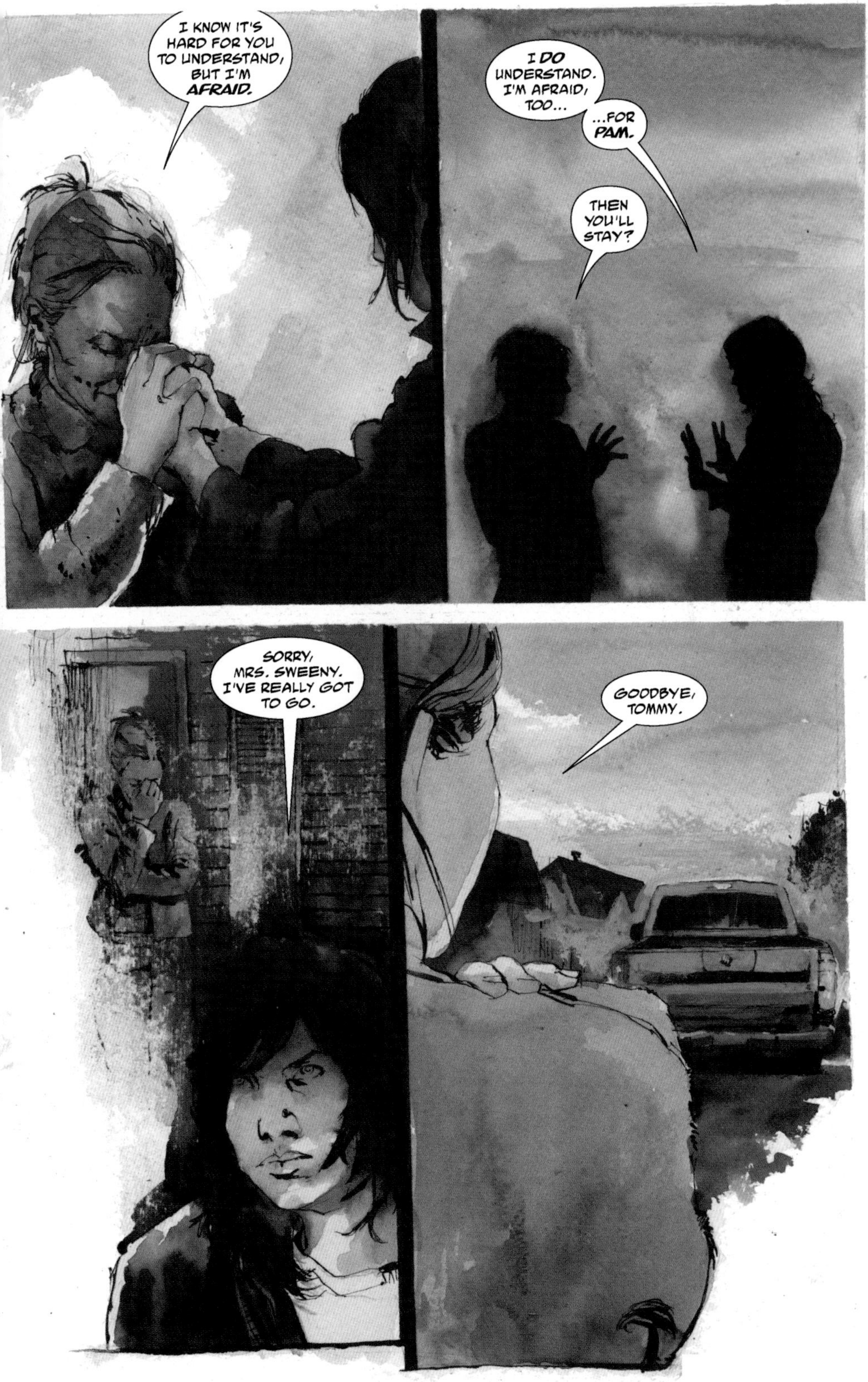
I KNOW IT'S HARD FOR YOU TO UNDERSTAND, BUT I'M AFRAID.
I DO UNDERSTAND. I'M AFRAID, TOO...
...FOR PAM.
THEN YOU'LL STAY?
SORRY, MRS. SWEENY. I'VE REALLY GOT TO GO.
GOODBYE, TOMMY.

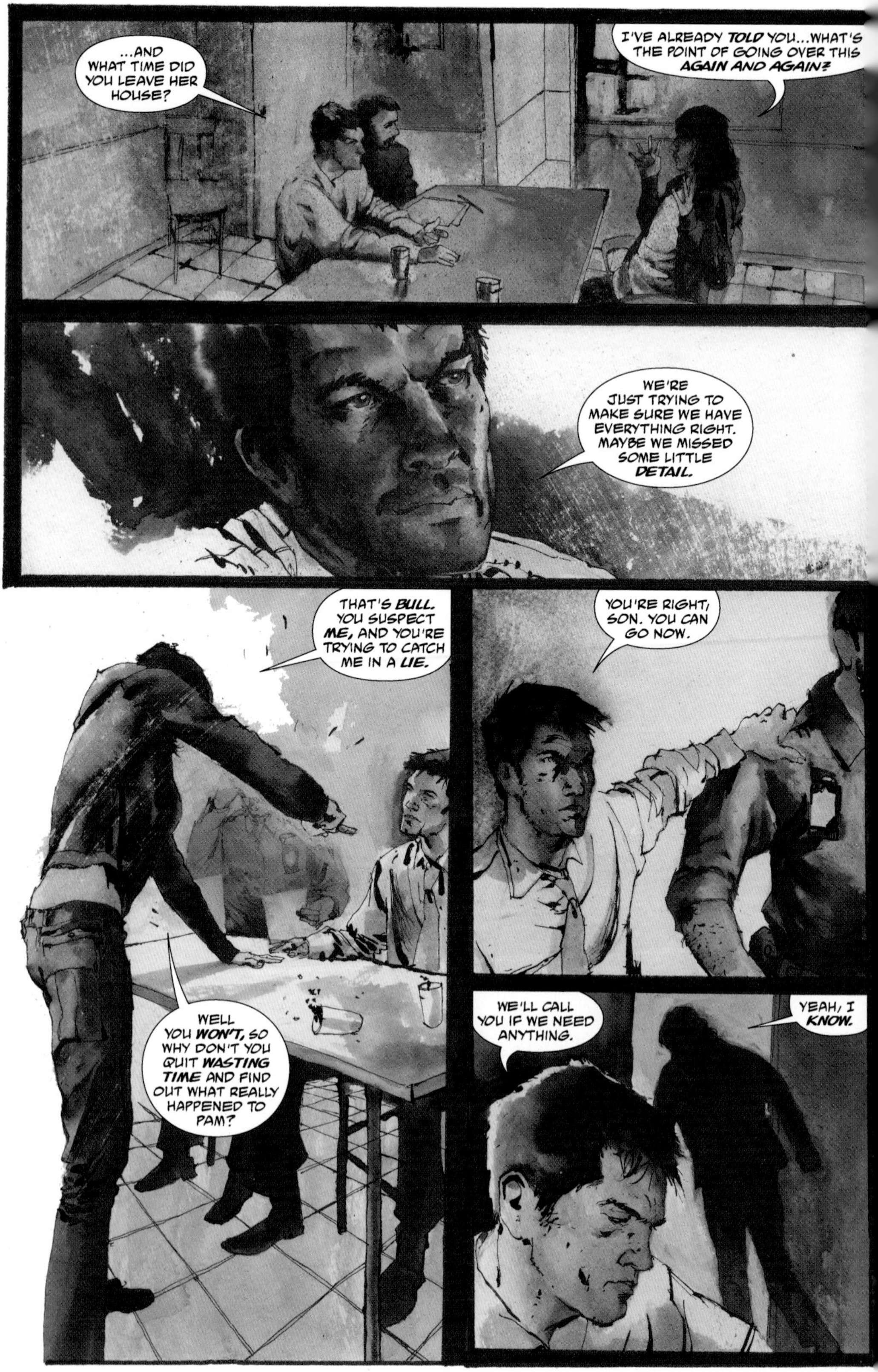
...AND WHAT TIME DID YOU LEAVE HER HOUSE?
I'VE ALREADY TOLD YOU...WHAT'S THE POINT OF GOING OVER THIS AGAIN AND AGAIN?
WE'RE JUST TRYING TO MAKE SURE WE HAVE EVERYTHING RIGHT. MAYBE WE MISSED SOME LITTLE DETAIL.
THAT'S BULL. YOU SUSPECT ME, AND YOU'RE TRYING TO CATCH ME IN A LIE.
WELL YOU WON'T, SO WHY DON'T YOU QUIT WASTING TIME AND FIND OUT WHAT REALLY HAPPENED TO PAM?
YOU'RE RIGHT, SON. YOU CAN GO NOW.
WE'LL CALL YOU IF WE NEED ANYTHING.
YEAH, I KNOW.

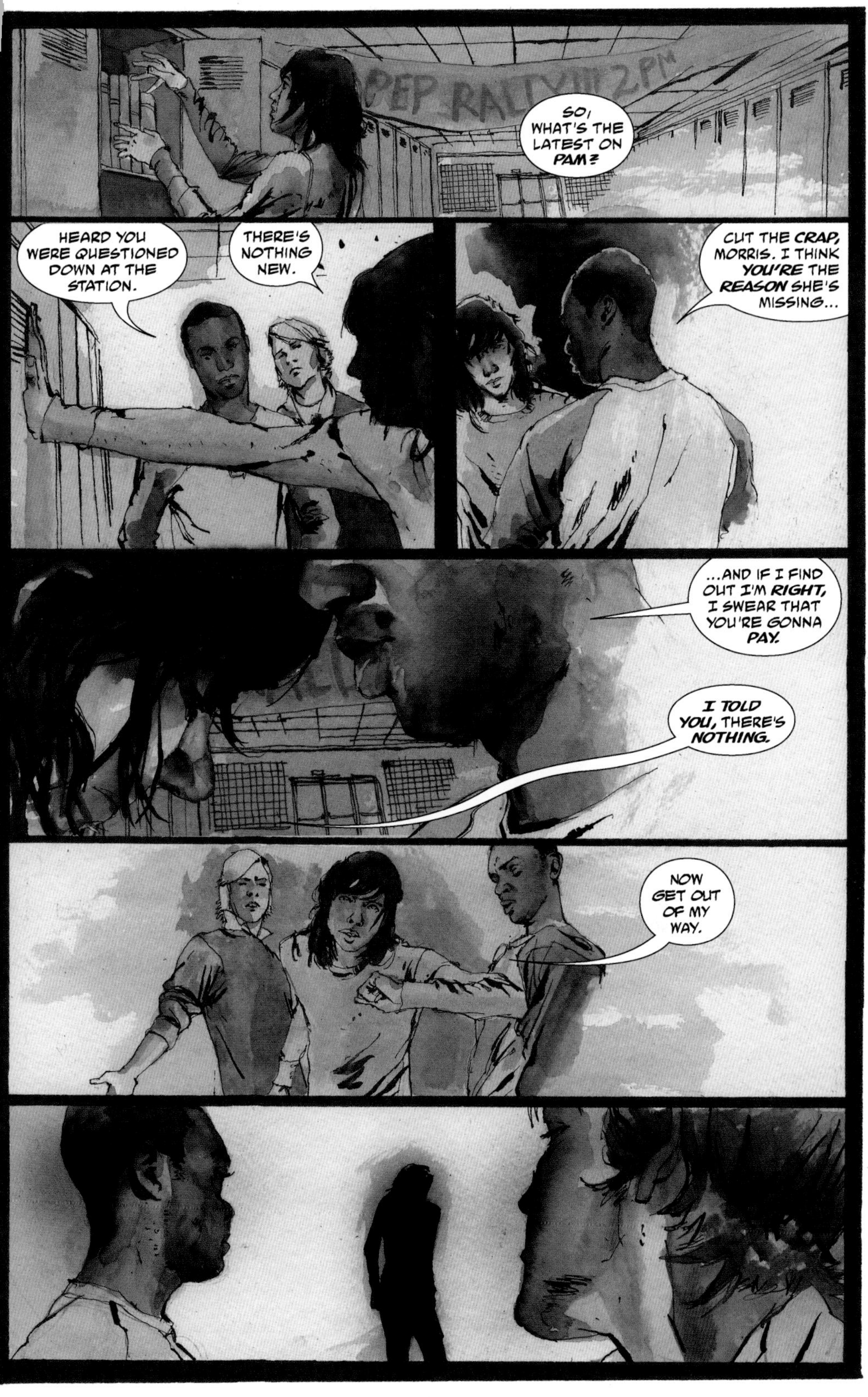
PEP RALLY!!! 2 PM
SO, WHAT'S THE LATEST ON PAM?
HEARD YOU WERE QUESTIONED DOWN AT THE STATION.
THERE'S NOTHING NEW.
CUT THE CRAP, MORRIS. I THINK YOU'RE THE REASON SHE'S MISSING...
...AND IF I FIND OUT I'M RIGHT, I SWEAR THAT YOU'RE GONNA PAY.
I TOLD YOU, THERE'S NOTHING.
NOW GET OUT OF MY WAY.

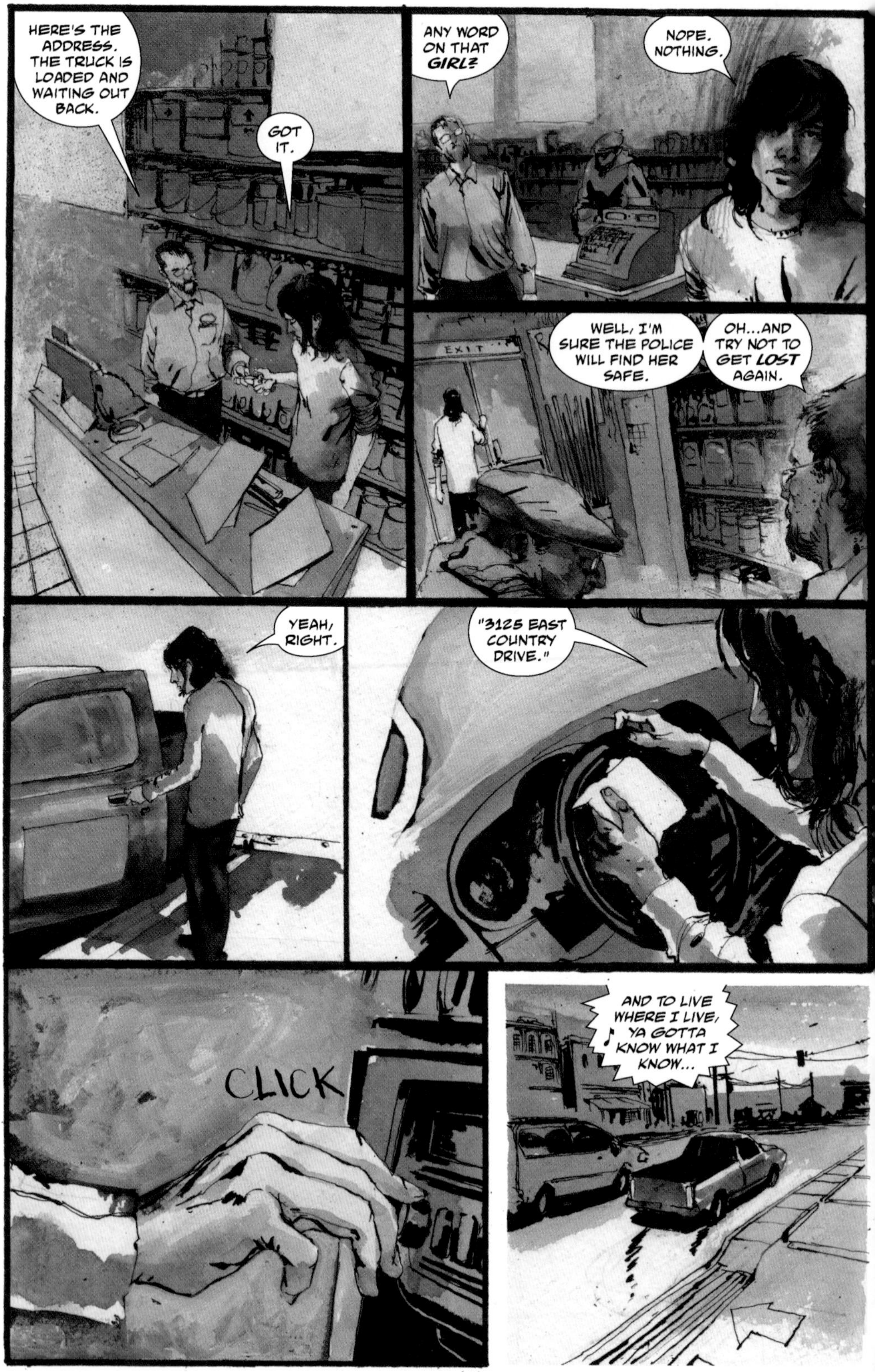
HERE'S THE ADDRESS. THE TRUCK IS LOADED AND WAITING OUT BACK.
GOT IT.
ANY WORD ON THAT GIRL?
NOPE. NOTHING.
WELL, I'M SURE THE POLICE WILL FIND HER SAFE.
OH...AND TRY NOT TO GET LOST AGAIN.
YEAH, RIGHT.
"3125 EAST COUNTRY DRIVE."
CLICK
AND TO LIVE WHERE I LIVE, YA GOTTA KNOW WHAT I KNOW...

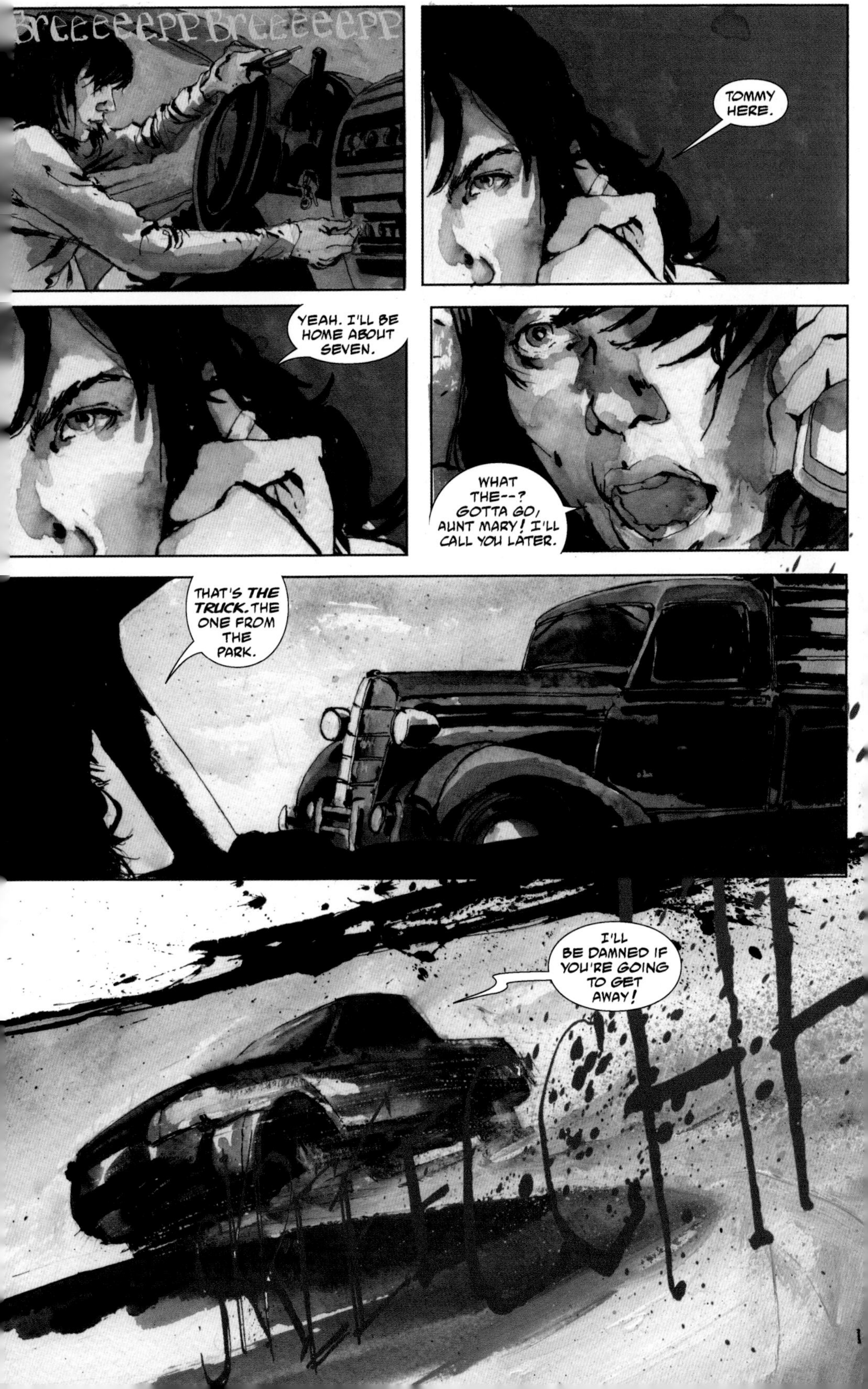
BreeeeePP BreeeeePP
TOMMY HERE.
YEAH. I'LL BE HOME ABOUT SEVEN.
WHAT THE--? GOTTA GO, AUNT MARY! I'LL CALL YOU LATER.
THAT'S **THE TRUCK.** THE ONE FROM THE PARK.
I'LL BE DAMNED IF YOU'RE GOING TO GET AWAY!

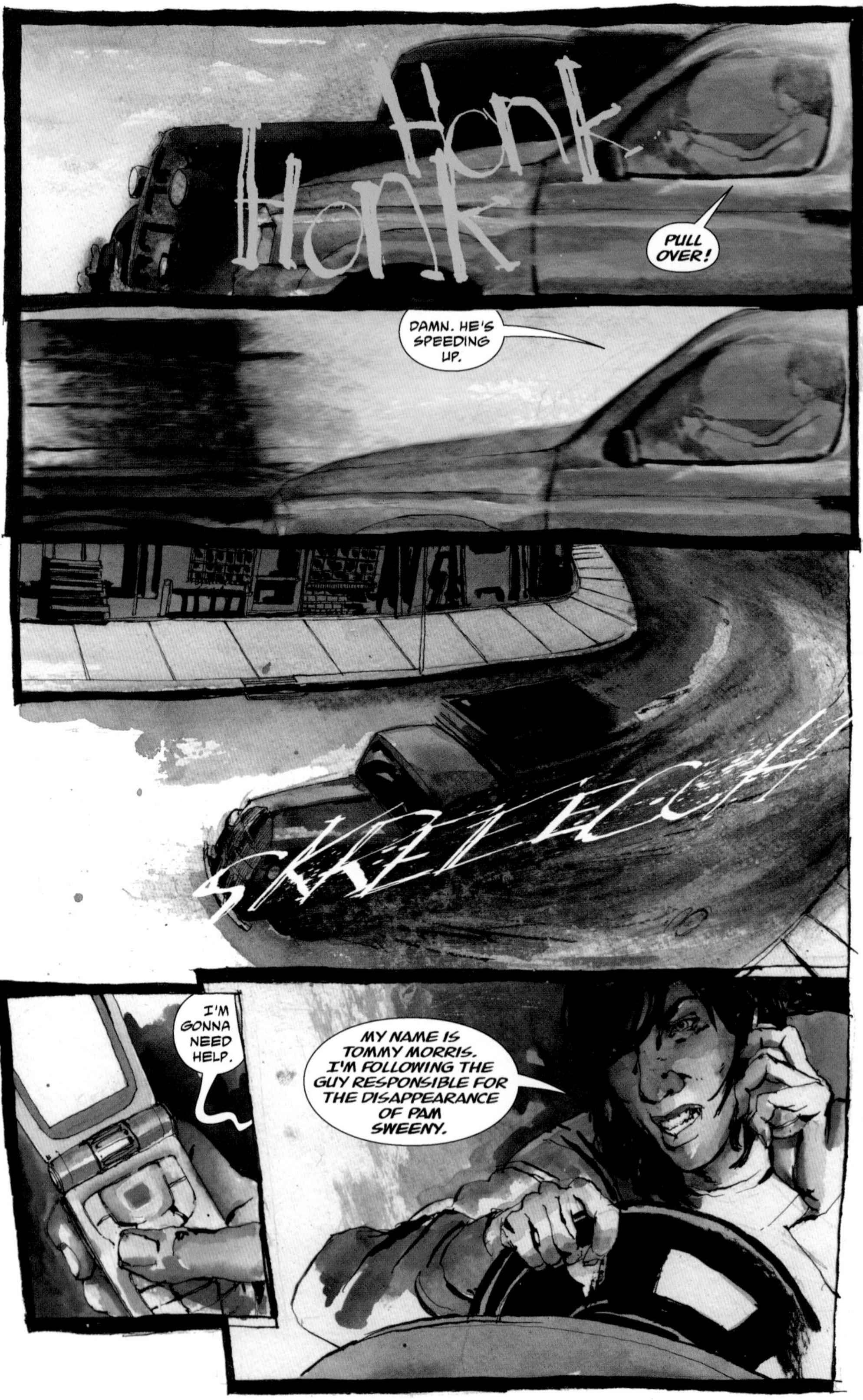
Honk
Honk
PULL OVER!
DAMN. HE'S SPEEDING UP.
SKREEECH
I'M GONNA NEED HELP.
MY NAME IS TOMMY MORRIS. I'M FOLLOWING THE GUY RESPONSIBLE FOR THE DISAPPEARANCE OF PAM SWEENY.

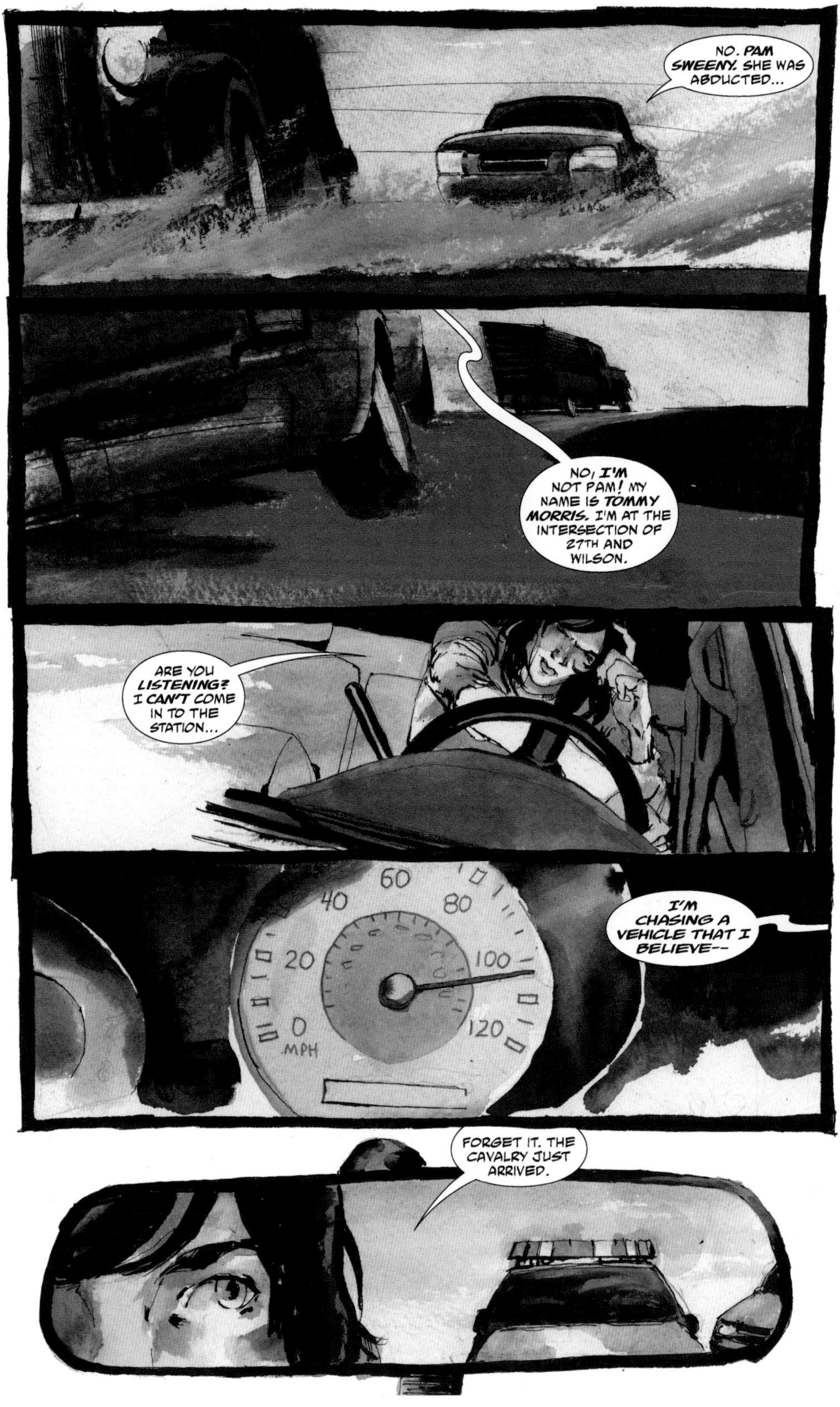
NO. PAM SWEENY. SHE WAS ABDUCTED...
NO, I'M NOT PAM! MY NAME IS TOMMY MORRIS. I'M AT THE INTERSECTION OF 27TH AND WILSON.
ARE YOU LISTENING? I CAN'T COME IN TO THE STATION...
40
60
80
20
100
0
120
MPH
I'M CHASING A VEHICLE THAT I BELIEVE--
FORGET IT. THE CAVALRY JUST ARRIVED.

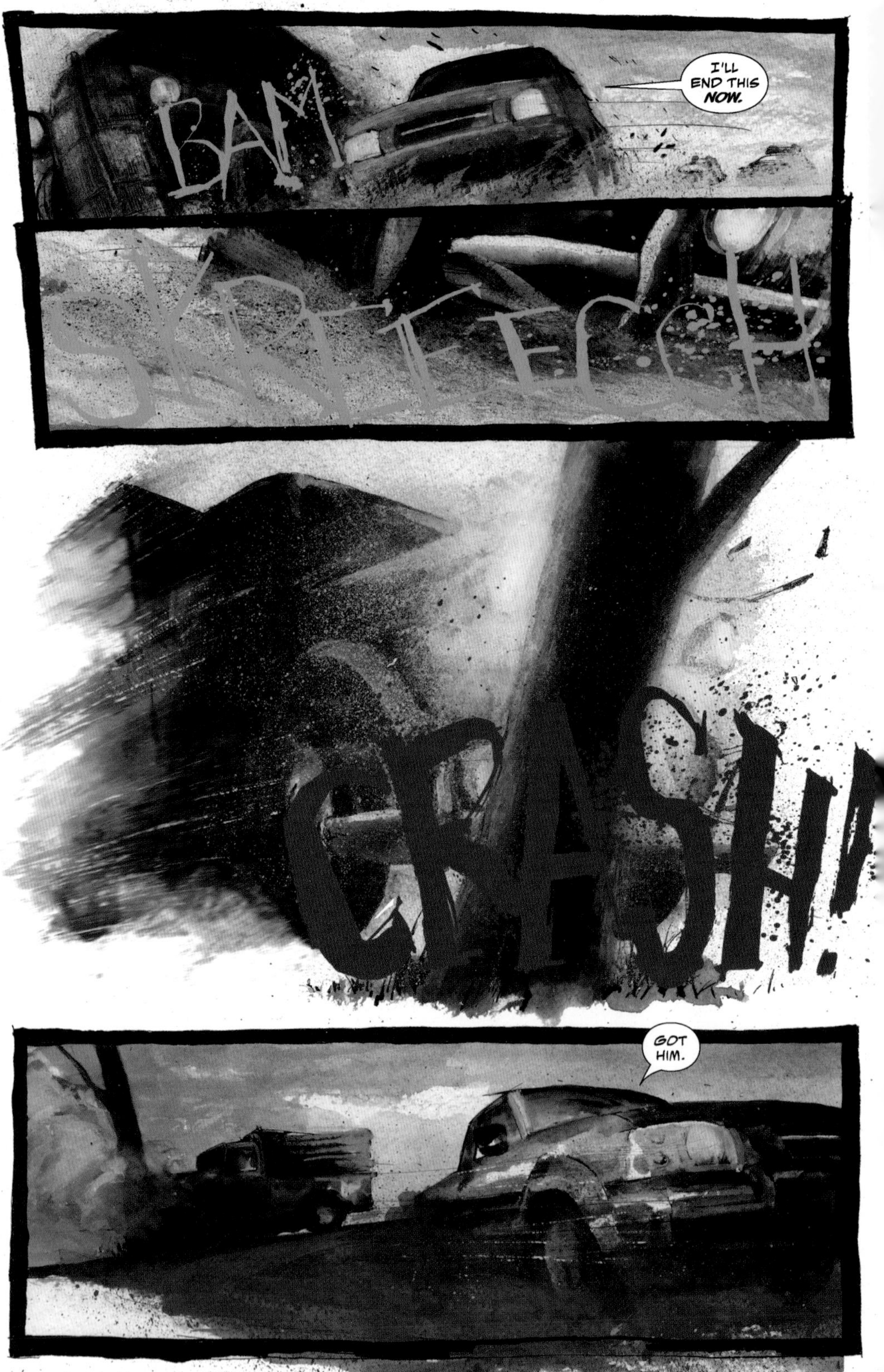
BAM
I'LL END THIS NOW.
SKREEECH!
CRASH!
GOT HIM.

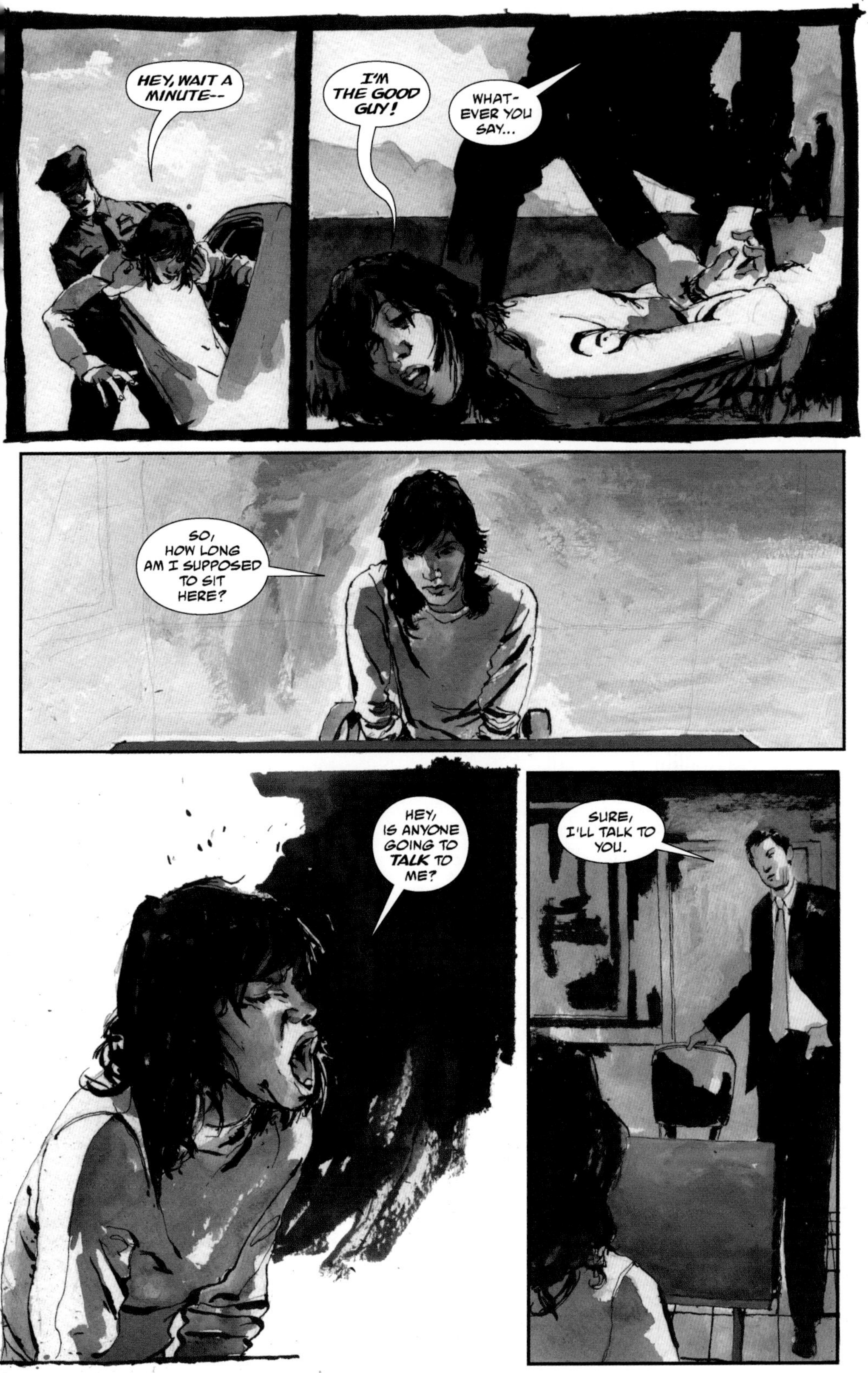
HEY, WAIT A MINUTE--
I'M THE GOOD GUY!
WHAT-EVER YOU SAY...
SO, HOW LONG AM I SUPPOSED TO SIT HERE?
HEY, IS ANYONE GOING TO TALK TO ME?
SURE, I'LL TALK TO YOU.

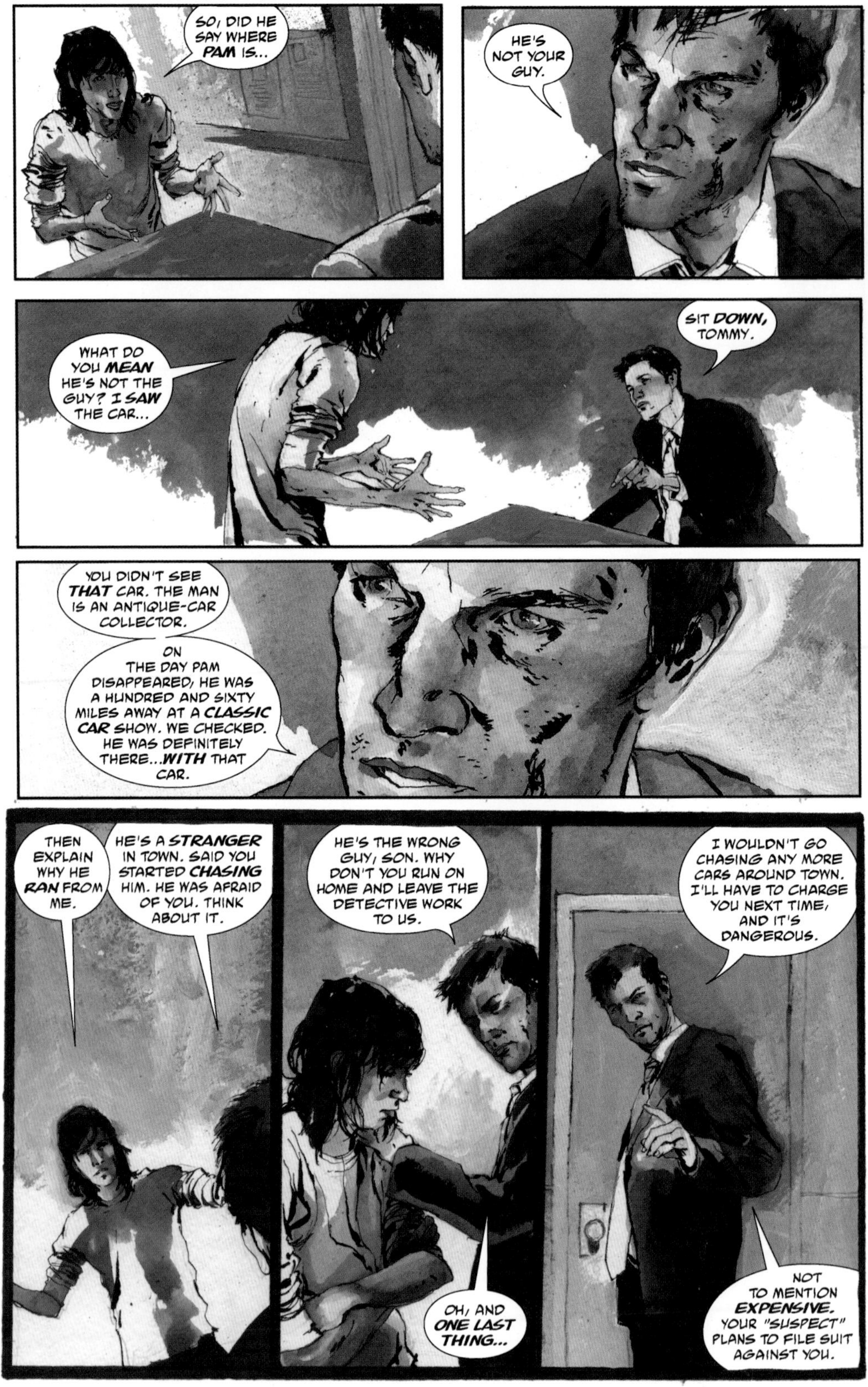
SO, DID HE SAY WHERE PAM IS...
HE'S NOT YOUR GUY.
WHAT DO YOU MEAN HE'S NOT THE GUY? I SAW THE CAR...
SIT DOWN, TOMMY.
YOU DIDN'T SEE THAT CAR. THE MAN IS AN ANTIQUE-CAR COLLECTOR.
ON THE DAY PAM DISAPPEARED, HE WAS A HUNDRED AND SIXTY MILES AWAY AT A CLASSIC CAR SHOW. WE CHECKED. HE WAS DEFINITELY THERE...WITH THAT CAR.
THEN EXPLAIN WHY HE RAN FROM ME.
HE'S A STRANGER IN TOWN. SAID YOU STARTED CHASING HIM. HE WAS AFRAID OF YOU. THINK ABOUT IT.
HE'S THE WRONG GUY, SON. WHY DON'T YOU RUN ON HOME AND LEAVE THE DETECTIVE WORK TO US.
OH, AND ONE LAST THING...
I WOULDN'T GO CHASING ANY MORE CARS AROUND TOWN. I'LL HAVE TO CHARGE YOU NEXT TIME, AND IT'S DANGEROUS.
NOT TO MENTION EXPENSIVE. YOUR "SUSPECT" PLANS TO FILE SUIT AGAINST YOU.

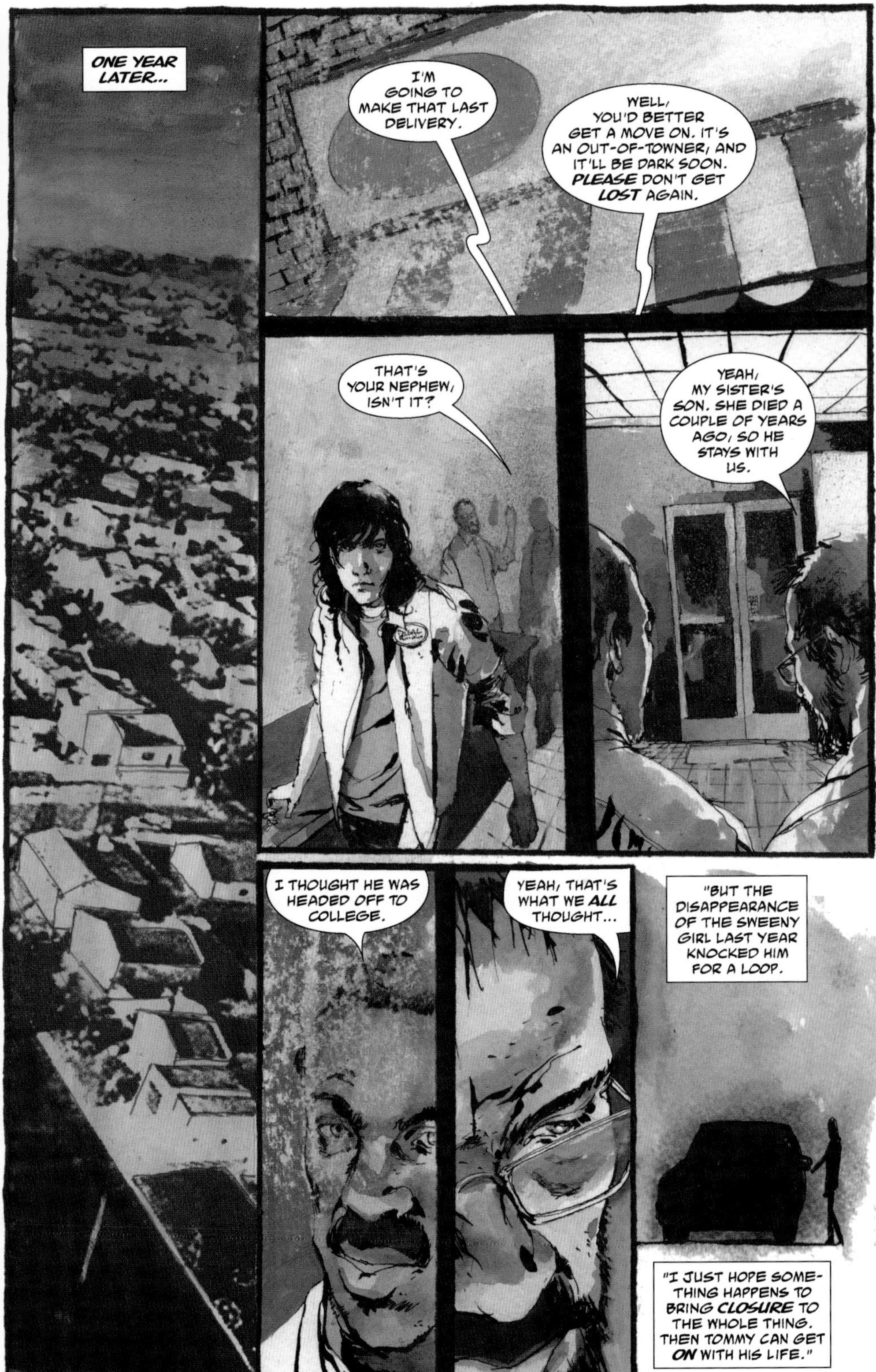
ONE YEAR LATER...
I'M GOING TO MAKE THAT LAST DELIVERY.
WELL, YOU'D BETTER GET A MOVE ON. IT'S AN OUT-OF-TOWNER, AND IT'LL BE DARK SOON. PLEASE DON'T GET LOST AGAIN.
THAT'S YOUR NEPHEW, ISN'T IT?
YEAH, MY SISTER'S SON. SHE DIED A COUPLE OF YEARS AGO, SO HE STAYS WITH US.
I THOUGHT HE WAS HEADED OFF TO COLLEGE.
YEAH, THAT'S WHAT WE ALL THOUGHT...
"BUT THE DISAPPEARANCE OF THE SWEENY GIRL LAST YEAR KNOCKED HIM FOR A LOOP.
"I JUST HOPE SOMETHING HAPPENS TO BRING CLOSURE TO THE WHOLE THING. THEN TOMMY CAN GET ON WITH HIS LIFE."

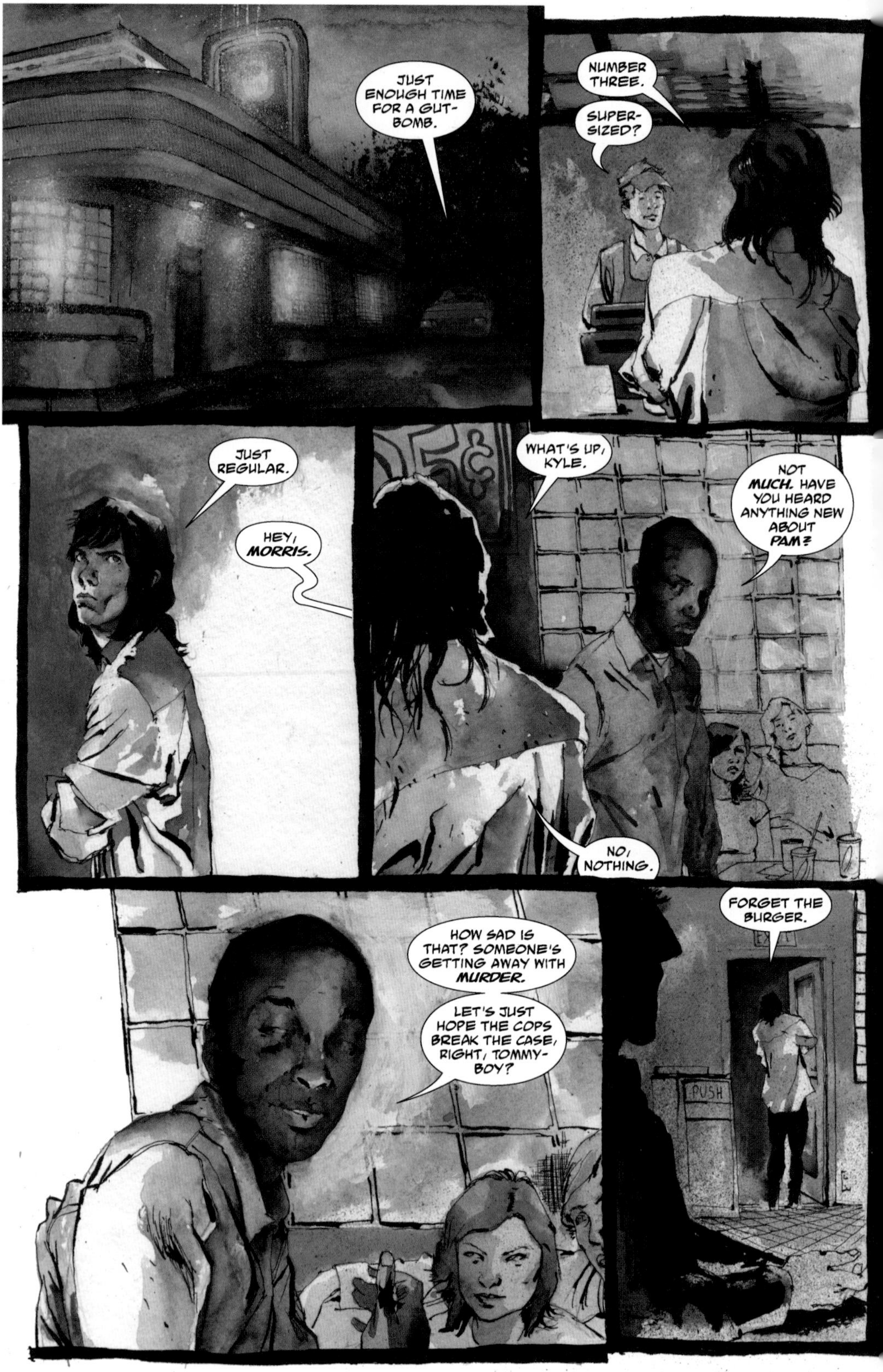
JUST ENOUGH TIME FOR A GUT-BOMB.
NUMBER THREE.
SUPER-SIZED?
JUST REGULAR.
HEY, MORRIS.
WHAT'S UP, KYLE.
NOT MUCH. HAVE YOU HEARD ANYTHING NEW ABOUT PAM?
NO, NOTHING.
HOW SAD IS THAT? SOMEONE'S GETTING AWAY WITH MURDER.
LET'S JUST HOPE THE COPS BREAK THE CASE, RIGHT, TOMMY-BOY?
FORGET THE BURGER.
PUSH

GREAT. I'M LOST AGAIN.

UNCLE PETE'S GONNA *KILL* ME.

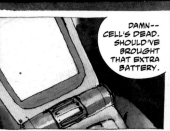

DAMN-- CELL'S DEAD. SHOULD'VE BROUGHT THAT EXTRA BATTERY.

I HAVE NO CLUE WHERE I'M AT...AND IT'S GETTING DARK.

MILLER ROAD...

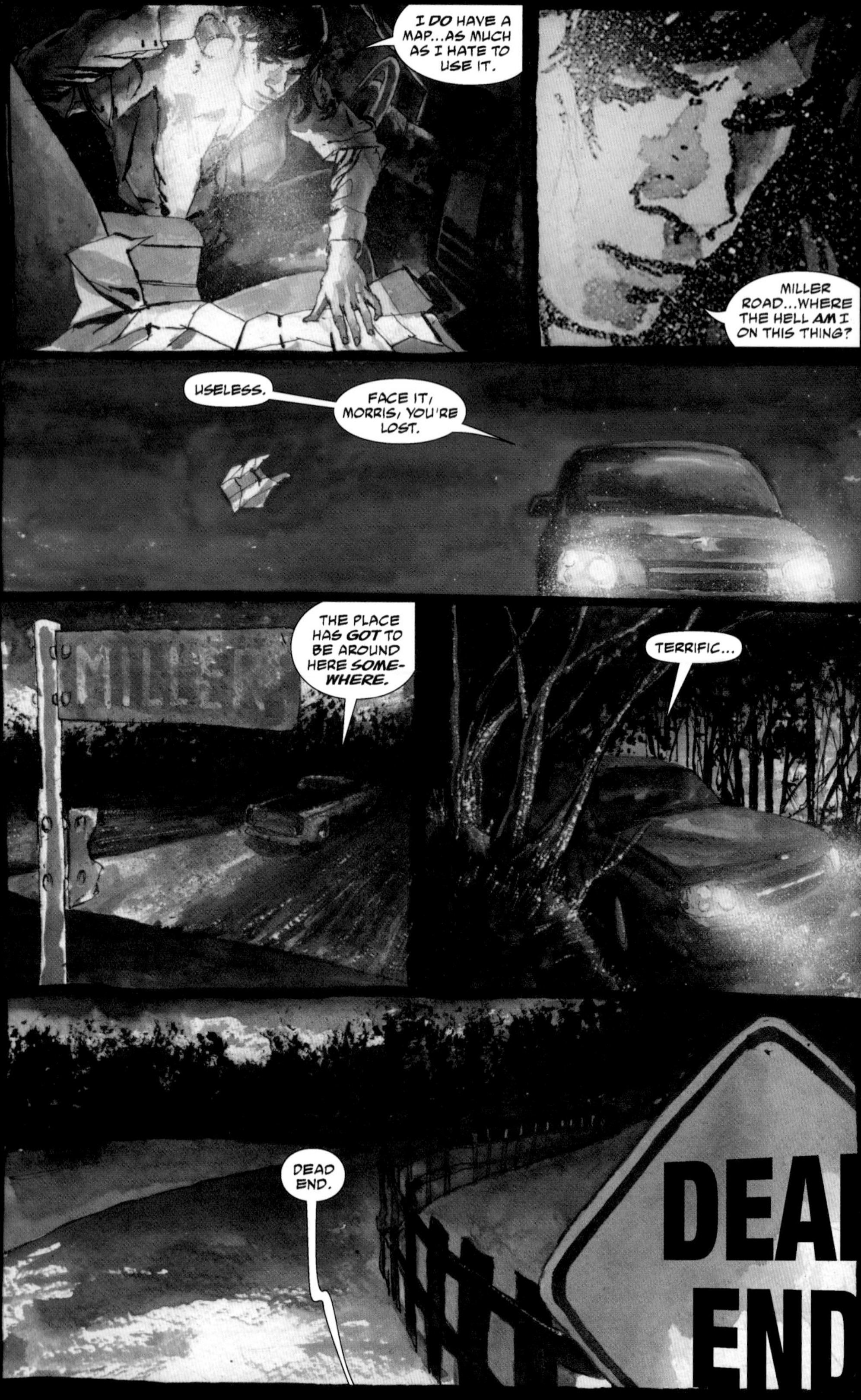

I DO HAVE A MAP...AS MUCH AS I HATE TO USE IT.
MILLER ROAD...WHERE THE HELL AM I ON THIS THING?
USELESS.
FACE IT, MORRIS, YOU'RE LOST.
MILLER
THE PLACE HAS GOT TO BE AROUND HERE SOME-WHERE.
TERRIFIC...
DEAD END.
DEAD END

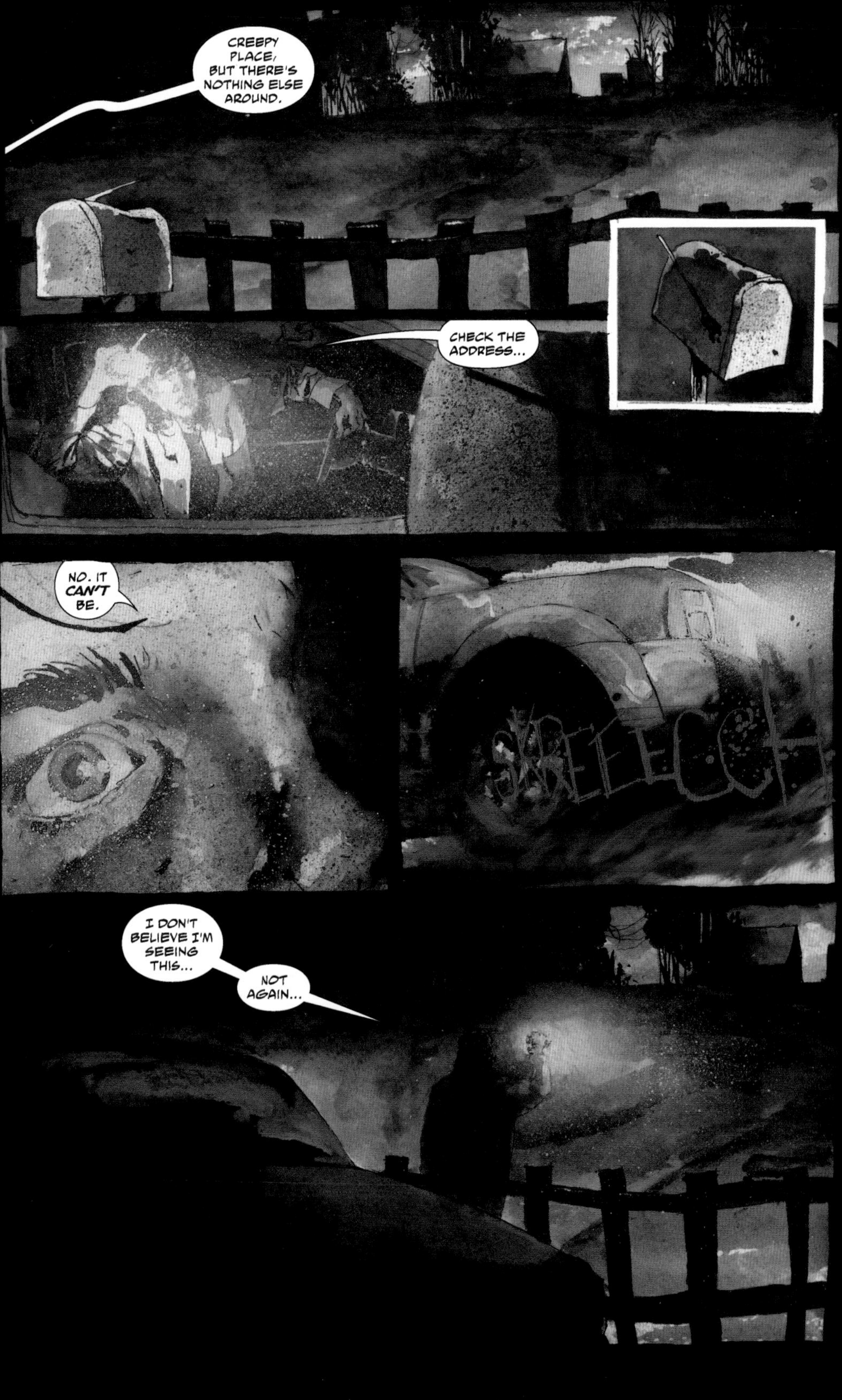
CREEPY PLACE, BUT THERE'S NOTHING ELSE AROUND.
CHECK THE ADDRESS...
NO. IT CAN'T BE.
SKREEECCH
I DON'T BELIEVE I'M SEEING THIS...
NOT AGAIN...

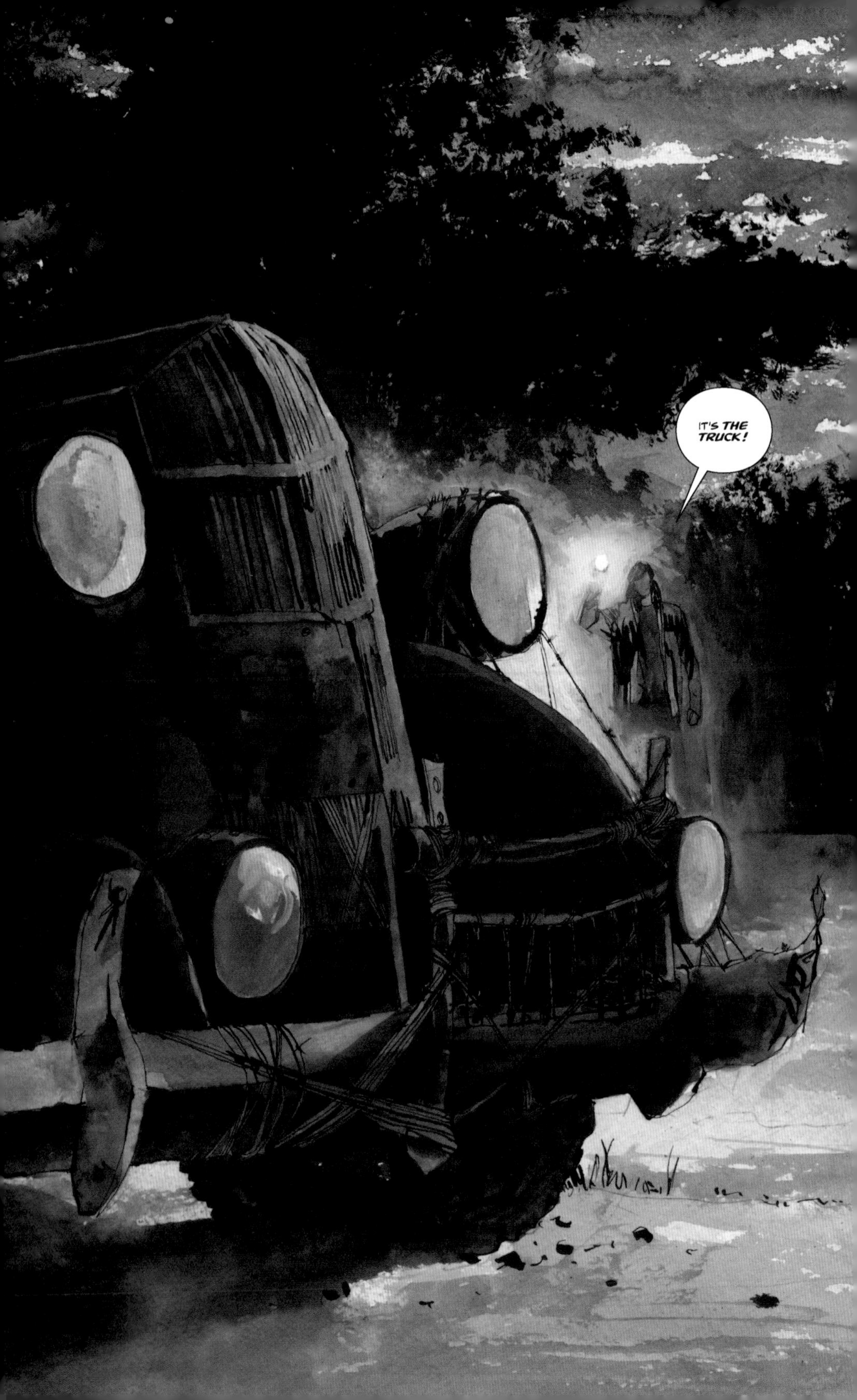
IT'S THE TRUCK!

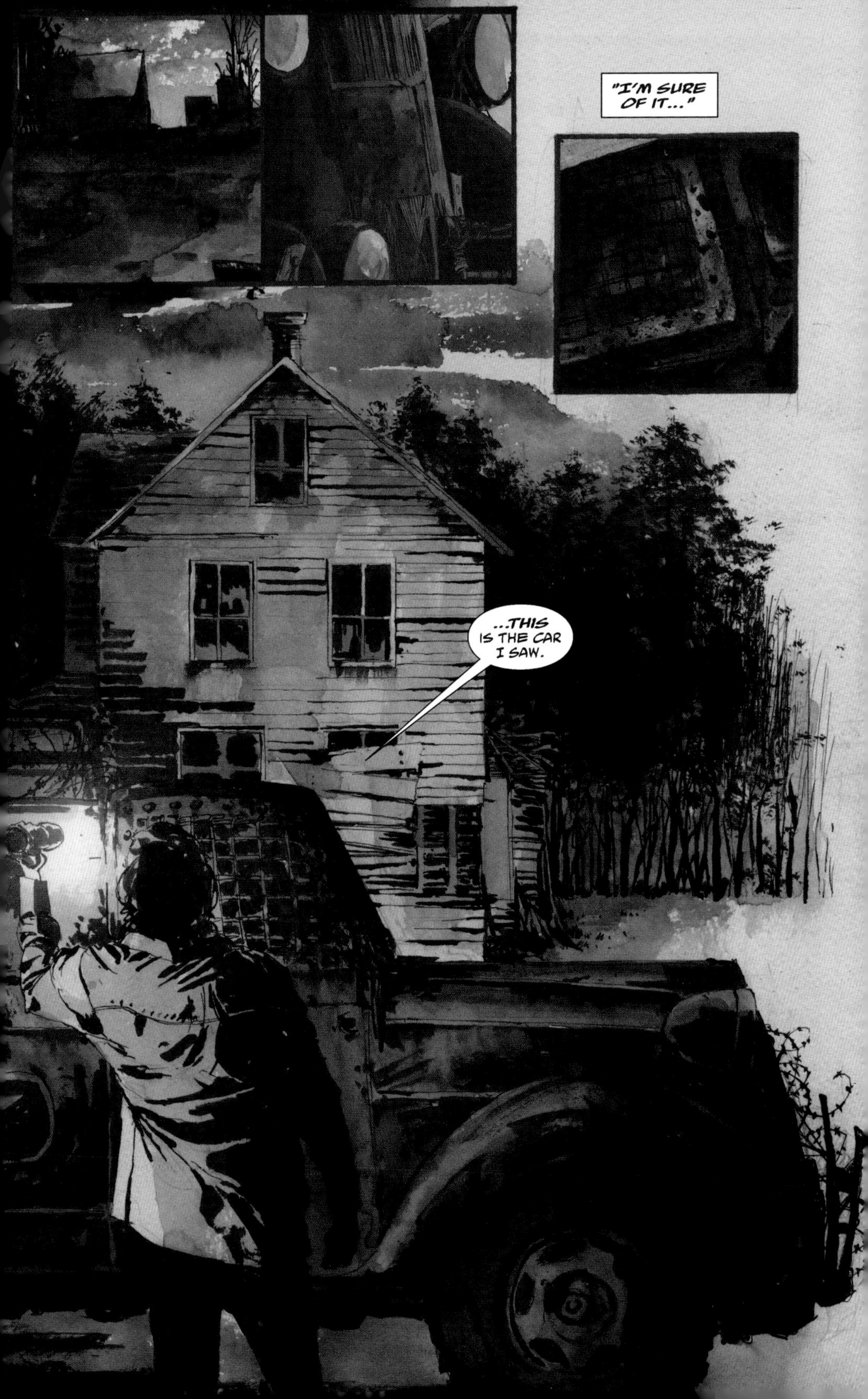
"I'M SURE OF IT..."
...THIS IS THE CAR I SAW.

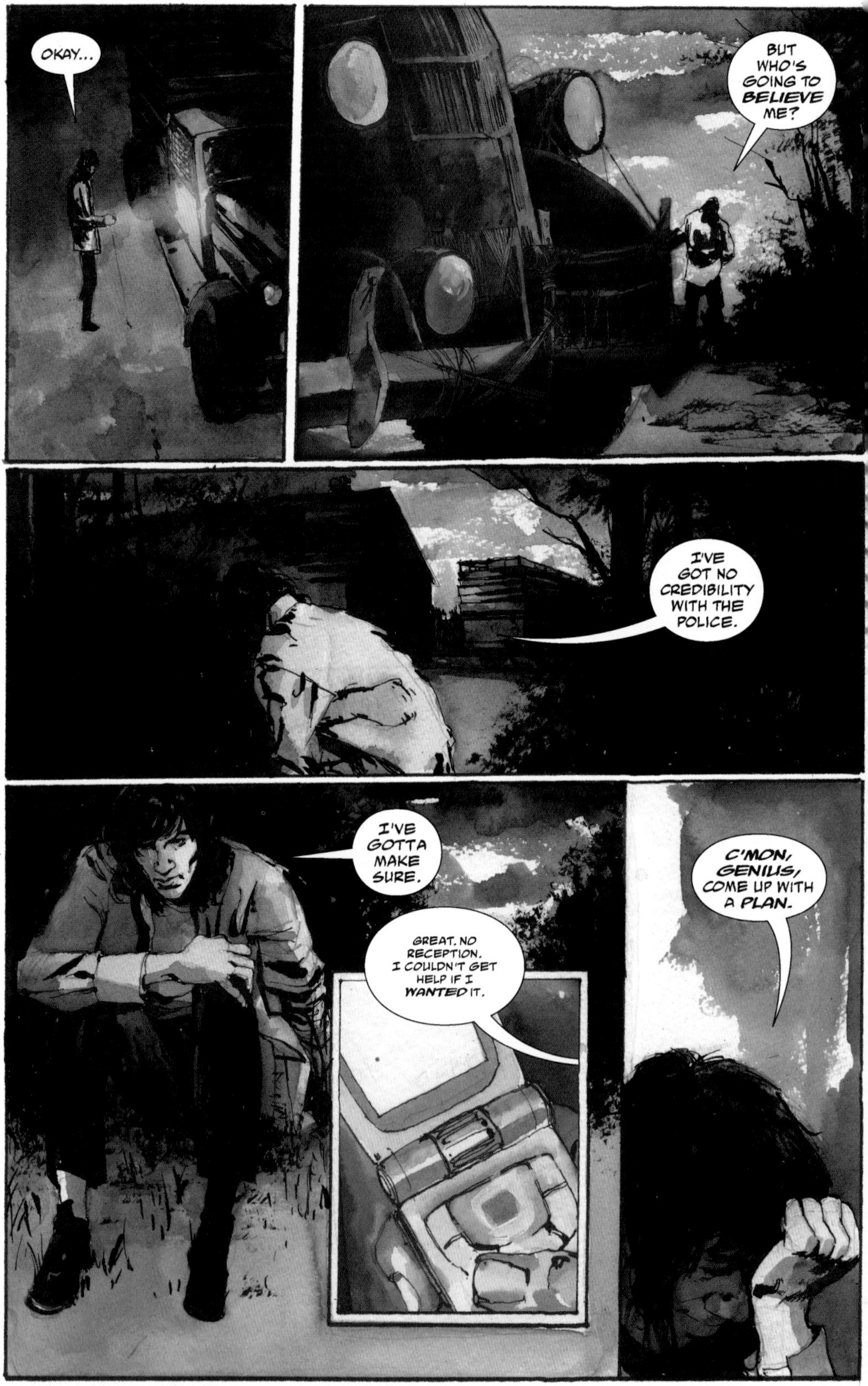
OKAY...
BUT WHO'S GOING TO *BELIEVE* ME?
I'VE GOT NO CREDIBILITY WITH THE POLICE.
I'VE GOTTA MAKE SURE.
GREAT. NO RECEPTION. I COULDN'T GET HELP IF I *WANTED* IT.
C'MON, GENIUS, COME UP WITH A *PLAN*.

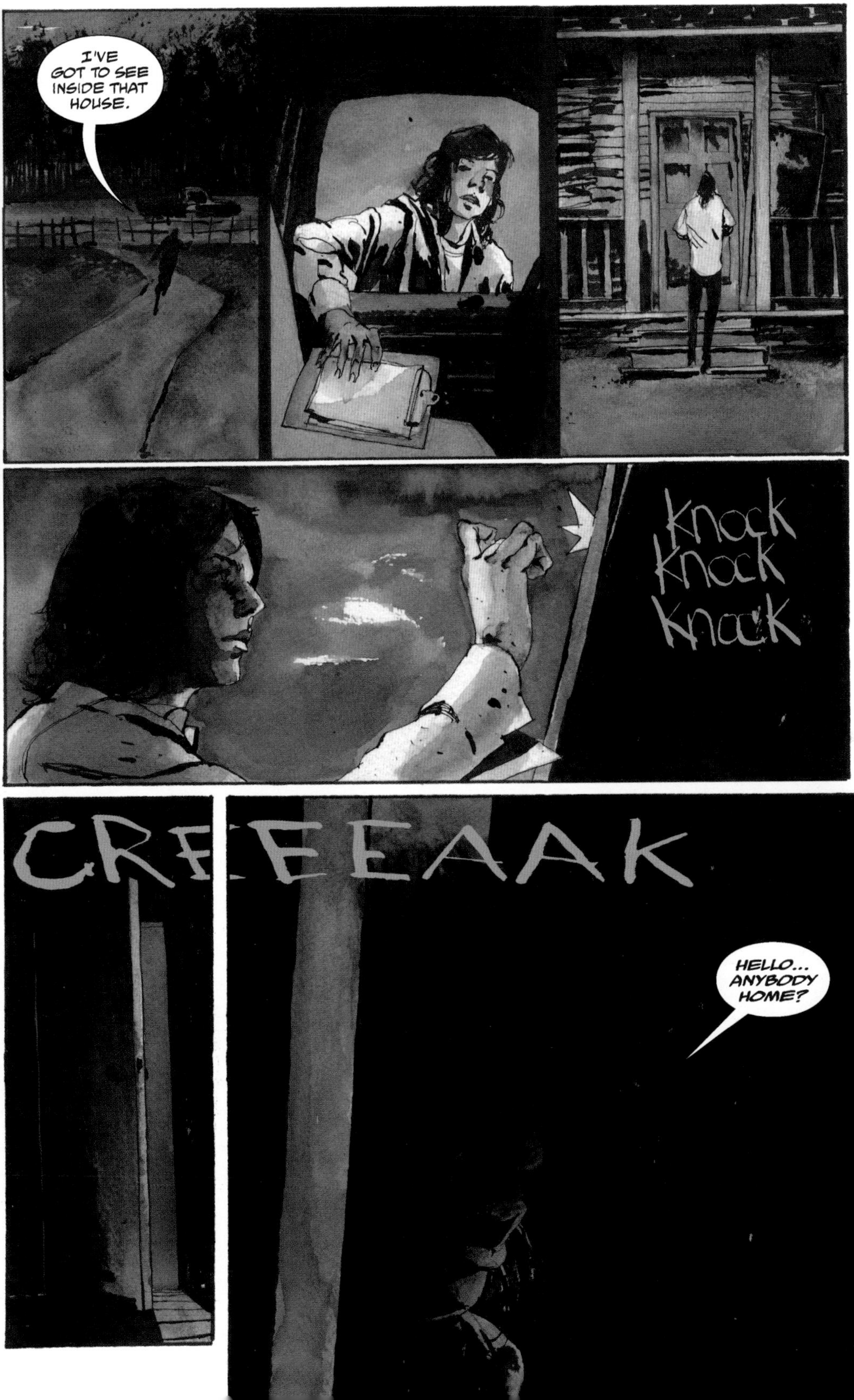
I'VE GOT TO SEE INSIDE THAT HOUSE.
Knock Knock Knock
CREEAAK
HELLO... ANYBODY HOME?

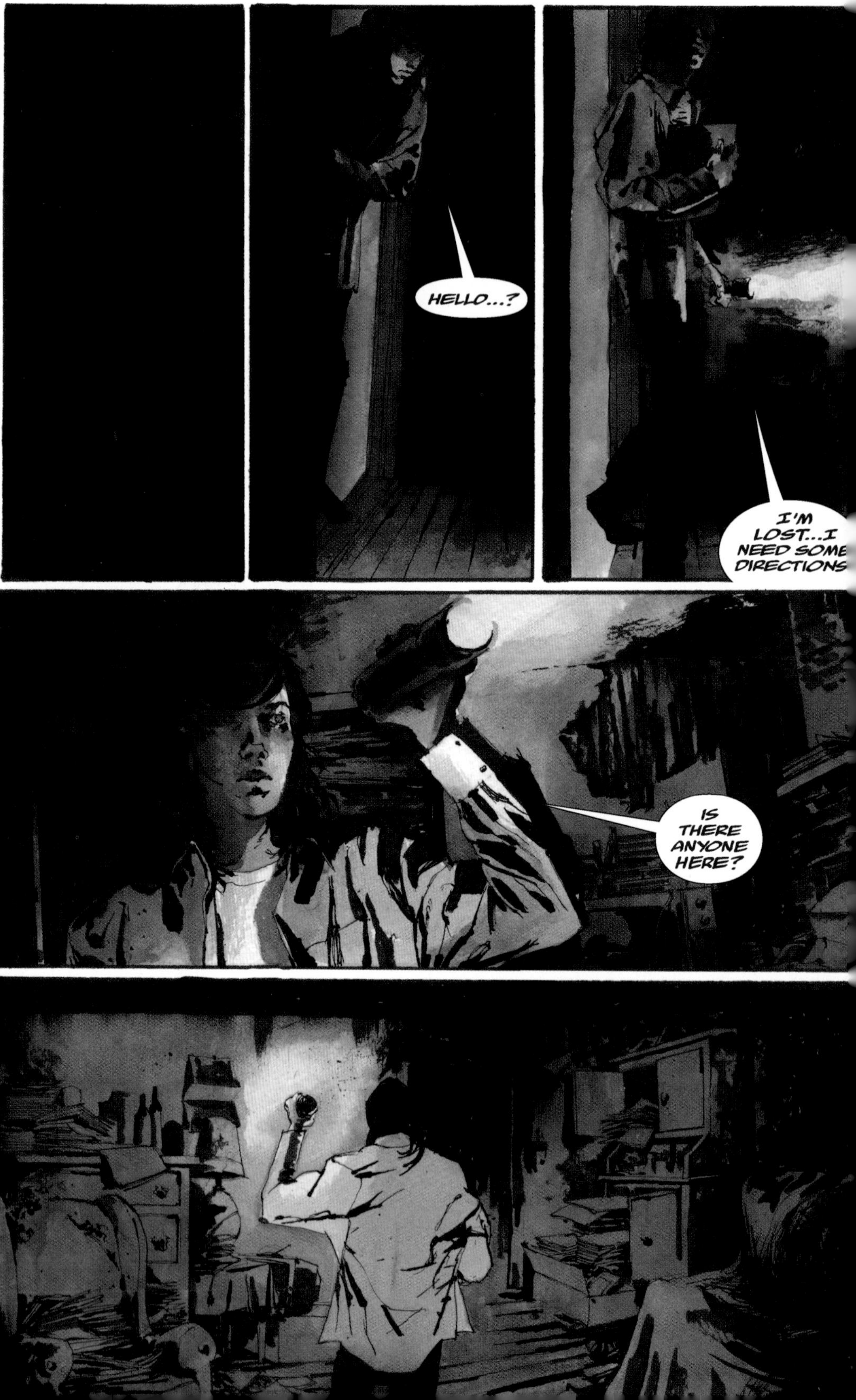
HELLO...?
I'M LOST...I NEED SOME DIRECTIONS
IS THERE ANYONE HERE?

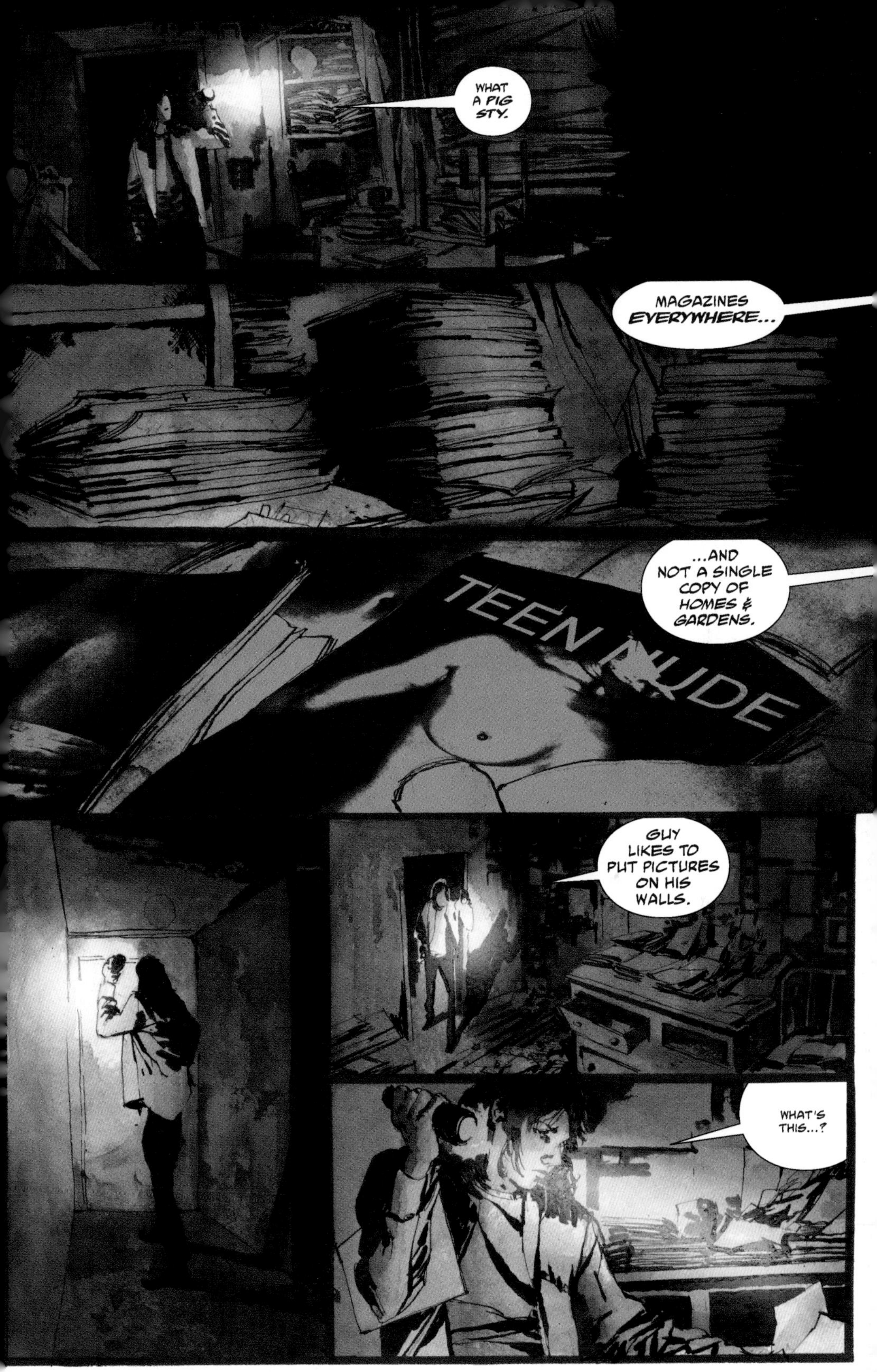
WHAT A PIG STY.
MAGAZINES EVERYWHERE...
...AND NOT A SINGLE COPY OF HOMES & GARDENS.
TEEN NUDE
GUY LIKES TO PUT PICTURES ON HIS WALLS.
WHAT'S THIS...?

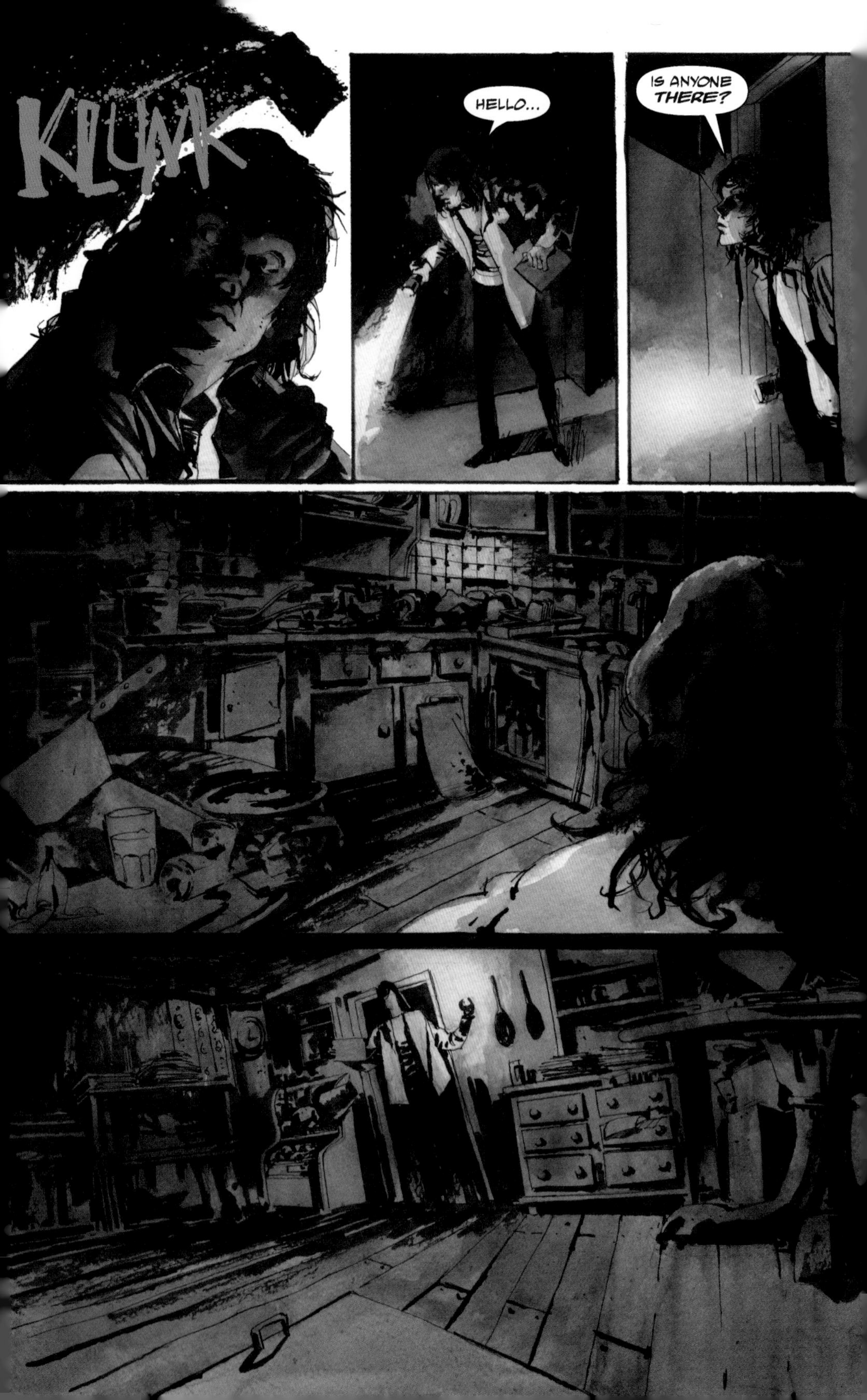
KLUNK
HELLO...
IS ANYONE THERE?

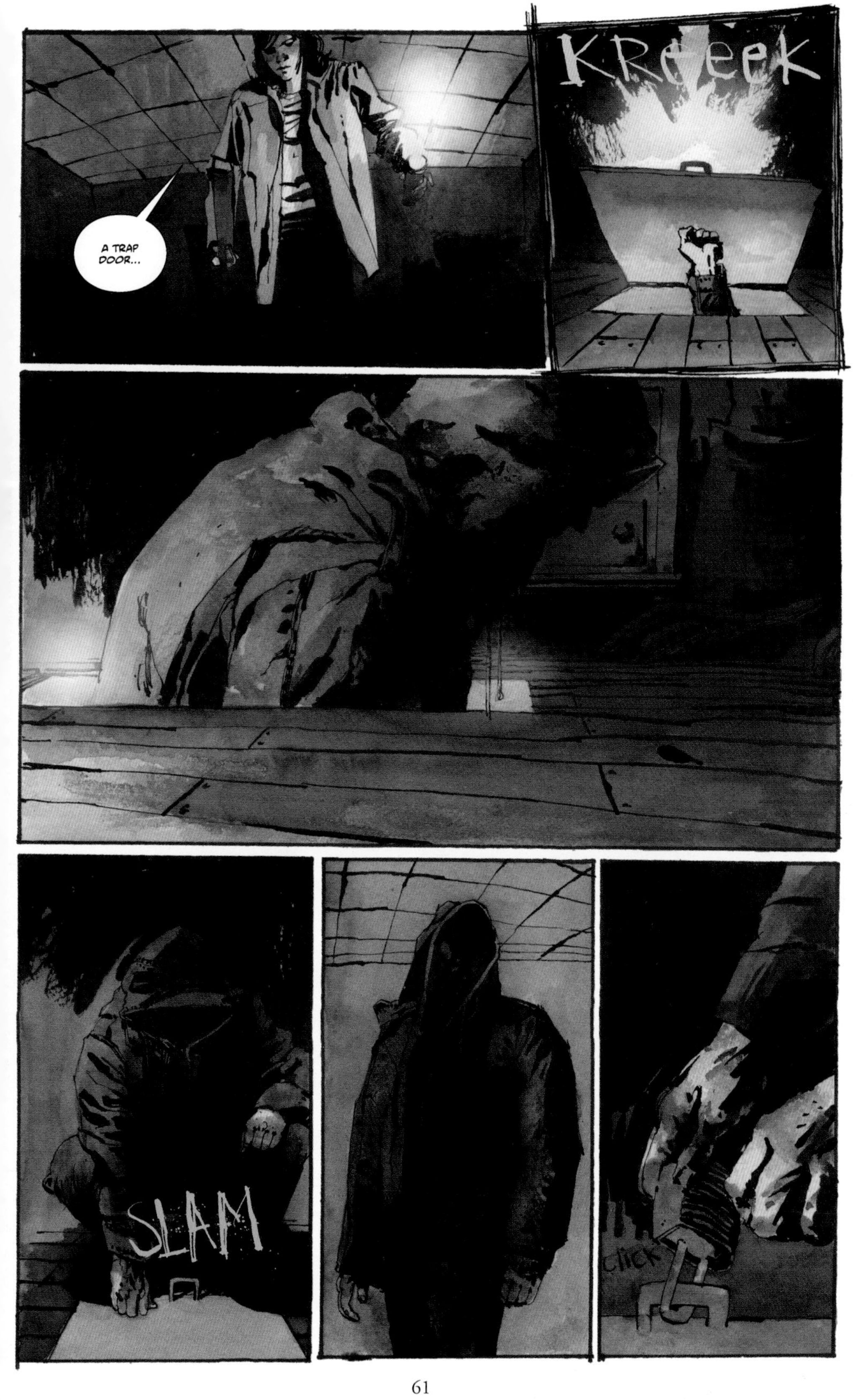
A TRAP DOOR...
KREEEK
SLAM
CLICK

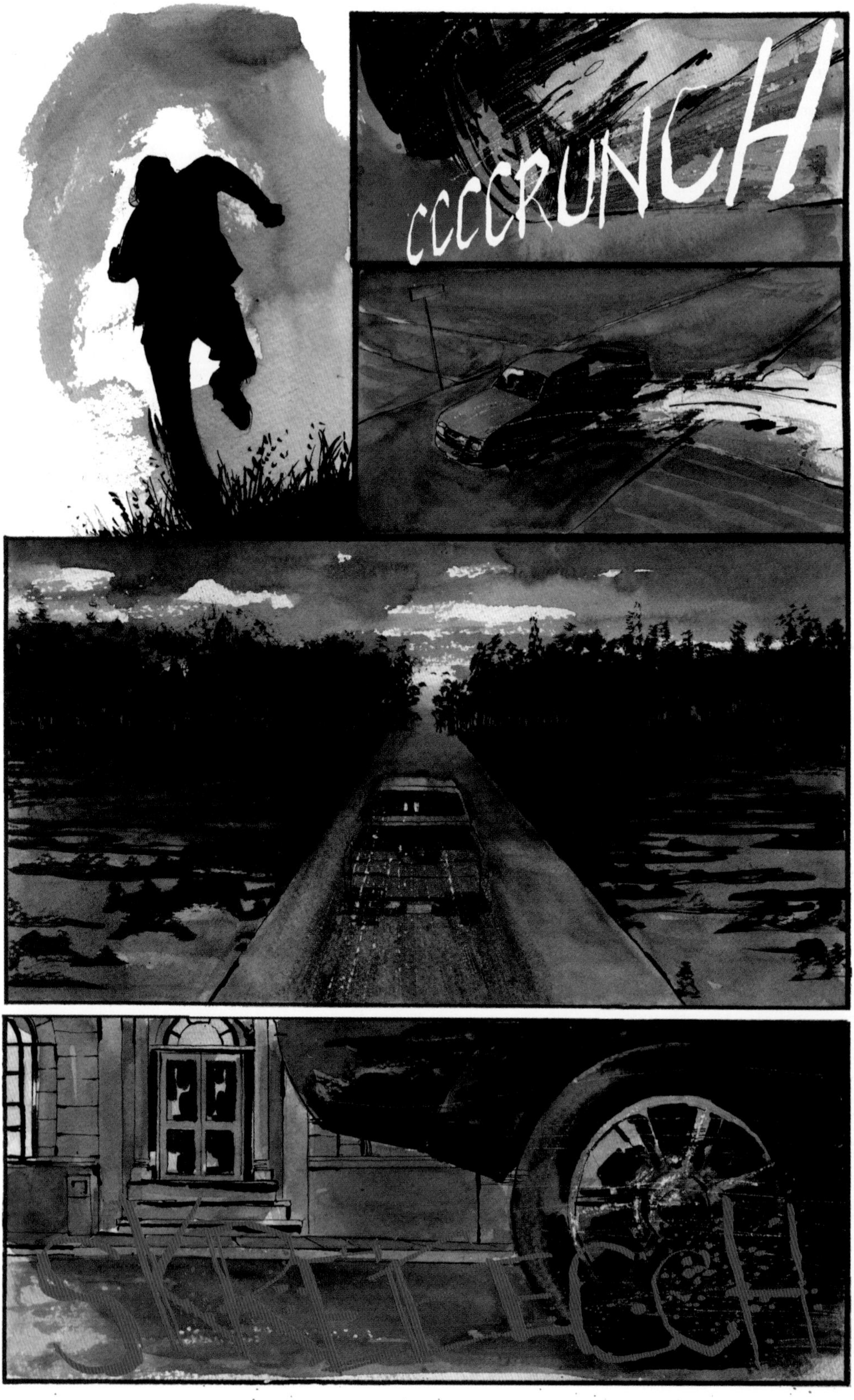
CCCCRUNCH

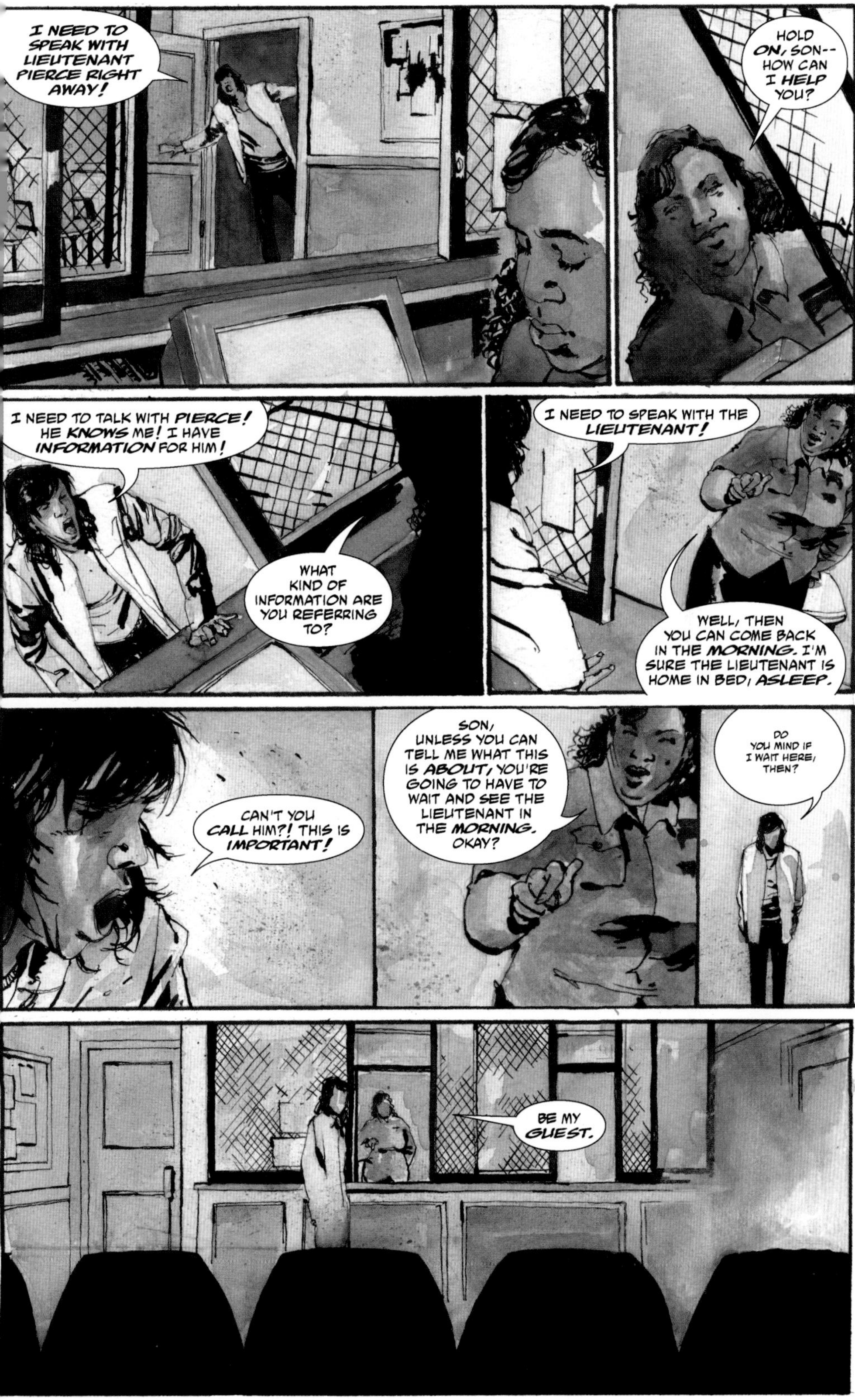
I NEED TO SPEAK WITH LIEUTENANT PIERCE RIGHT AWAY!
HOLD ON, SON-- HOW CAN I HELP YOU?
I NEED TO TALK WITH PIERCE! HE KNOWS ME! I HAVE INFORMATION FOR HIM!
WHAT KIND OF INFORMATION ARE YOU REFERRING TO?
I NEED TO SPEAK WITH THE LIEUTENANT!
WELL, THEN YOU CAN COME BACK IN THE MORNING. I'M SURE THE LIEUTENANT IS HOME IN BED, ASLEEP.
CAN'T YOU CALL HIM?! THIS IS IMPORTANT!
SON, UNLESS YOU CAN TELL ME WHAT THIS IS ABOUT, YOU'RE GOING TO HAVE TO WAIT AND SEE THE LIEUTENANT IN THE MORNING. OKAY?
DO YOU MIND IF I WAIT HERE, THEN?
BE MY GUEST.

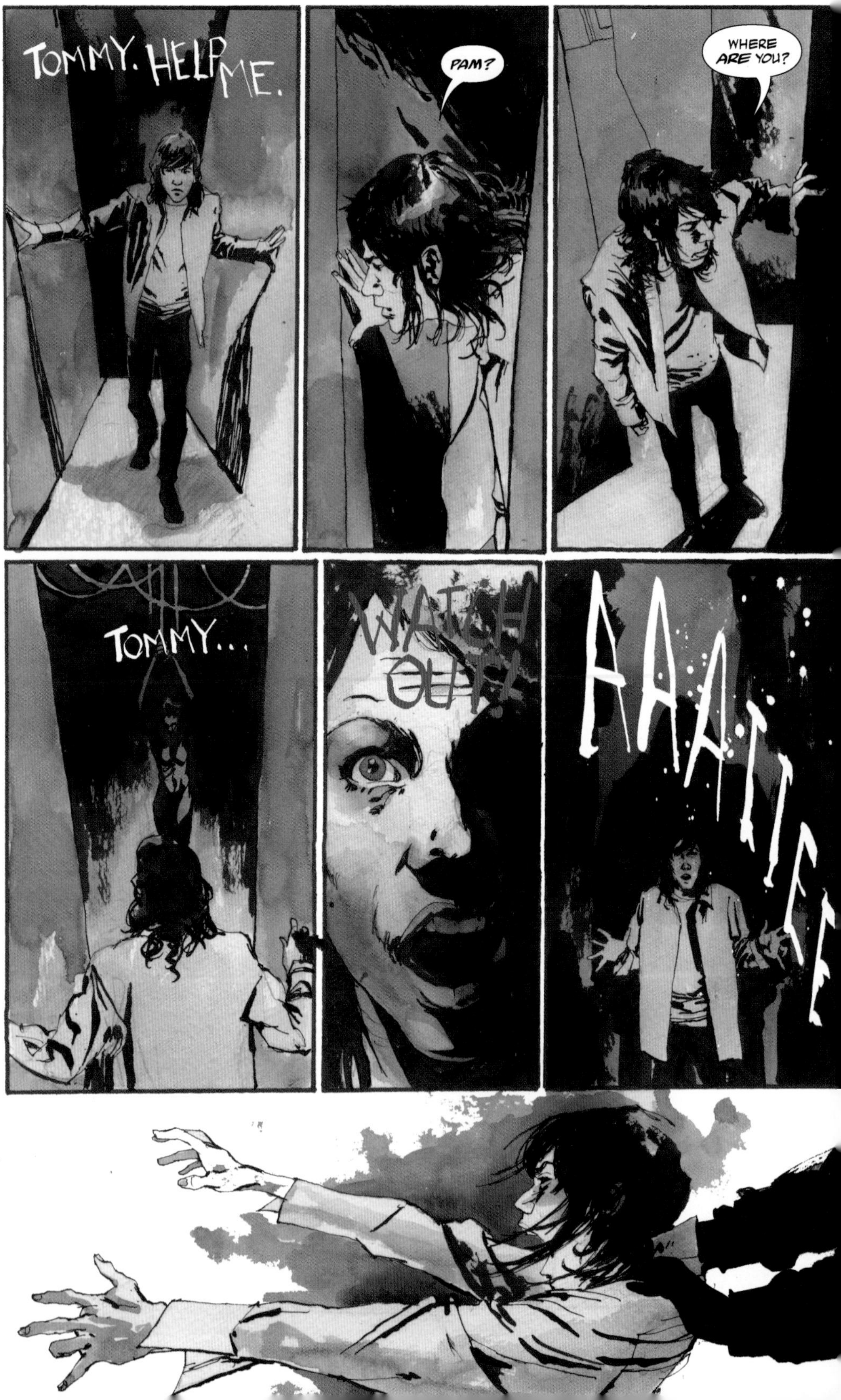
TOMMY. HELP ME.
PAM?
WHERE ARE YOU?
TOMMY...
WATCH OUT!
AAAIIEE

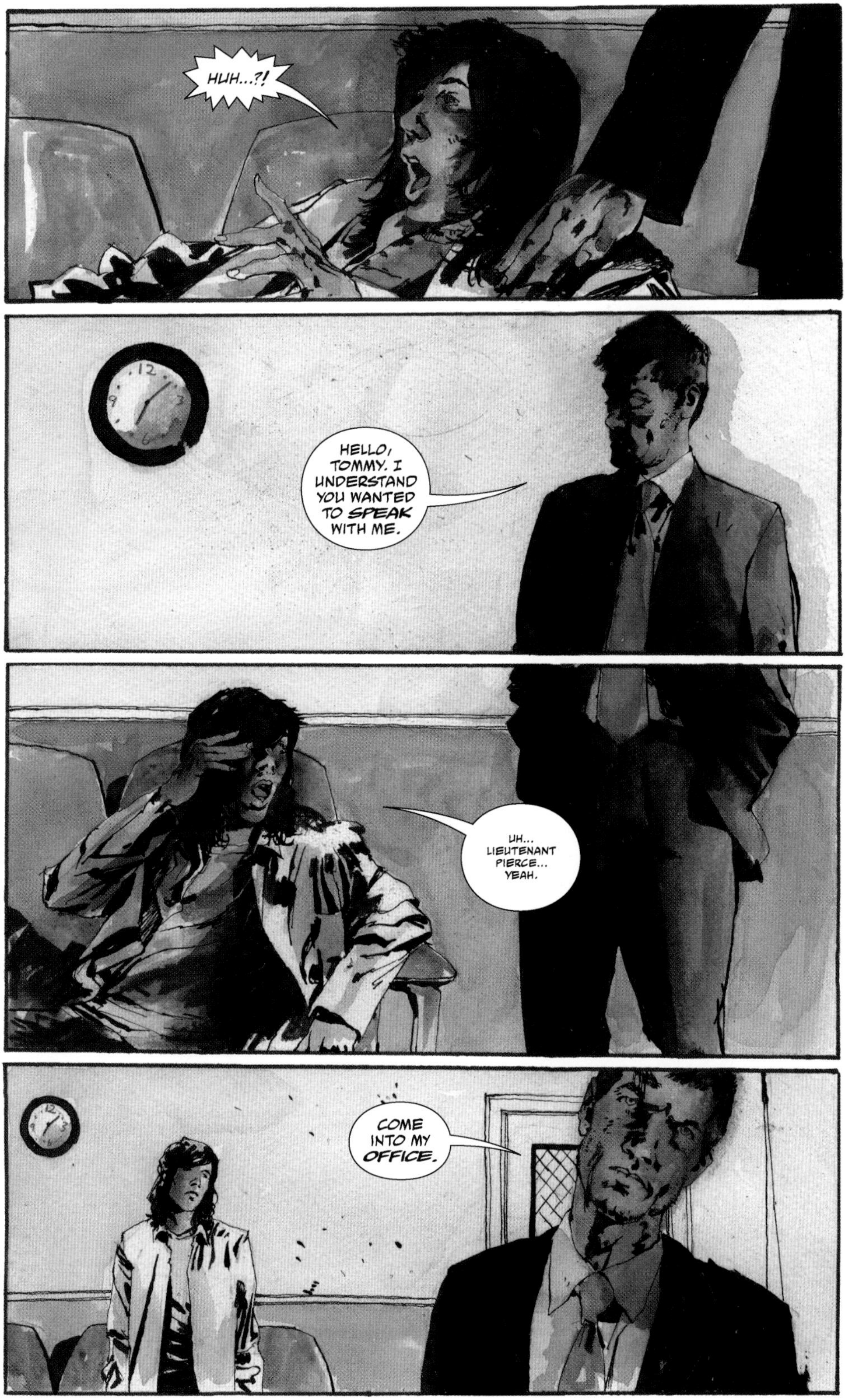
HUH...?!
HELLO, TOMMY. I UNDERSTAND YOU WANTED TO SPEAK WITH ME.
UH... LIEUTENANT PIERCE... YEAH.
COME INTO MY OFFICE.

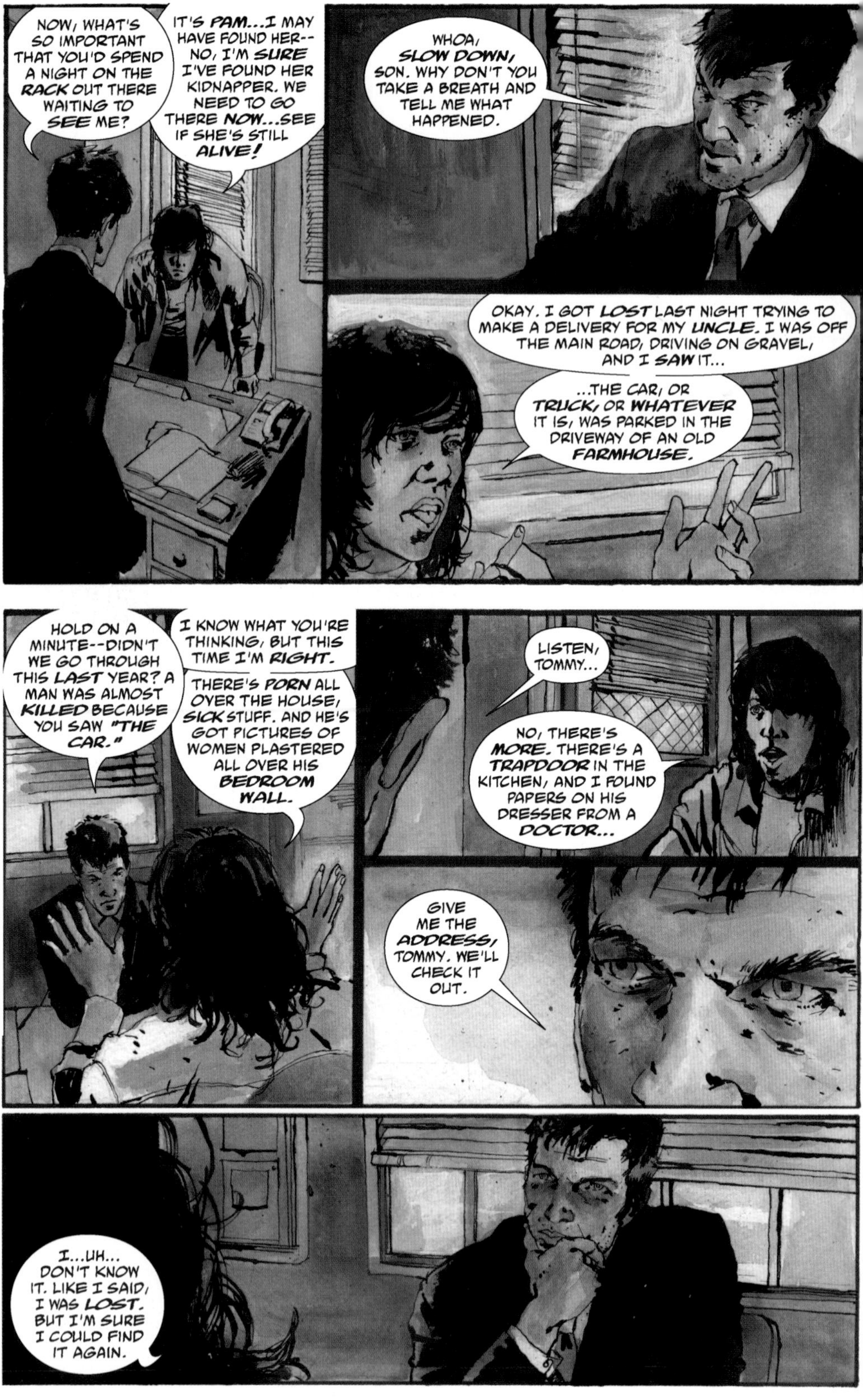
NOW, WHAT'S SO IMPORTANT THAT YOU'D SPEND A NIGHT ON THE RACK OUT THERE WAITING TO SEE ME?
IT'S PAM...I MAY HAVE FOUND HER--NO, I'M SURE I'VE FOUND HER KIDNAPPER. WE NEED TO GO THERE NOW...SEE IF SHE'S STILL ALIVE!
WHOA, SLOW DOWN, SON. WHY DON'T YOU TAKE A BREATH AND TELL ME WHAT HAPPENED.
OKAY. I GOT LOST LAST NIGHT TRYING TO MAKE A DELIVERY FOR MY UNCLE. I WAS OFF THE MAIN ROAD, DRIVING ON GRAVEL, AND I SAW IT...
...THE CAR, OR TRUCK, OR WHATEVER IT IS, WAS PARKED IN THE DRIVEWAY OF AN OLD FARMHOUSE.
HOLD ON A MINUTE--DIDN'T WE GO THROUGH THIS LAST YEAR? A MAN WAS ALMOST KILLED BECAUSE YOU SAW "THE CAR."
I KNOW WHAT YOU'RE THINKING, BUT THIS TIME I'M RIGHT.
THERE'S PORN ALL OVER THE HOUSE, SICK STUFF. AND HE'S GOT PICTURES OF WOMEN PLASTERED ALL OVER HIS BEDROOM WALL.
LISTEN, TOMMY...
NO, THERE'S MORE. THERE'S A TRAPDOOR IN THE KITCHEN, AND I FOUND PAPERS ON HIS DRESSER FROM A DOCTOR...
GIVE ME THE ADDRESS, TOMMY. WE'LL CHECK IT OUT.
I...UH... DON'T KNOW IT. LIKE I SAID, I WAS LOST. BUT I'M SURE I COULD FIND IT AGAIN.

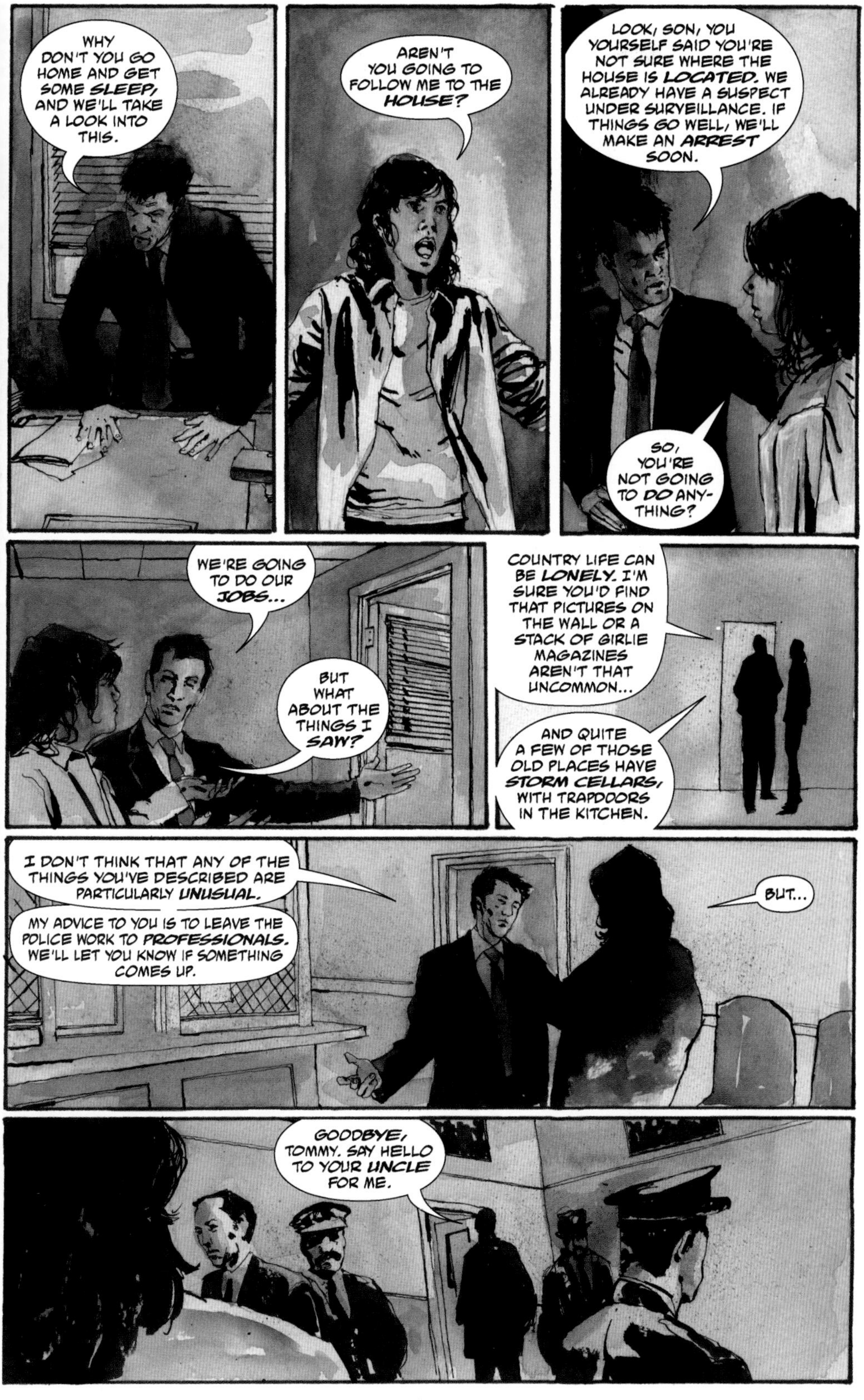
WHY DON'T YOU GO HOME AND GET SOME SLEEP, AND WE'LL TAKE A LOOK INTO THIS.
AREN'T YOU GOING TO FOLLOW ME TO THE HOUSE?
LOOK, SON, YOU YOURSELF SAID YOU'RE NOT SURE WHERE THE HOUSE IS LOCATED. WE ALREADY HAVE A SUSPECT UNDER SURVEILLANCE. IF THINGS GO WELL, WE'LL MAKE AN ARREST SOON.
SO, YOU'RE NOT GOING TO DO ANYTHING?
WE'RE GOING TO DO OUR JOBS...
BUT WHAT ABOUT THE THINGS I SAW?
COUNTRY LIFE CAN BE LONELY. I'M SURE YOU'D FIND THAT PICTURES ON THE WALL OR A STACK OF GIRLIE MAGAZINES AREN'T THAT UNCOMMON...
AND QUITE A FEW OF THOSE OLD PLACES HAVE STORM CELLARS, WITH TRAPDOORS IN THE KITCHEN.
I DON'T THINK THAT ANY OF THE THINGS YOU'VE DESCRIBED ARE PARTICULARLY UNUSUAL.
MY ADVICE TO YOU IS TO LEAVE THE POLICE WORK TO PROFESSIONALS. WE'LL LET YOU KNOW IF SOMETHING COMES UP.
BUT...
GOODBYE, TOMMY. SAY HELLO TO YOUR UNCLE FOR ME.

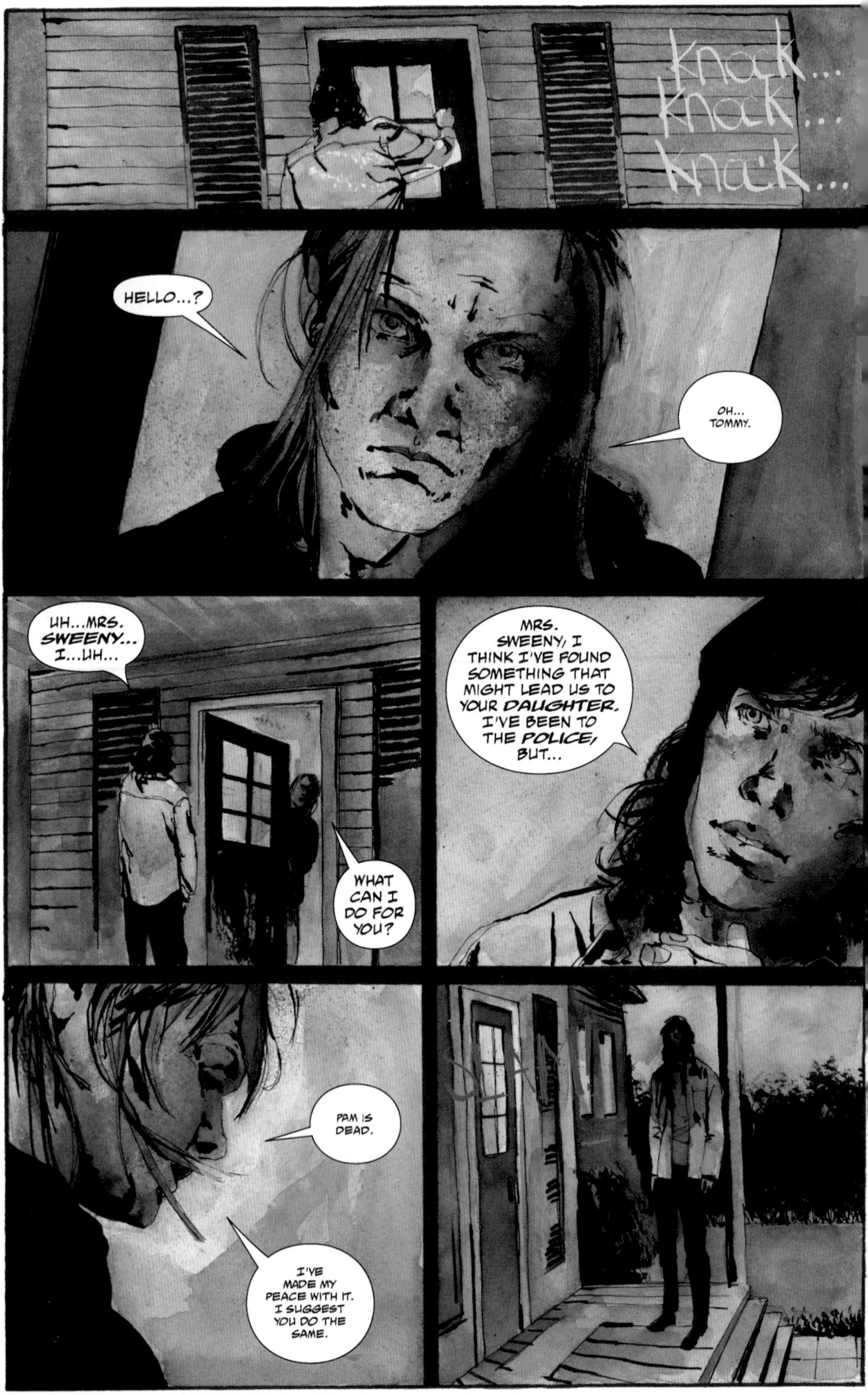
Knock... Knock... Knock...
HELLO...?
OH... TOMMY.
UH...MRS. SWEENY... I...UH...
WHAT CAN I DO FOR YOU?
MRS. SWEENY, I THINK I'VE FOUND SOMETHING THAT MIGHT LEAD US TO YOUR DAUGHTER. I'VE BEEN TO THE POLICE, BUT...
PAM IS DEAD.
I'VE MADE MY PEACE WITH IT. I SUGGEST YOU DO THE SAME.

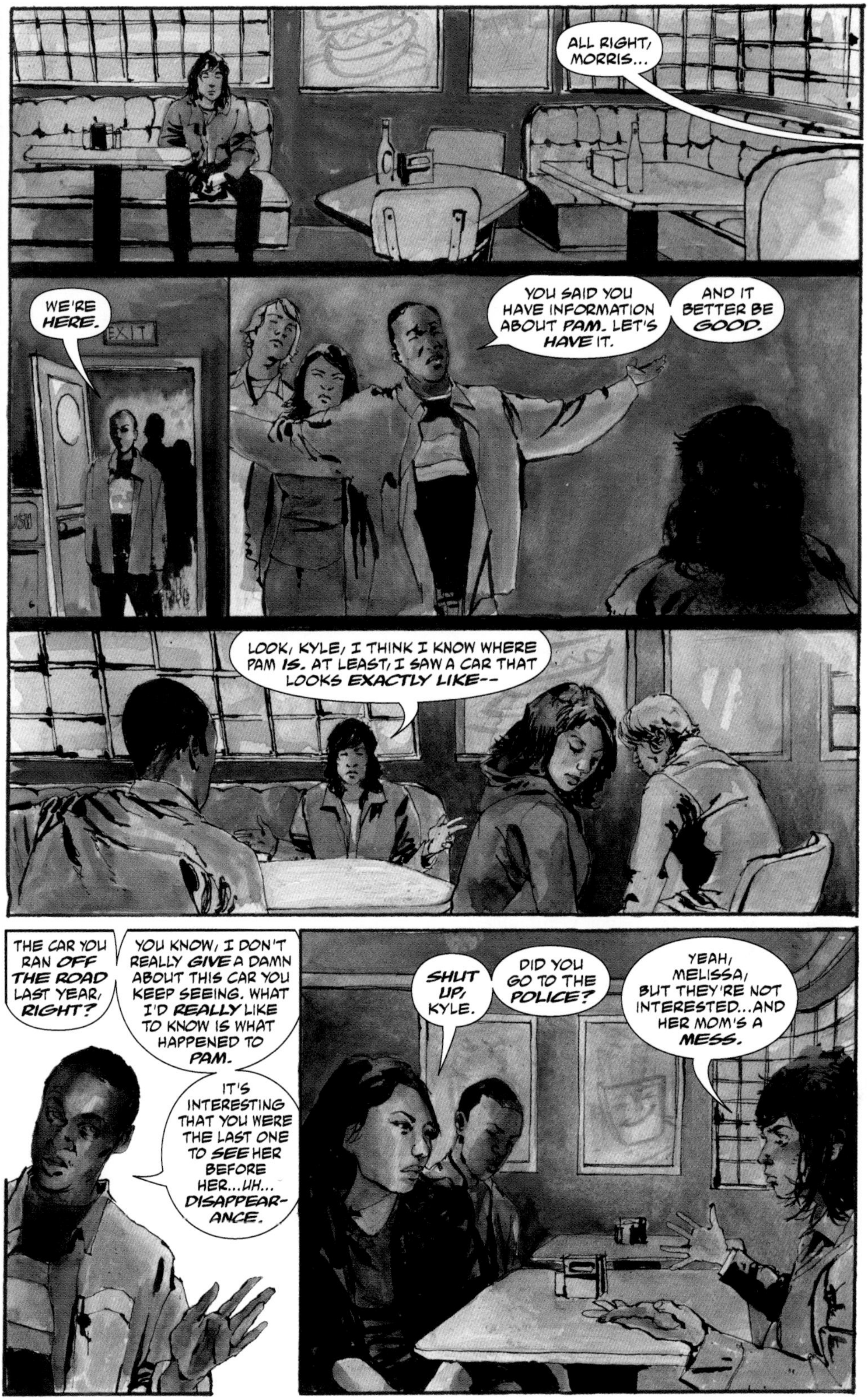
ALL RIGHT, MORRIS...
WE'RE HERE.
EXIT
YOU SAID YOU HAVE INFORMATION ABOUT PAM. LET'S HAVE IT.
AND IT BETTER BE GOOD.
LOOK, KYLE, I THINK I KNOW WHERE PAM IS. AT LEAST, I SAW A CAR THAT LOOKS EXACTLY LIKE--
THE CAR YOU RAN OFF THE ROAD LAST YEAR, RIGHT?
YOU KNOW, I DON'T REALLY GIVE A DAMN ABOUT THIS CAR YOU KEEP SEEING. WHAT I'D REALLY LIKE TO KNOW IS WHAT HAPPENED TO PAM.
IT'S INTERESTING THAT YOU WERE THE LAST ONE TO SEE HER BEFORE HER...UH... DISAPPEARANCE.
SHUT UP, KYLE.
DID YOU GO TO THE POLICE?
YEAH, MELISSA, BUT THEY'RE NOT INTERESTED...AND HER MOM'S A MESS.

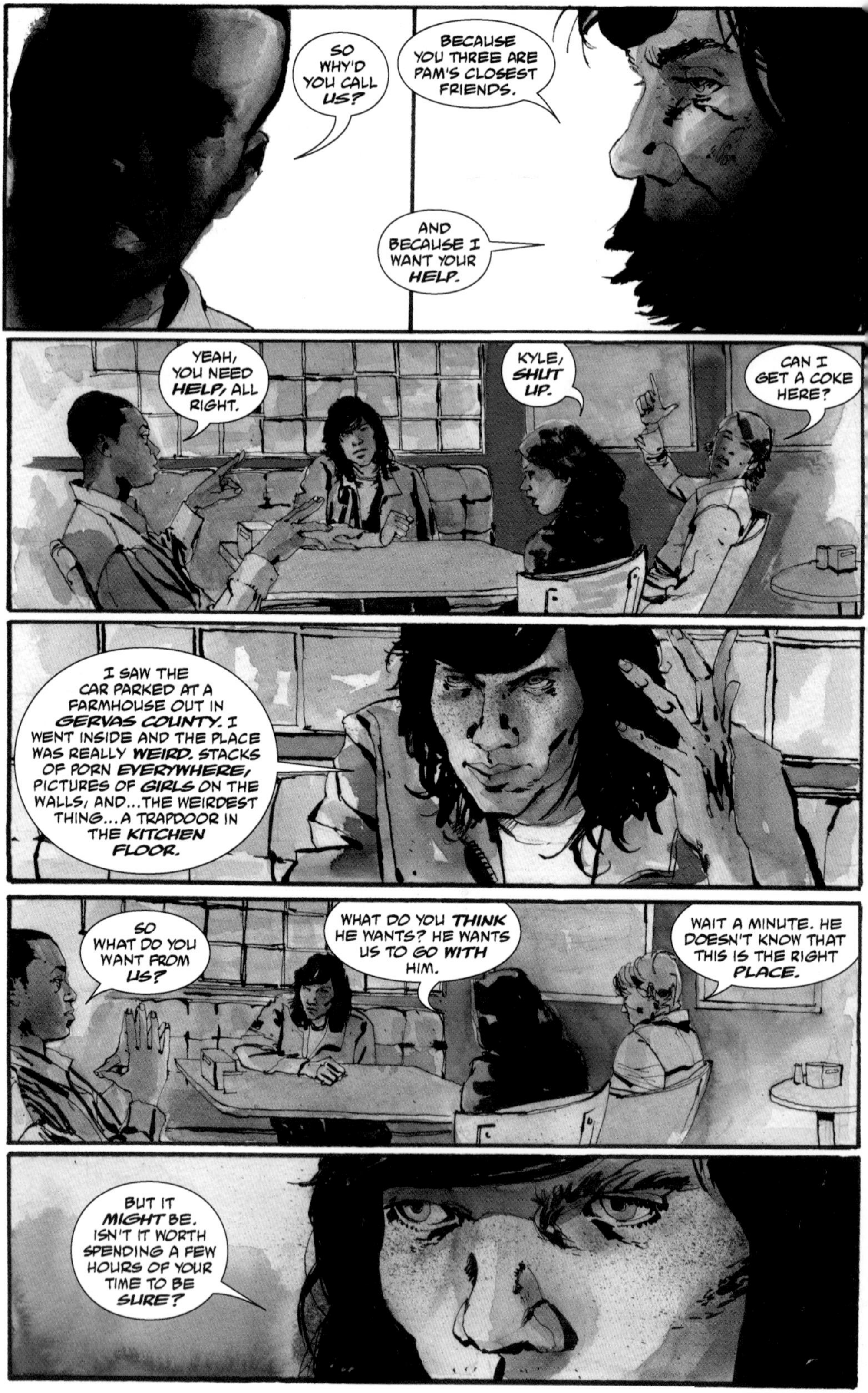
SO WHY'D YOU CALL US?
BECAUSE YOU THREE ARE PAM'S CLOSEST FRIENDS.
AND BECAUSE I WANT YOUR HELP.
YEAH, YOU NEED HELP, ALL RIGHT.
KYLE, SHUT UP.
CAN I GET A COKE HERE?
I SAW THE CAR PARKED AT A FARMHOUSE OUT IN GERVAS COUNTY. I WENT INSIDE AND THE PLACE WAS REALLY WEIRD. STACKS OF PORN EVERYWHERE, PICTURES OF GIRLS ON THE WALLS, AND...THE WEIRDEST THING...A TRAPDOOR IN THE KITCHEN FLOOR.
SO WHAT DO YOU WANT FROM US?
WHAT DO YOU THINK HE WANTS? HE WANTS US TO GO WITH HIM.
WAIT A MINUTE. HE DOESN'T KNOW THAT THIS IS THE RIGHT PLACE.
BUT IT MIGHT BE. ISN'T IT WORTH SPENDING A FEW HOURS OF YOUR TIME TO BE SURE?

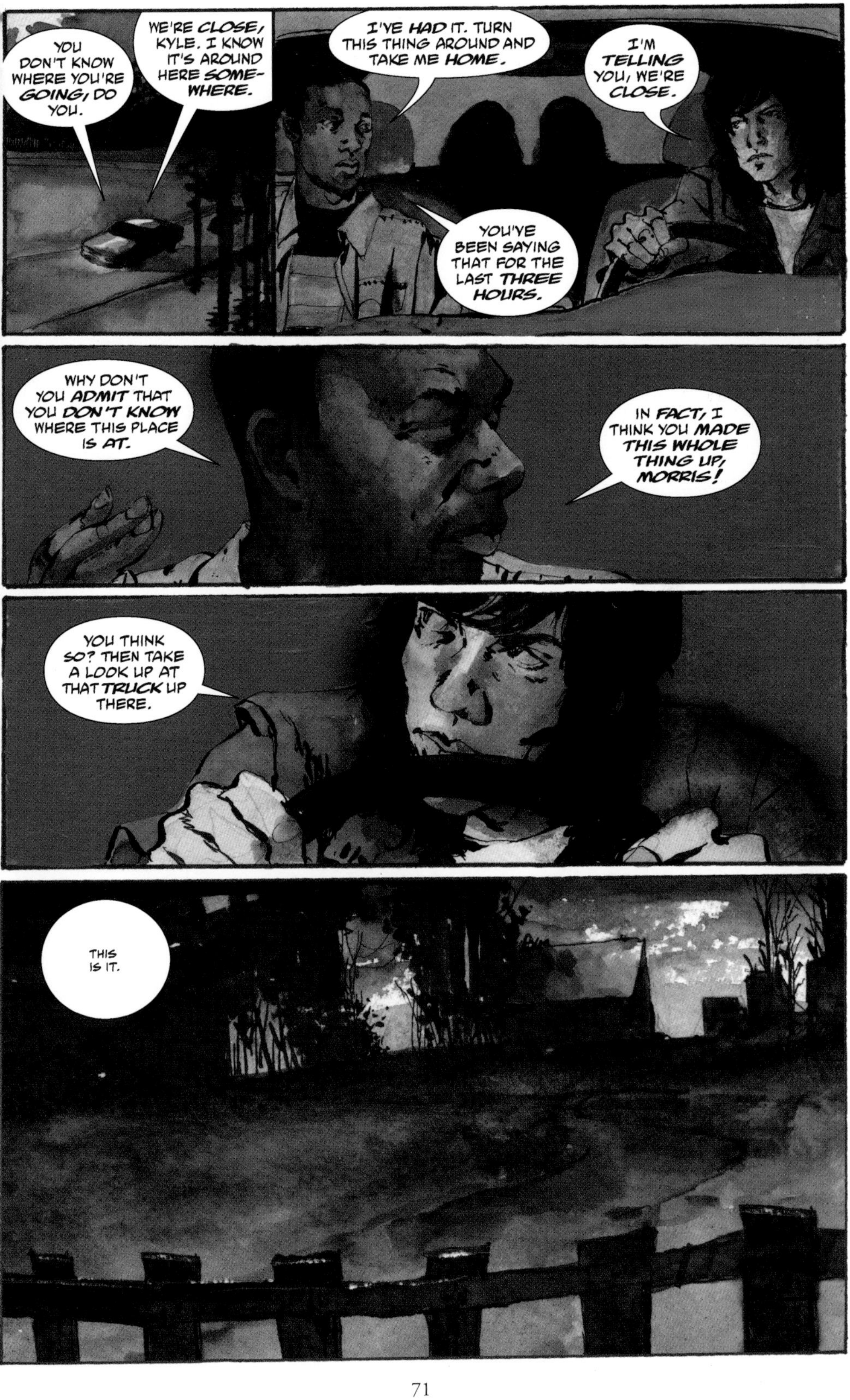
YOU DON'T KNOW WHERE YOU'RE GOING, DO YOU.
WE'RE CLOSE, KYLE. I KNOW IT'S AROUND HERE SOME-WHERE.
I'VE HAD IT. TURN THIS THING AROUND AND TAKE ME HOME.
I'M TELLING YOU, WE'RE CLOSE.
YOU'VE BEEN SAYING THAT FOR THE LAST THREE HOURS.
WHY DON'T YOU ADMIT THAT YOU DON'T KNOW WHERE THIS PLACE IS AT.
IN FACT, I THINK YOU MADE THIS WHOLE THING UP, MORRIS!
YOU THINK SO? THEN TAKE A LOOK UP AT THAT TRUCK UP THERE.
THIS IS IT.

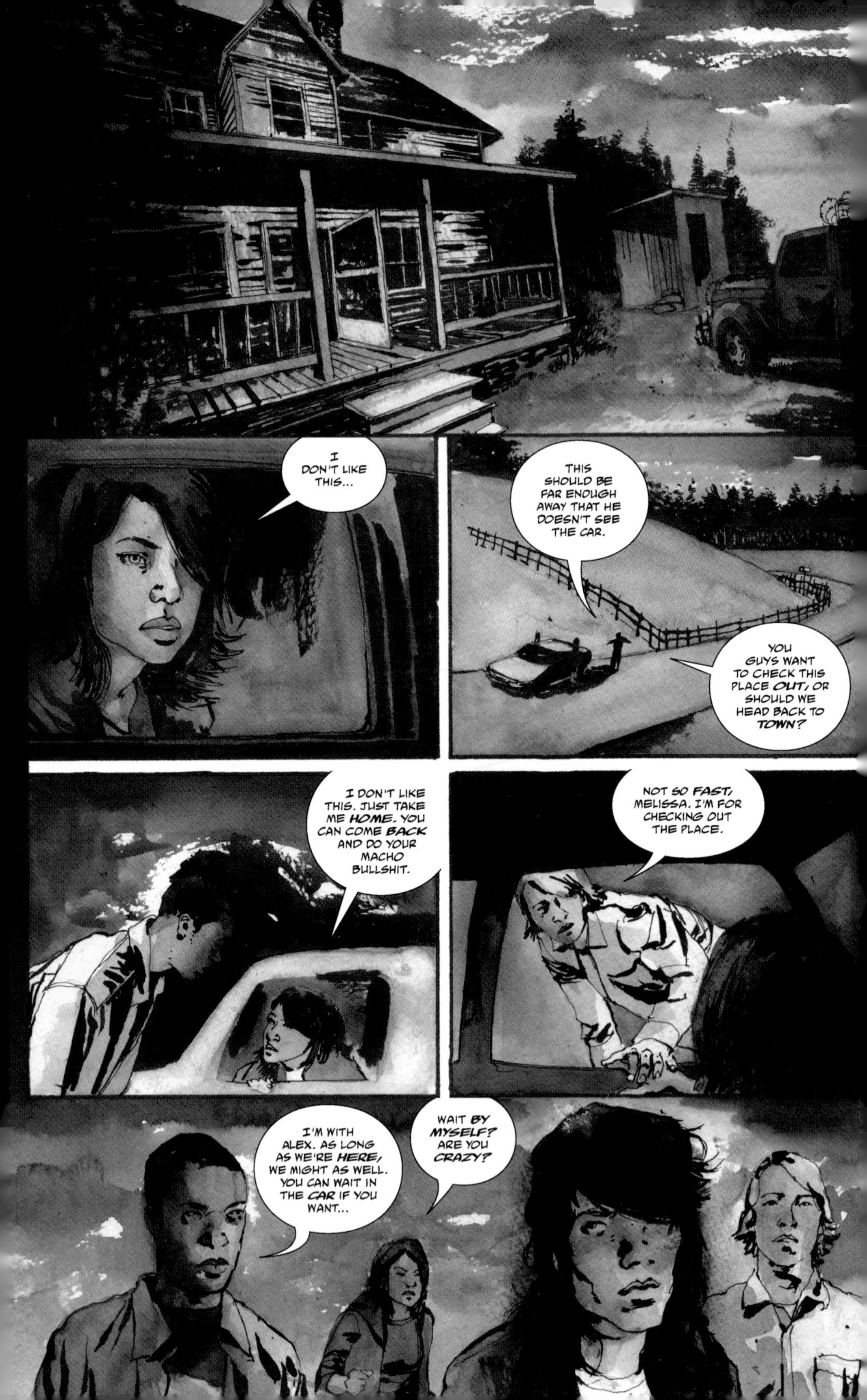
I DON'T LIKE THIS...
THIS SHOULD BE FAR ENOUGH AWAY THAT HE DOESN'T SEE THE CAR.
YOU GUYS WANT TO CHECK THIS PLACE OUT, OR SHOULD WE HEAD BACK TO TOWN?
I DON'T LIKE THIS. JUST TAKE ME HOME. YOU CAN COME BACK AND DO YOUR MACHO BULLSHIT.
NOT SO FAST, MELISSA. I'M FOR CHECKING OUT THE PLACE.
I'M WITH ALEX. AS LONG AS WE'RE HERE, WE MIGHT AS WELL. YOU CAN WAIT IN THE CAR IF YOU WANT...
WAIT BY MYSELF? ARE YOU CRAZY?

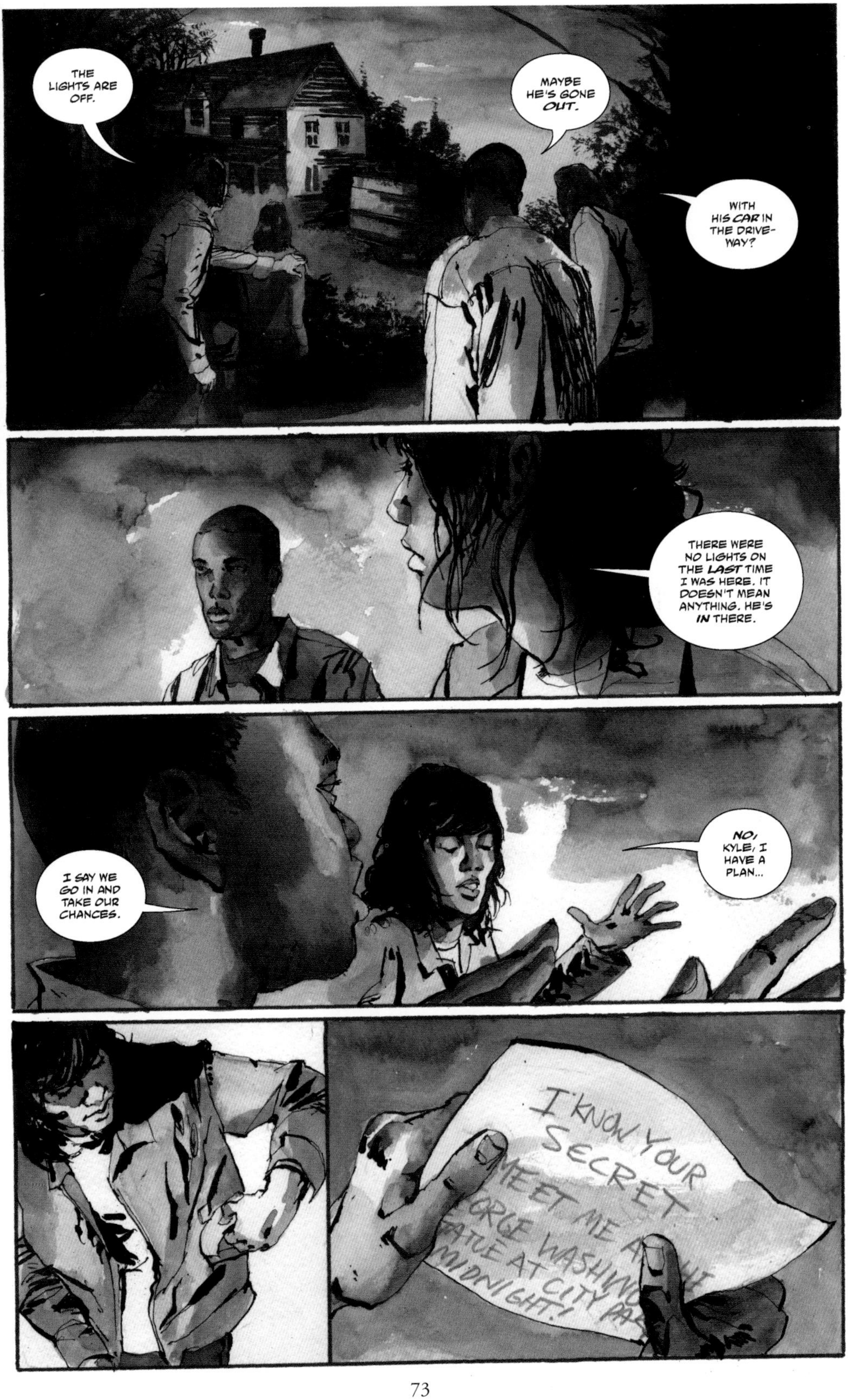
THE LIGHTS ARE OFF.
MAYBE HE'S GONE OUT.
WITH HIS CAR IN THE DRIVE-WAY?
THERE WERE NO LIGHTS ON THE LAST TIME I WAS HERE. IT DOESN'T MEAN ANYTHING. HE'S IN THERE.
I SAY WE GO IN AND TAKE OUR CHANCES.
NO, KYLE, I HAVE A PLAN...
I KNOW YOUR SECRET

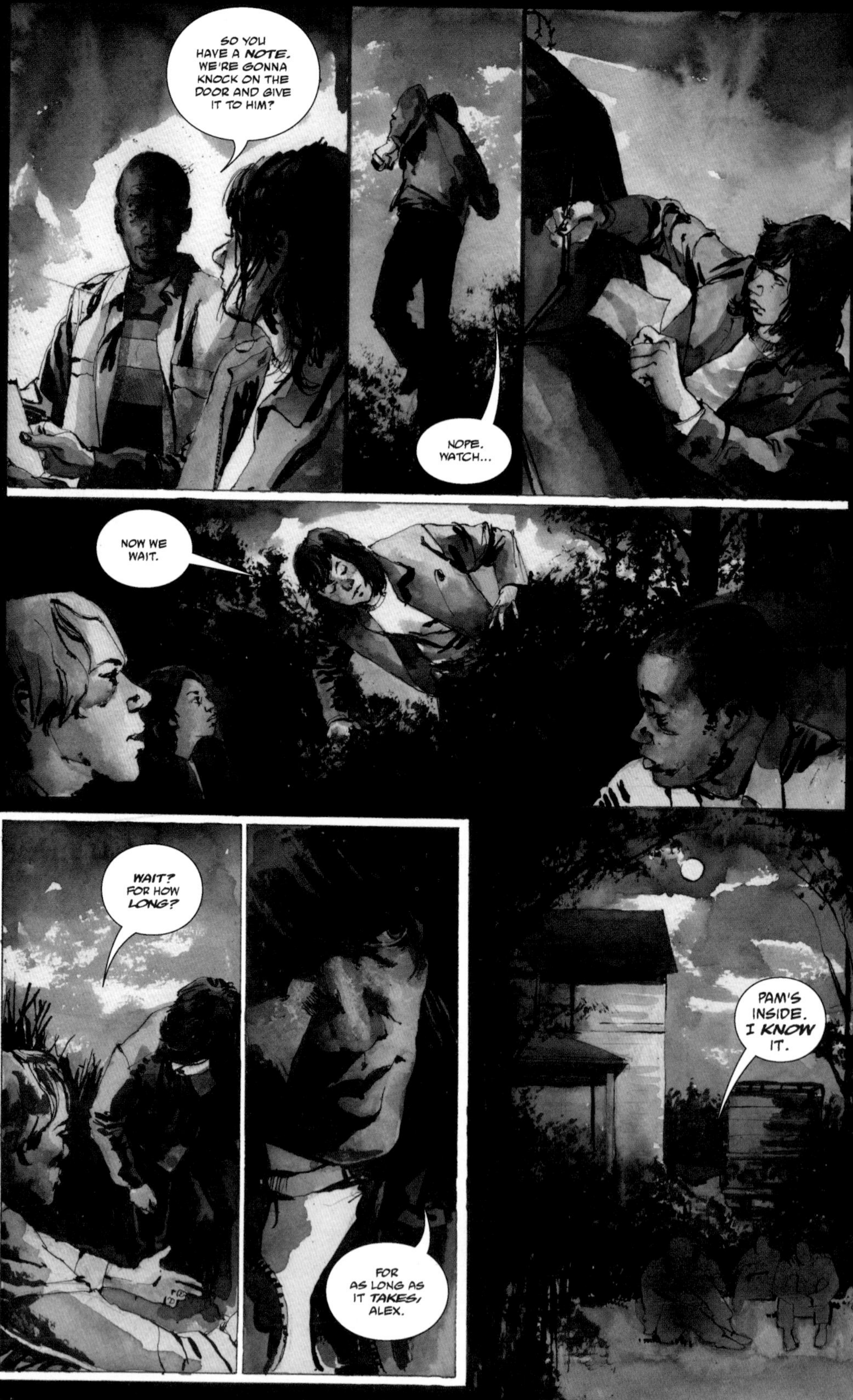
SO YOU HAVE A NOTE. WE'RE GONNA KNOCK ON THE DOOR AND GIVE IT TO HIM?
NOPE. WATCH...
NOW WE WAIT.
WAIT? FOR HOW LONG?
FOR AS LONG AS IT TAKES, ALEX.
PAM'S INSIDE. I KNOW IT.

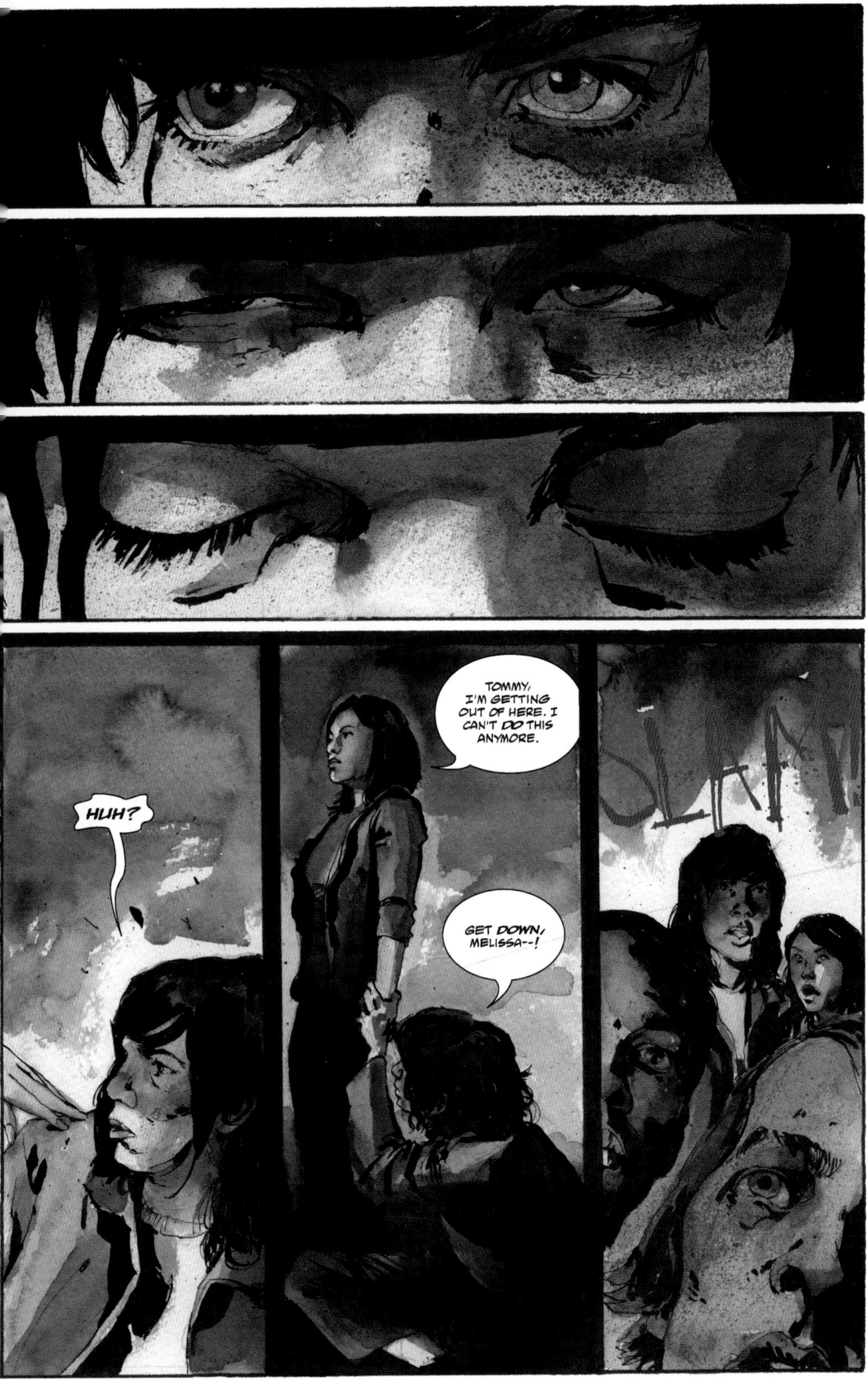
HUH?
TOMMY, I'M GETTING OUT OF HERE. I CAN'T DO THIS ANYMORE.
GET DOWN, MELISSA--!
SLAM!

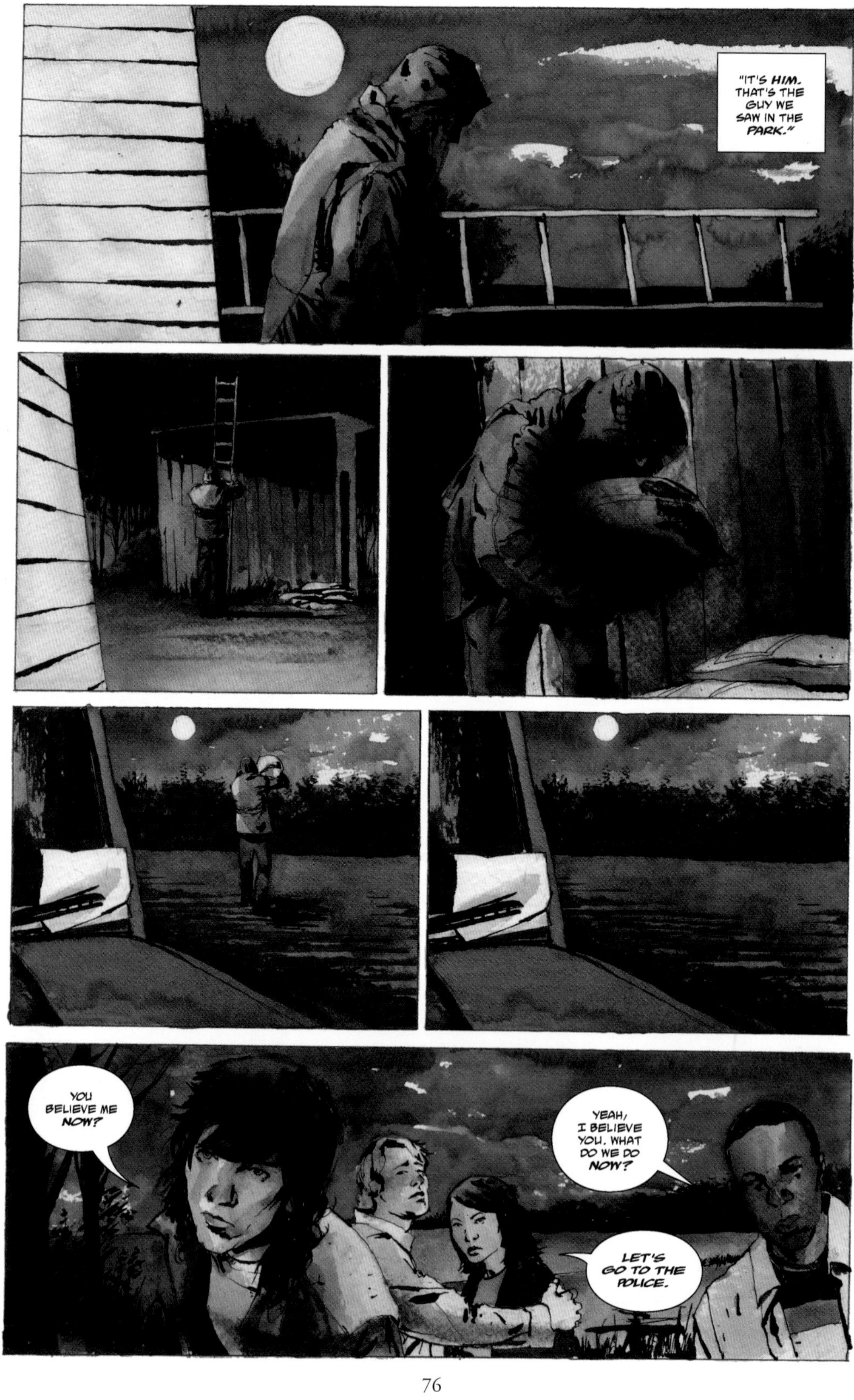
"IT'S HIM. THAT'S THE GUY WE SAW IN THE PARK."
YOU BELIEVE ME NOW?
YEAH, I BELIEVE YOU. WHAT DO WE DO NOW?
LET'S GO TO THE POLICE.

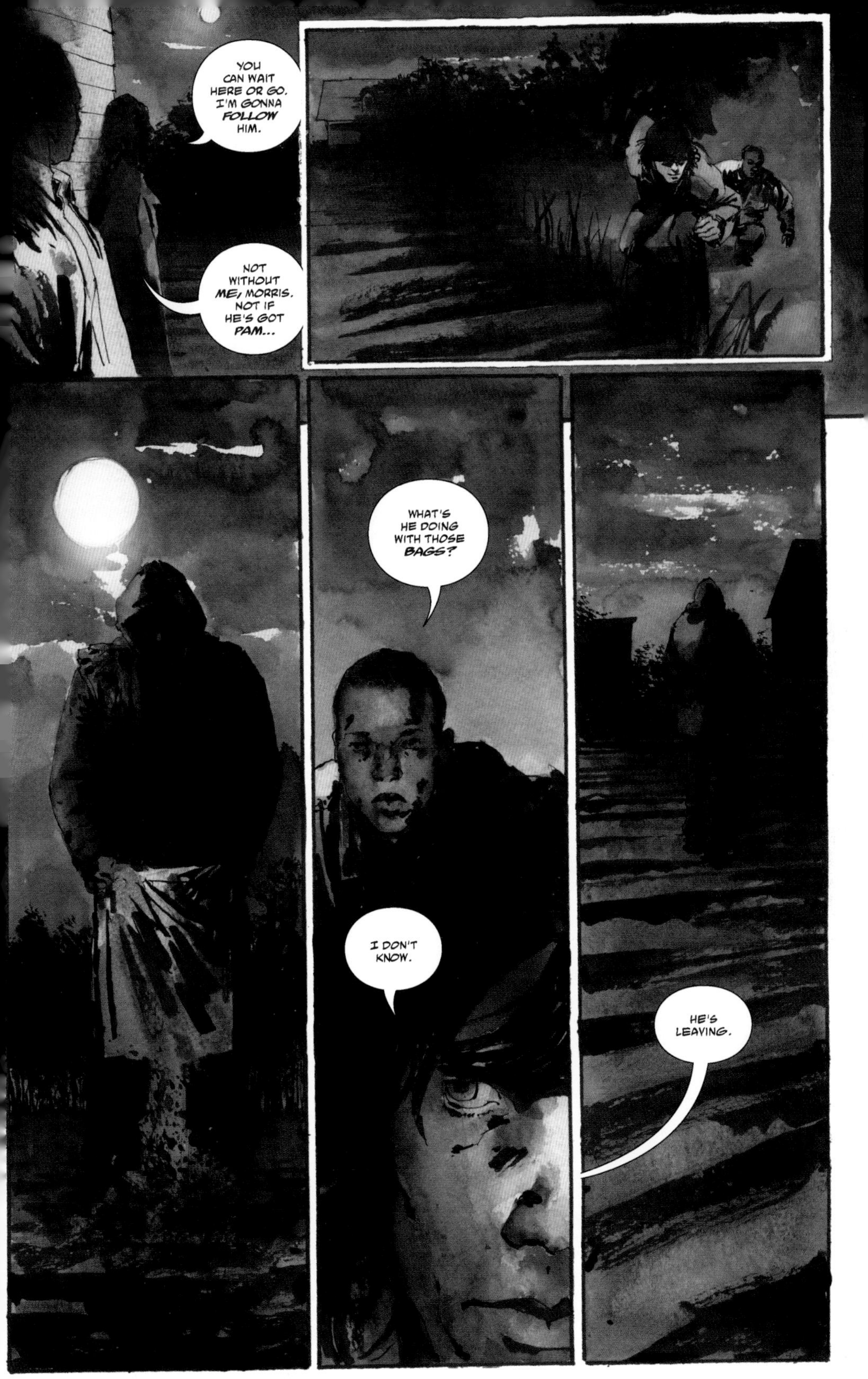
YOU CAN WAIT HERE OR GO. I'M GONNA FOLLOW HIM.
NOT WITHOUT ME, MORRIS. NOT IF HE'S GOT PAM...
WHAT'S HE DOING WITH THOSE BAGS?
I DON'T KNOW.
HE'S LEAVING.

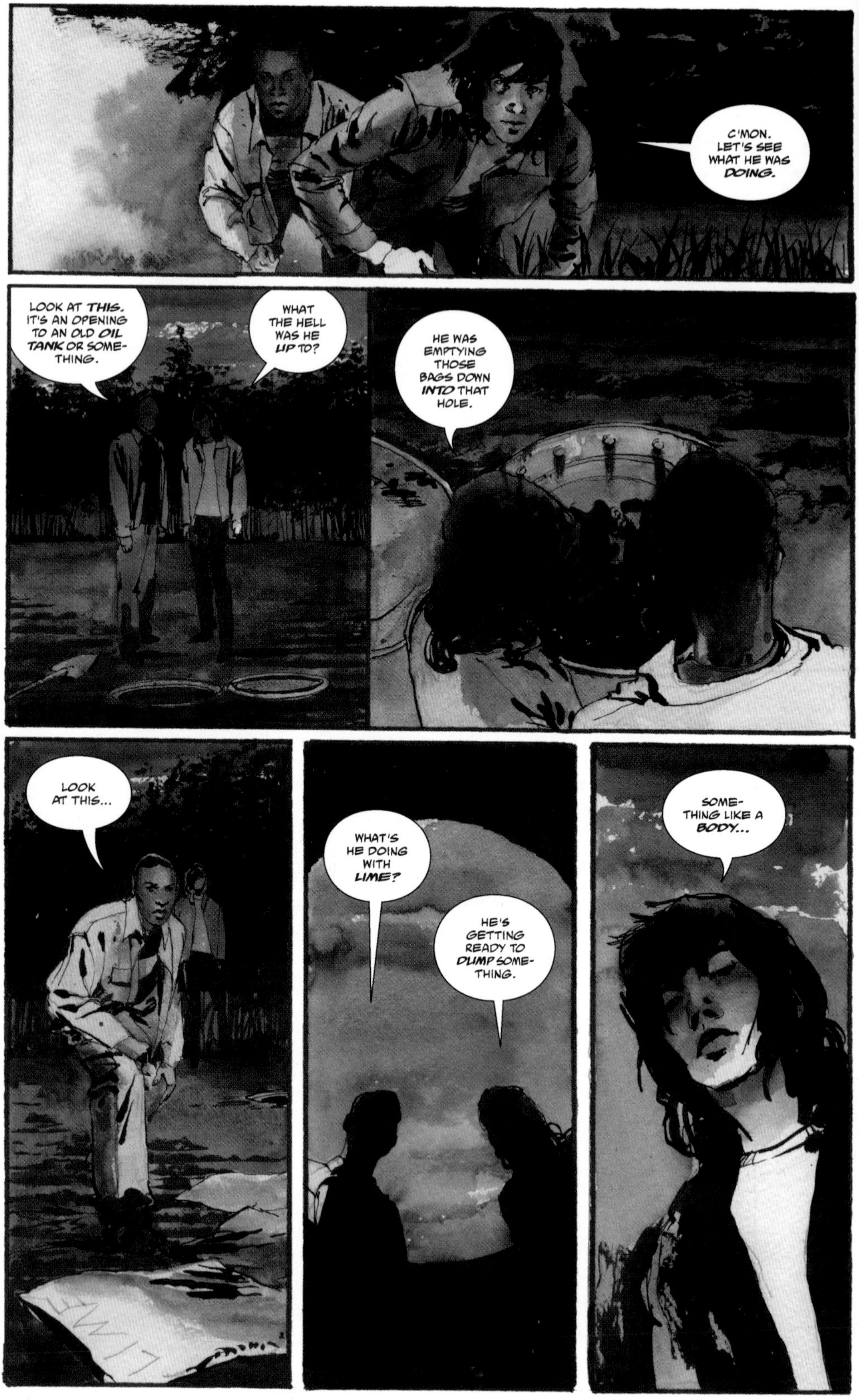
C'MON. LET'S SEE WHAT HE WAS DOING.
LOOK AT THIS. IT'S AN OPENING TO AN OLD OIL TANK OR SOME-THING.
WHAT THE HELL WAS HE UP TO?
HE WAS EMPTYING THOSE BAGS DOWN INTO THAT HOLE.
LOOK AT THIS...
WHAT'S HE DOING WITH LIME?
HE'S GETTING READY TO DUMP SOME-THING.
SOME-THING LIKE A BODY...

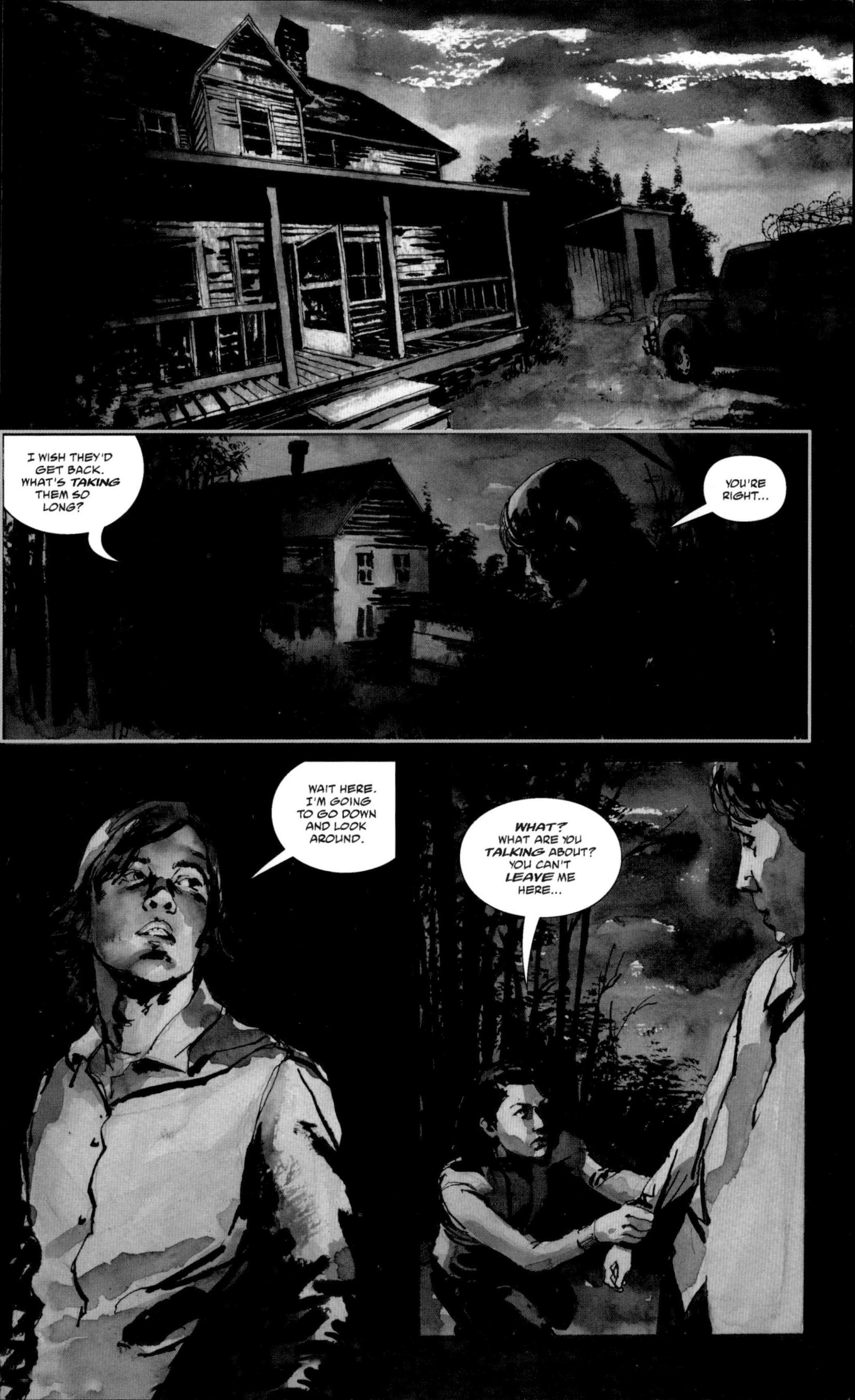
I WISH THEY'D GET BACK. WHAT'S TAKING THEM SO LONG?
YOU'RE RIGHT...
WAIT HERE. I'M GOING TO GO DOWN AND LOOK AROUND.
WHAT? WHAT ARE YOU TALKING ABOUT? YOU CAN'T LEAVE ME HERE...

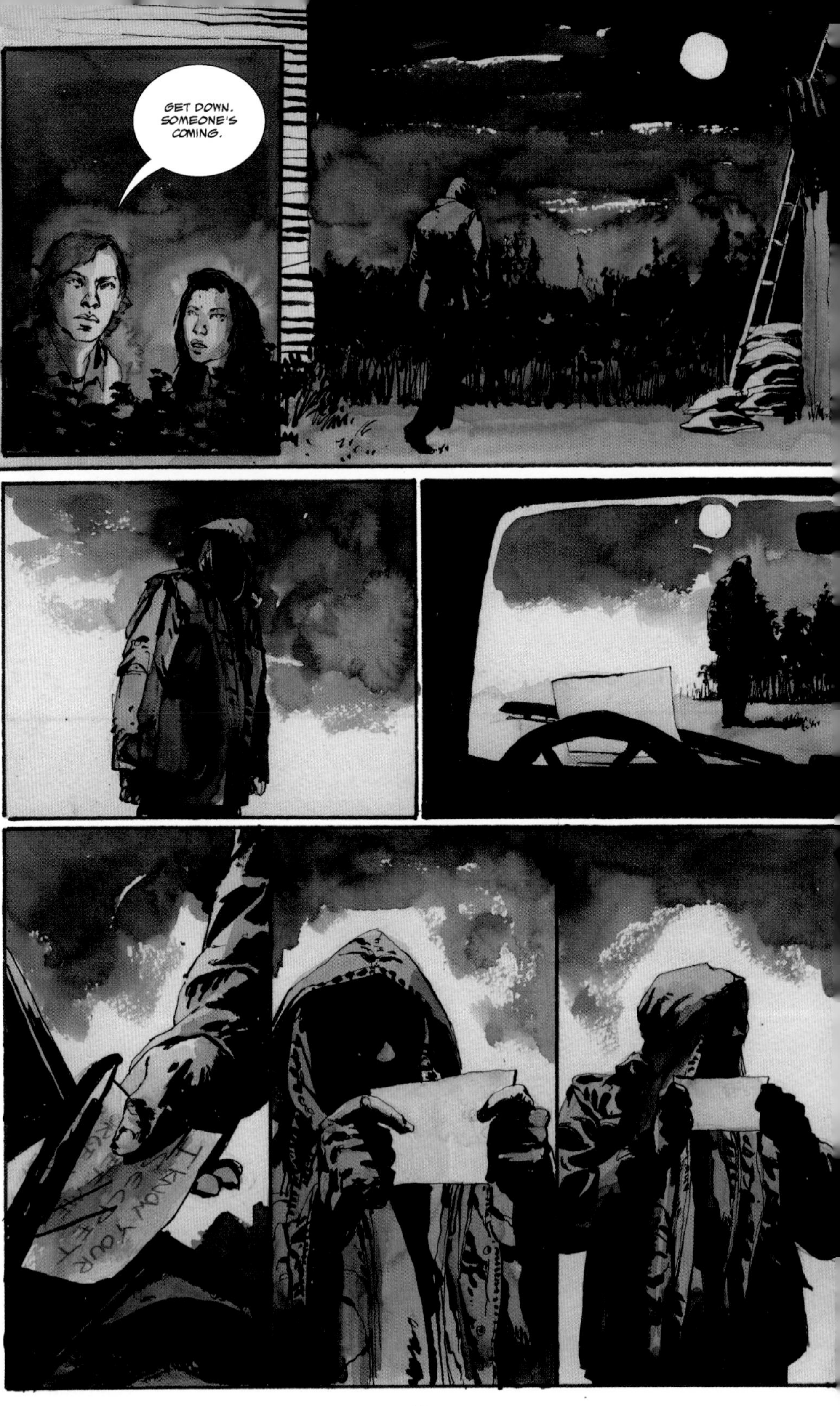
GET DOWN. SOMEONE'S COMING.
I KNOW YOUR

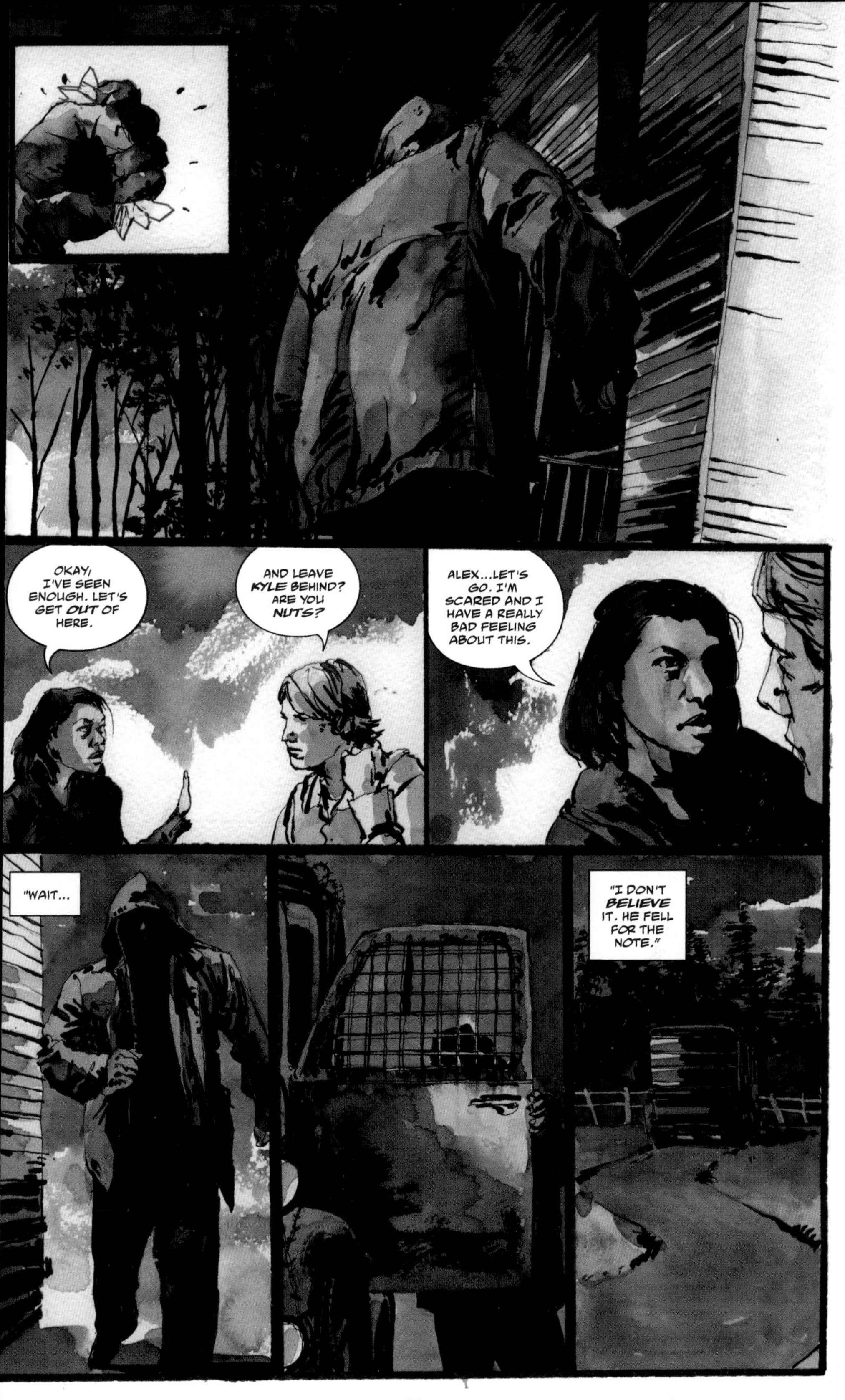

OKAY, I'VE SEEN ENOUGH. LET'S GET OUT OF HERE.
AND LEAVE KYLE BEHIND? ARE YOU NUTS?
ALEX...LET'S GO. I'M SCARED AND I HAVE A REALLY BAD FEELING ABOUT THIS.
"WAIT...
"I DON'T BELIEVE IT. HE FELL FOR THE NOTE."

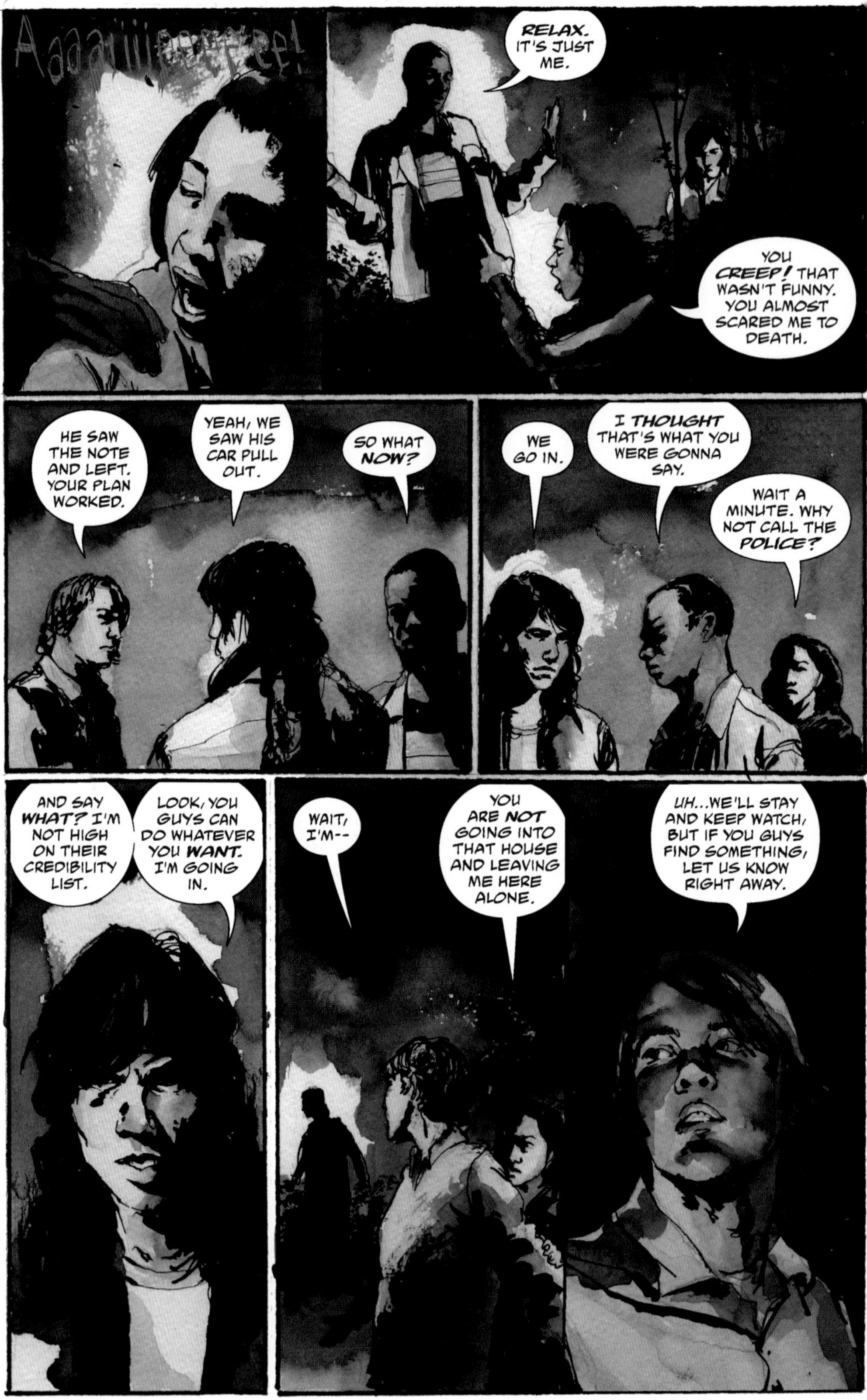
Aaaaiiiieeeeee!
RELAX. IT'S JUST ME.
YOU CREEP! THAT WASN'T FUNNY. YOU ALMOST SCARED ME TO DEATH.
HE SAW THE NOTE AND LEFT. YOUR PLAN WORKED.
YEAH, WE SAW HIS CAR PULL OUT.
SO WHAT NOW?
WE GO IN.
I THOUGHT THAT'S WHAT YOU WERE GONNA SAY.
WAIT A MINUTE. WHY NOT CALL THE POLICE?
AND SAY WHAT? I'M NOT HIGH ON THEIR CREDIBILITY LIST.
LOOK, YOU GUYS CAN DO WHATEVER YOU WANT. I'M GOING IN.
WAIT, I'M--
YOU ARE NOT GOING INTO THAT HOUSE AND LEAVING ME HERE ALONE.
UH...WE'LL STAY AND KEEP WATCH, BUT IF YOU GUYS FIND SOMETHING, LET US KNOW RIGHT AWAY.

YEAH, RIGHT. WE'LL CALL YOU IF WE NEED HELP.

DON'T FLIP ANY SWITCHES. I'VE GOT A PEN-LIGHT THAT'LL WORK.

SOME-BODY ACTUALLY LIVES IN THIS PLACE?

WHOOOEEE. LOOK AT THESE MAGAZINES. I AIN'T NEVER SEEN GIRLS LIKE THESE.

PUT 'EM DOWN. WE'VE GOT TO SEARCH THIS PLACE FAST.

OKAY, BUT I'M GONNA HAVE TO BORROW A FEW ON THE WAY OUT.

HOW 'BOUT THIS...

GUY LIKES TO TAKE PICTURES OF NAKED WOMEN... AND THEY DON'T SEEM TOO HAPPY ABOUT IT.

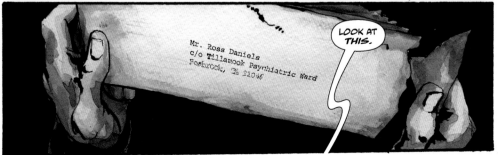

Mr. Ross Daniels
c/o Tillamook Psychiatric Ward
Foxbrook, PA 21046

LOOK AT THIS.

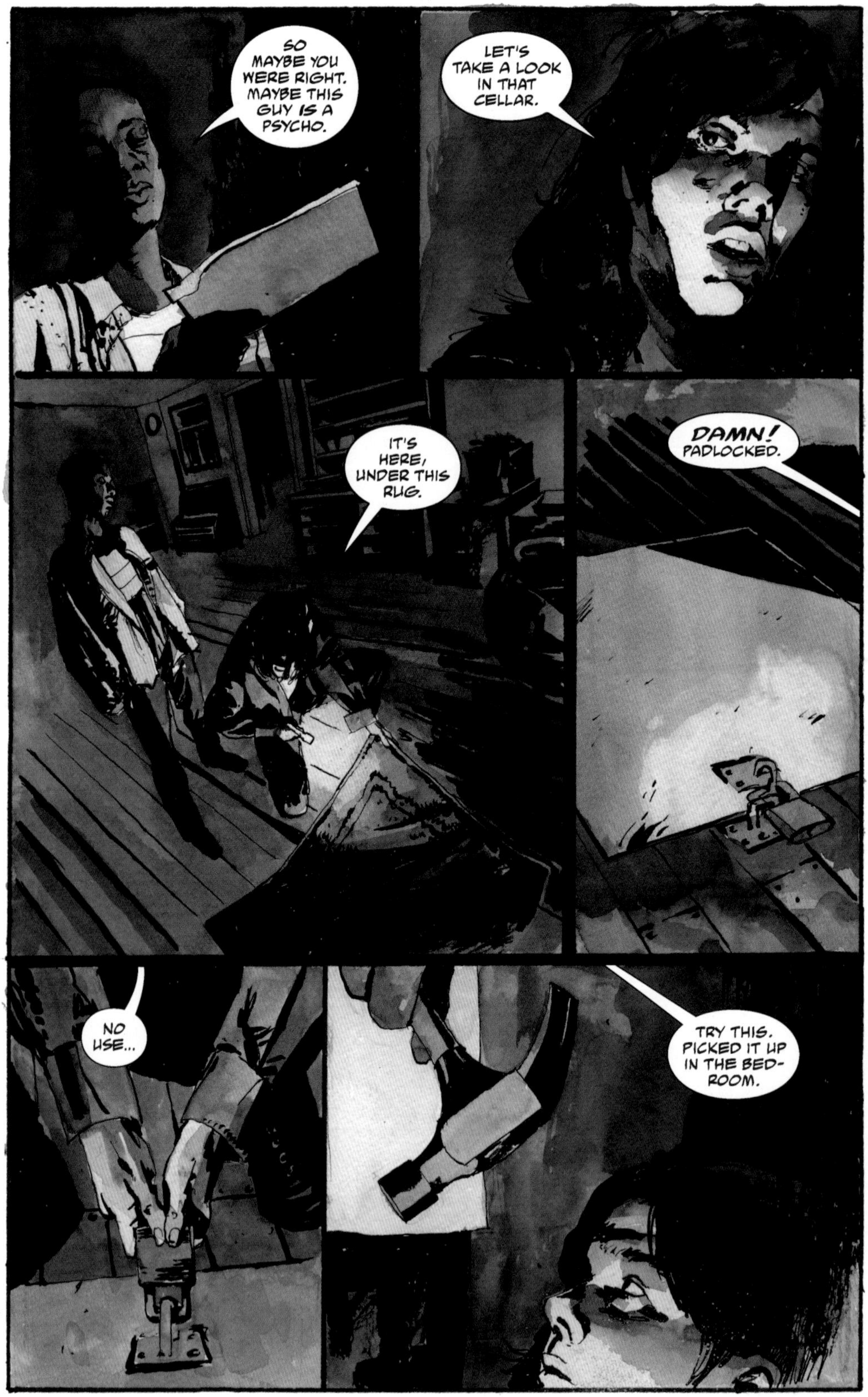
SO MAYBE YOU WERE RIGHT. MAYBE THIS GUY IS A PSYCHO.
LET'S TAKE A LOOK IN THAT CELLAR.
IT'S HERE, UNDER THIS RUG.
DAMN! PADLOCKED.
NO USE...
TRY THIS. PICKED IT UP IN THE BED-ROOM.

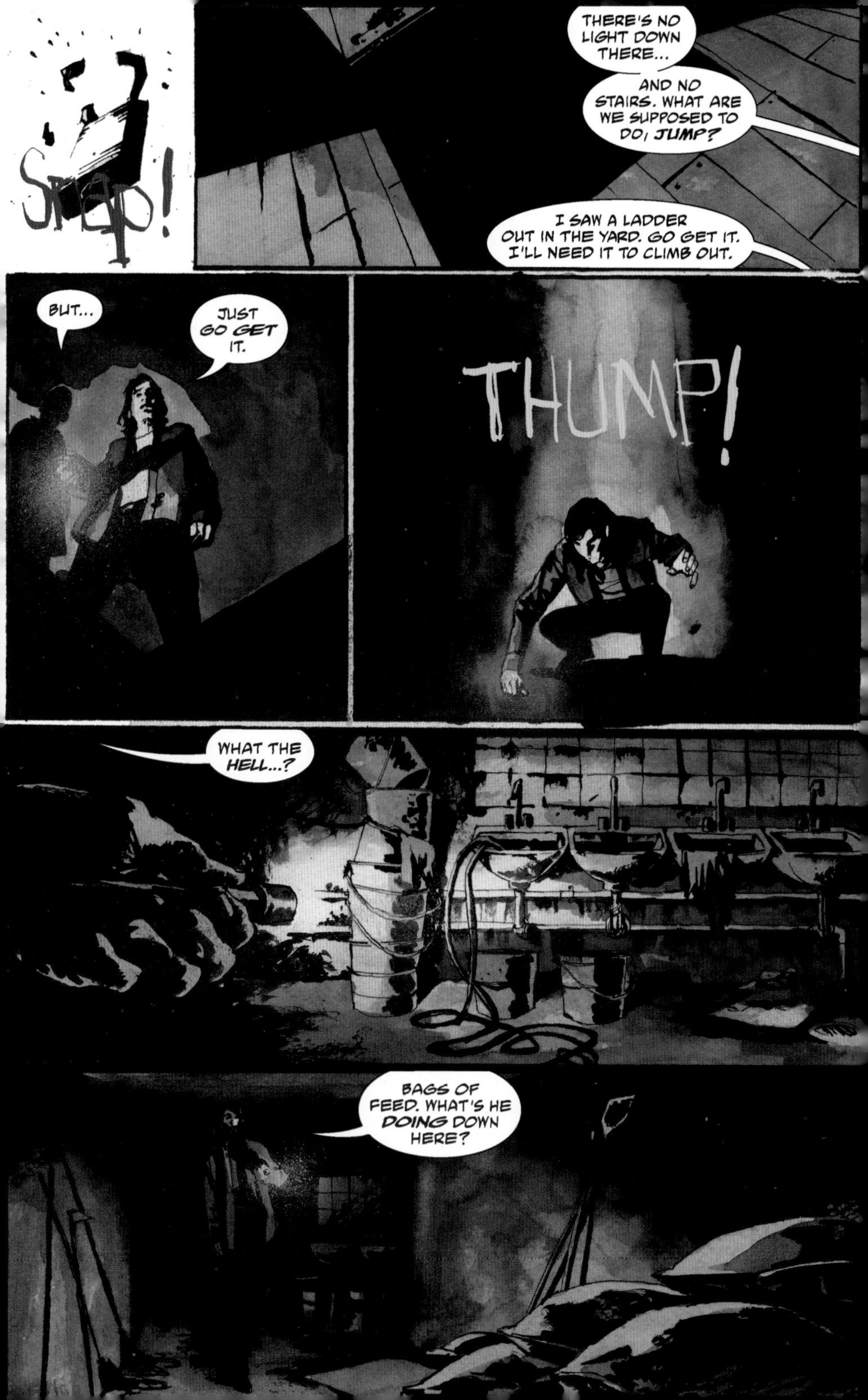

SNAP!
THERE'S NO LIGHT DOWN THERE...
AND NO STAIRS. WHAT ARE WE SUPPOSED TO DO, JUMP?
I SAW A LADDER OUT IN THE YARD. GO GET IT. I'LL NEED IT TO CLIMB OUT.
BUT...
JUST GO GET IT.
THUMP!
WHAT THE HELL...?
BAGS OF FEED. WHAT'S HE DOING DOWN HERE?

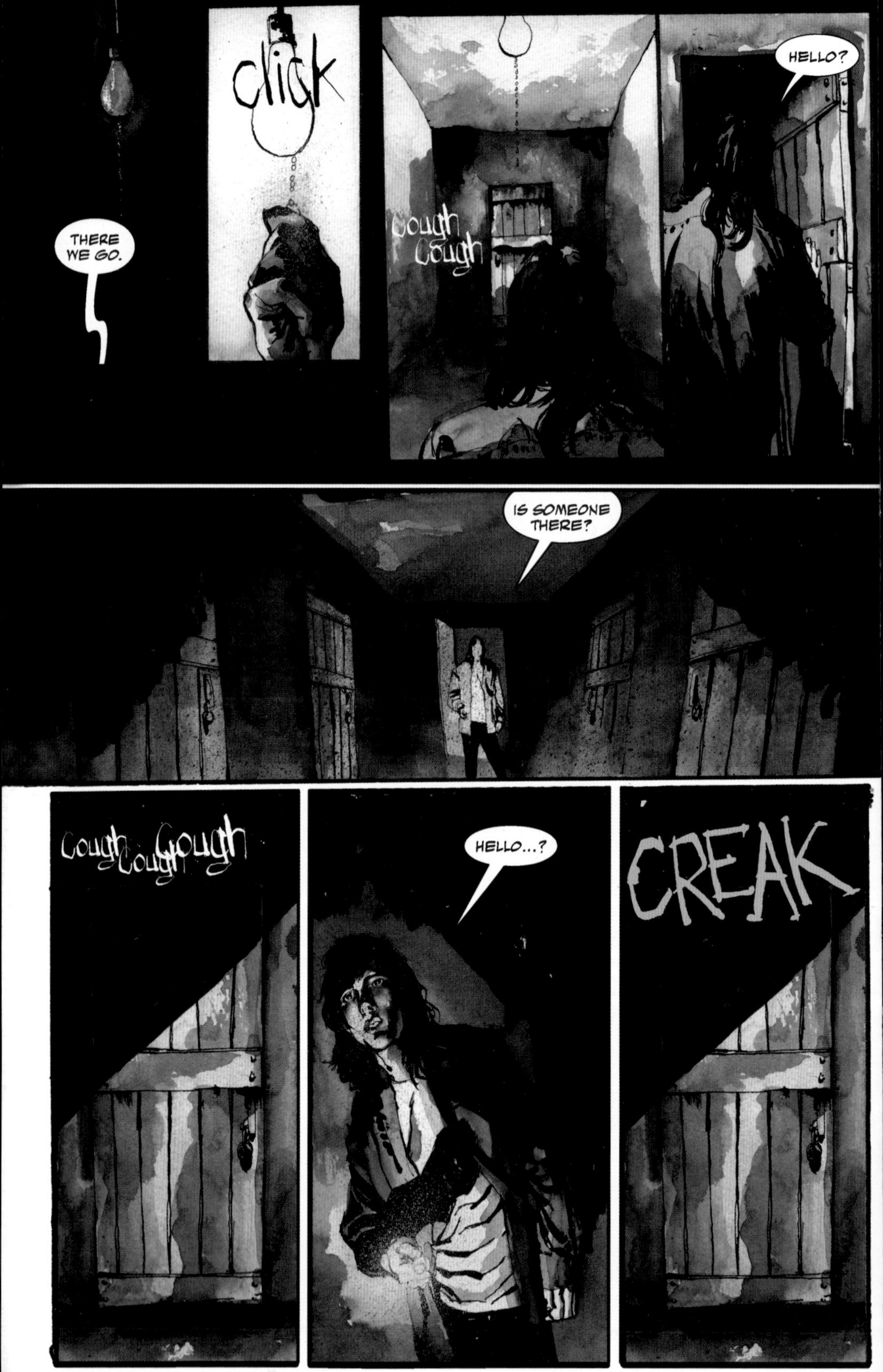

THERE WE GO.
CLICK
COUGH COUGH
HELLO?
IS SOMEONE THERE?
COUGH COUGH COUGH
HELLO...?
CREAK

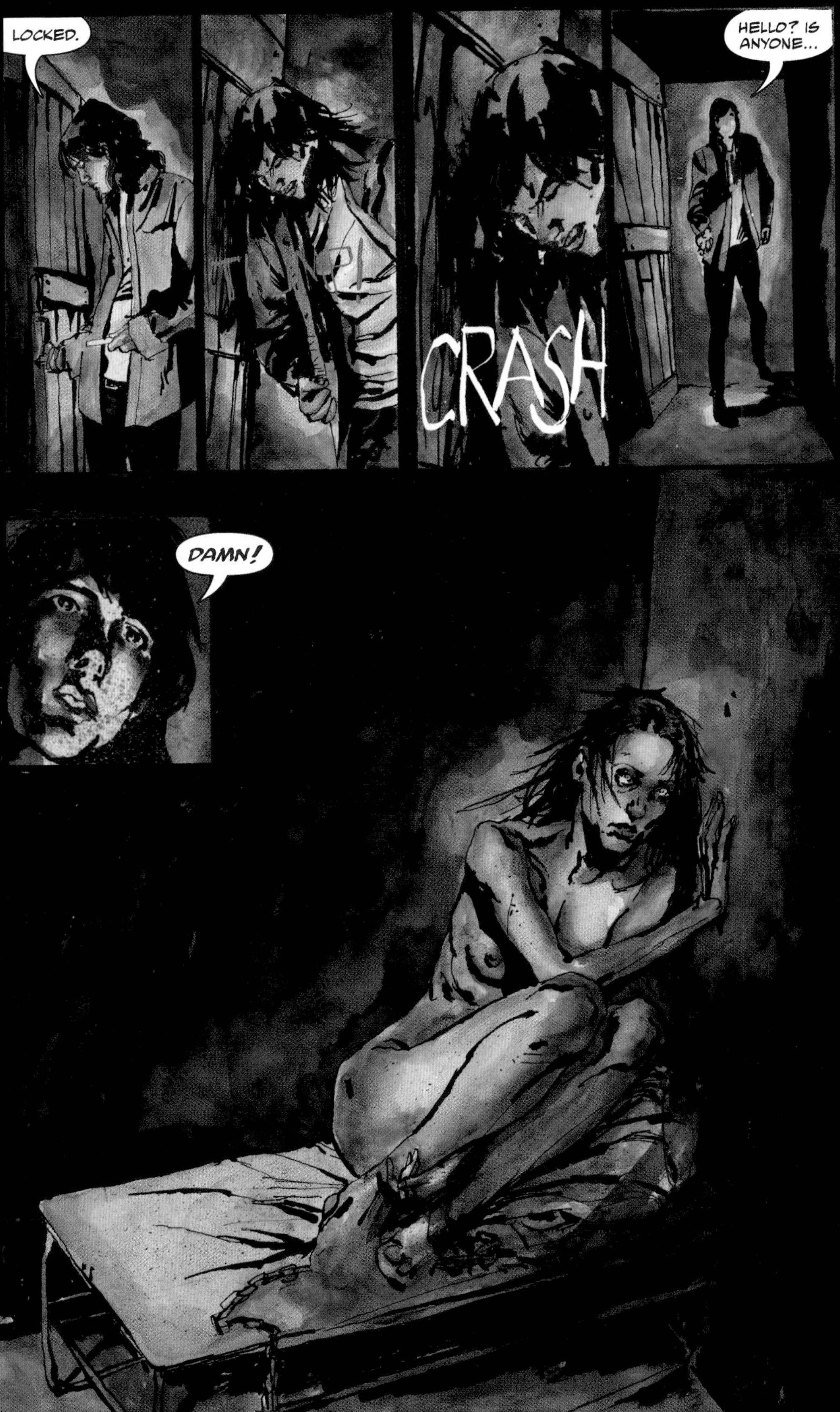
LOCKED.
CRASH
HELLO? IS ANYONE...
DAMN!

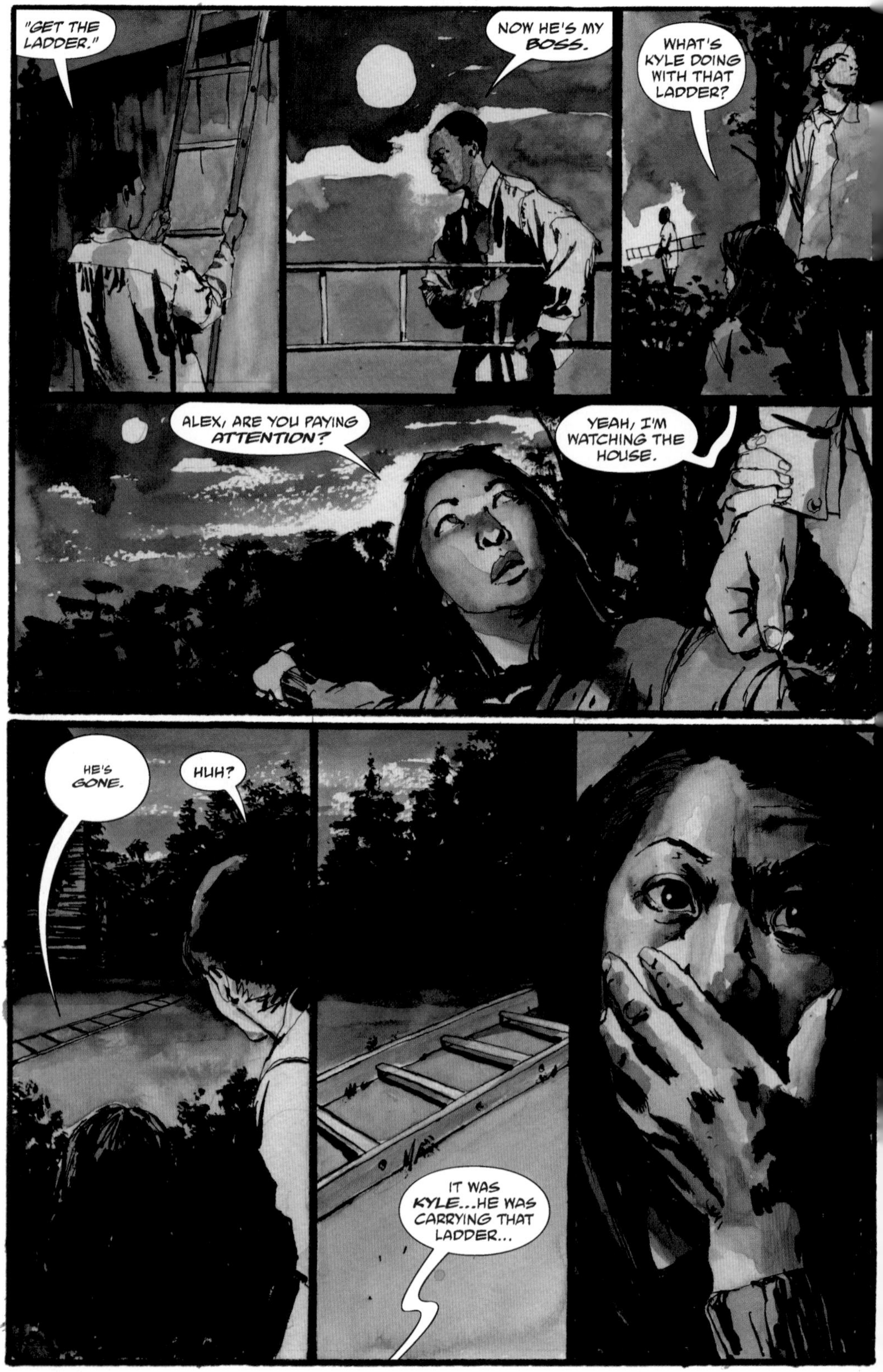
"GET THE LADDER."
NOW HE'S MY BOSS.
WHAT'S KYLE DOING WITH THAT LADDER?
ALEX, ARE YOU PAYING ATTENTION?
YEAH, I'M WATCHING THE HOUSE.
HE'S GONE.
HUH?
IT WAS KYLE...HE WAS CARRYING THAT LADDER...

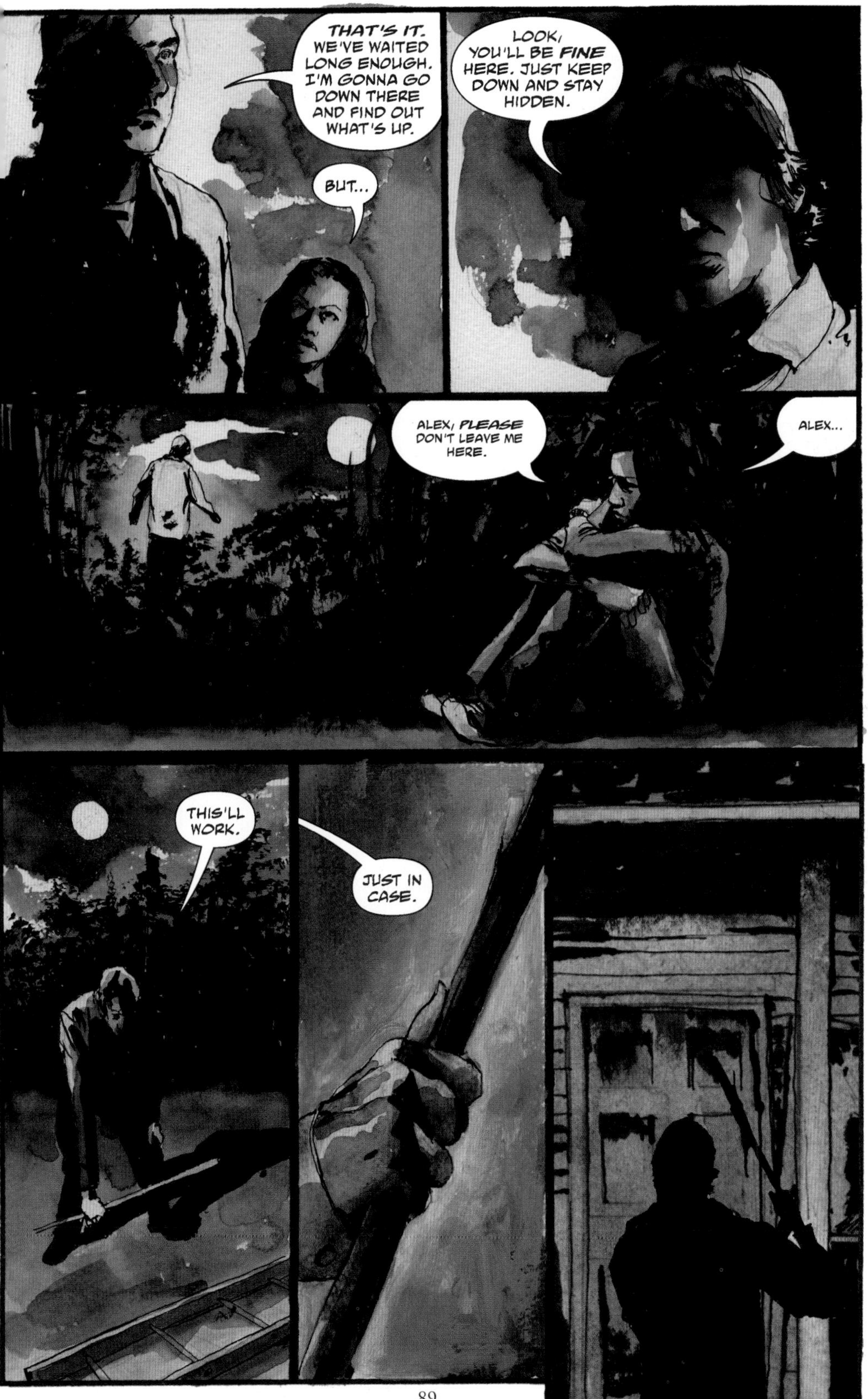
THAT'S IT. WE'VE WAITED LONG ENOUGH. I'M GONNA GO DOWN THERE AND FIND OUT WHAT'S UP.
BUT...
LOOK, YOU'LL BE FINE HERE. JUST KEEP DOWN AND STAY HIDDEN.
ALEX, PLEASE DON'T LEAVE ME HERE.
ALEX...
THIS'LL WORK.
JUST IN CASE.

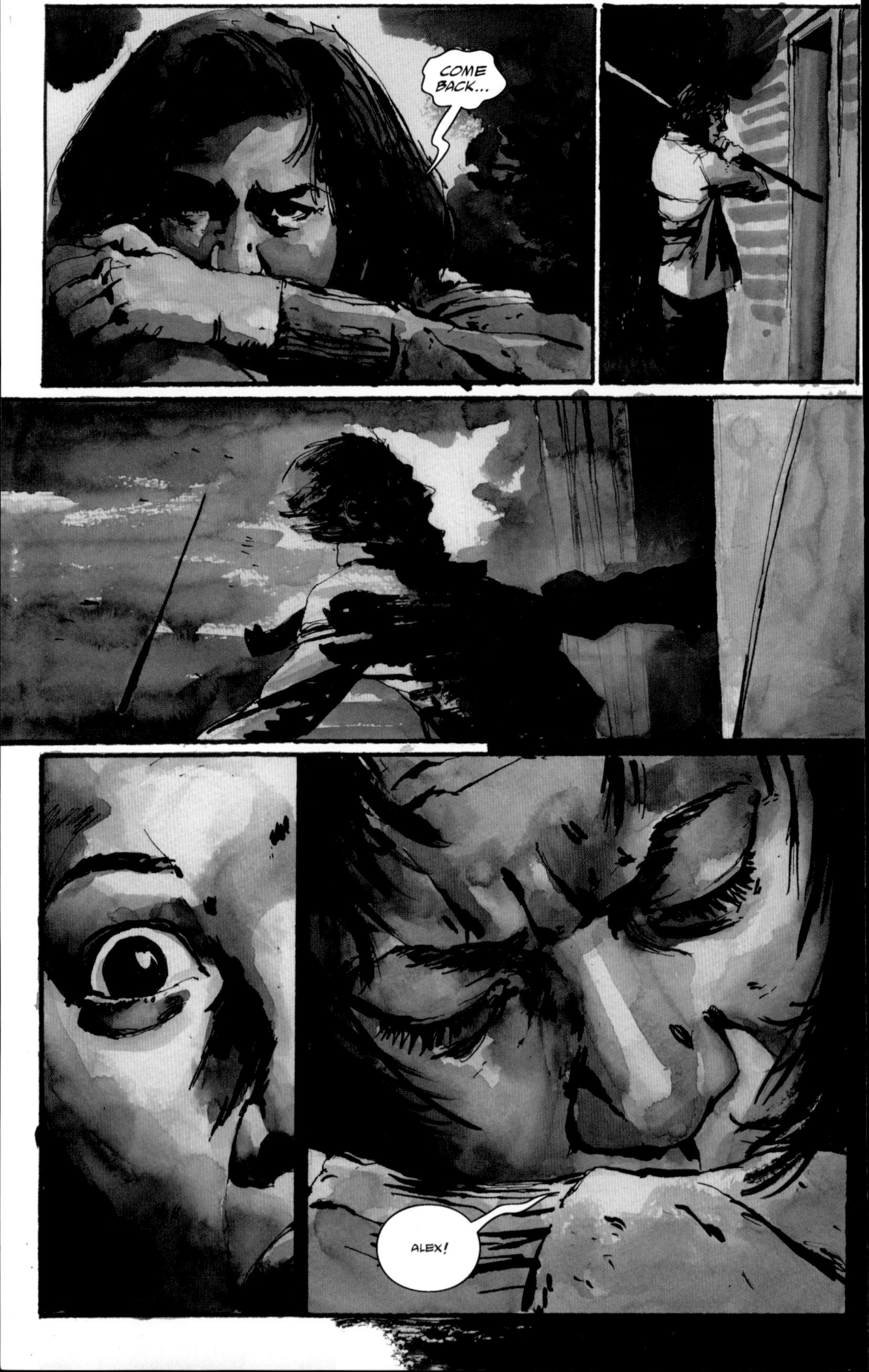
COME BACK...
ALEX!

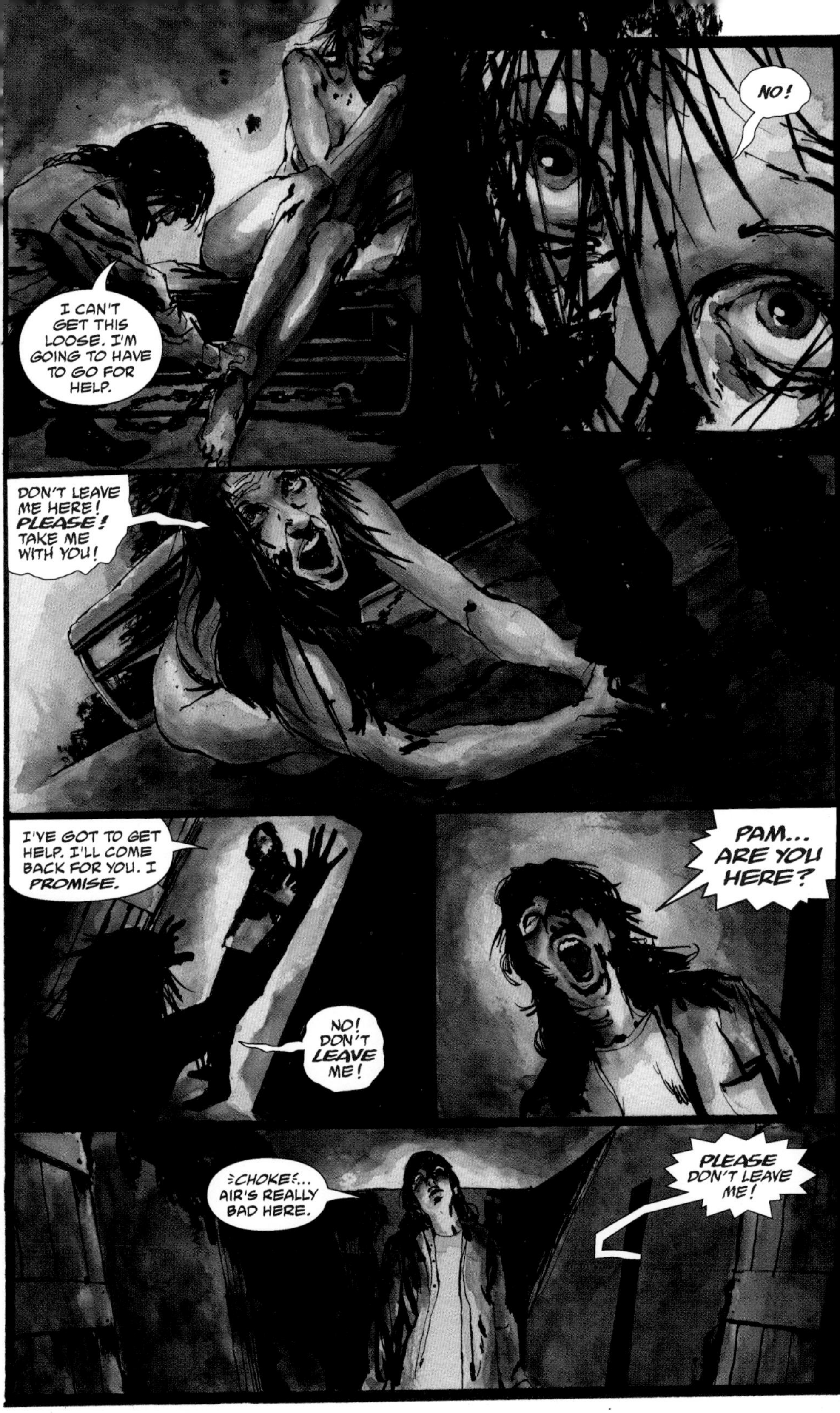
I CAN'T GET THIS LOOSE. I'M GOING TO HAVE TO GO FOR HELP.
NO!
DON'T LEAVE ME HERE! PLEASE! TAKE ME WITH YOU!
I'VE GOT TO GET HELP. I'LL COME BACK FOR YOU. I PROMISE.
NO! DON'T LEAVE ME!
PAM... ARE YOU HERE?
CHOKE... AIR'S REALLY BAD HERE.
PLEASE DON'T LEAVE ME!

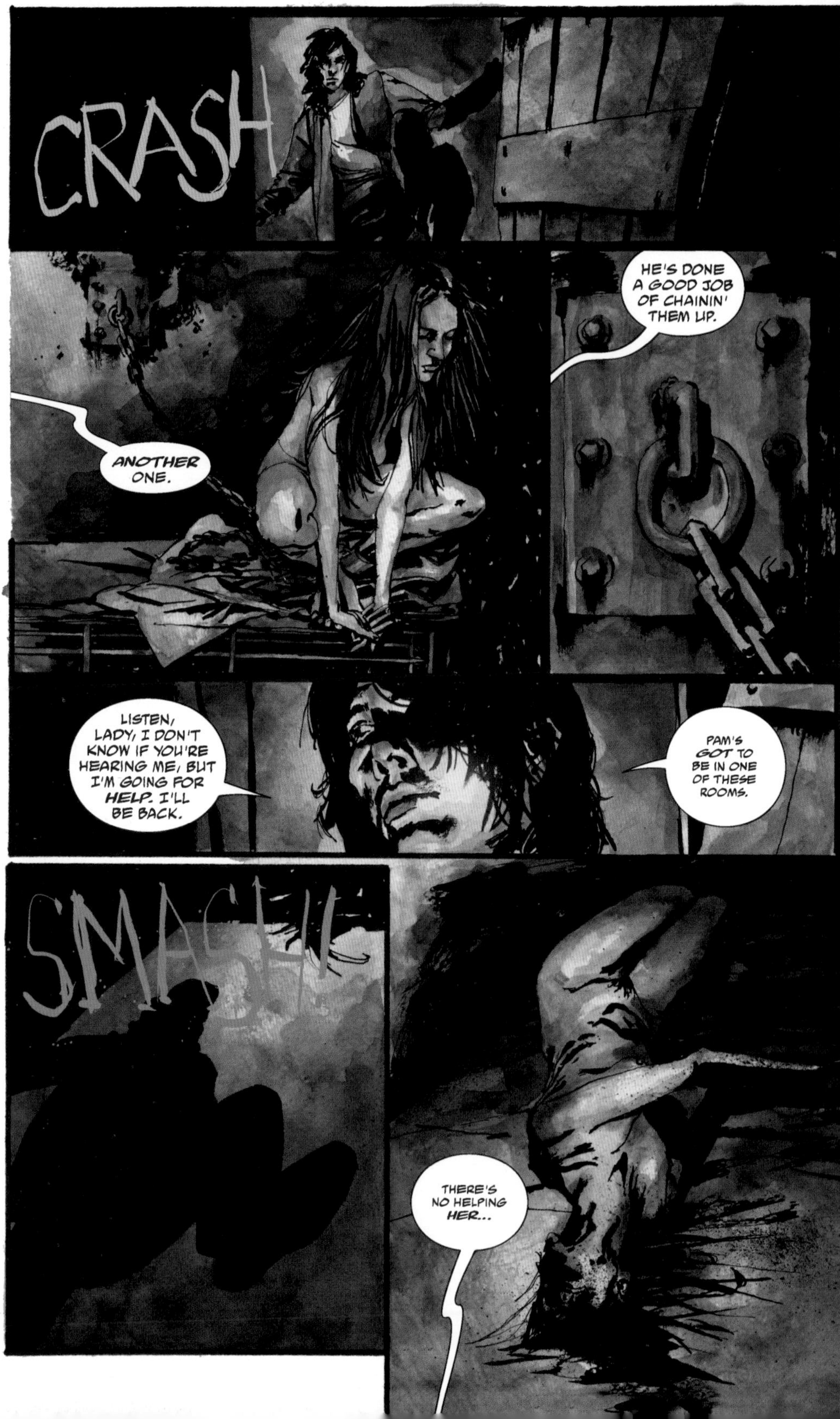
CRASH
ANOTHER ONE.
HE'S DONE A GOOD JOB OF CHAININ' THEM UP.
LISTEN, LADY, I DON'T KNOW IF YOU'RE HEARING ME, BUT I'M GOING FOR HELP. I'LL BE BACK.
PAM'S GOT TO BE IN ONE OF THESE ROOMS.
SMASH
THERE'S NO HELPING HER...

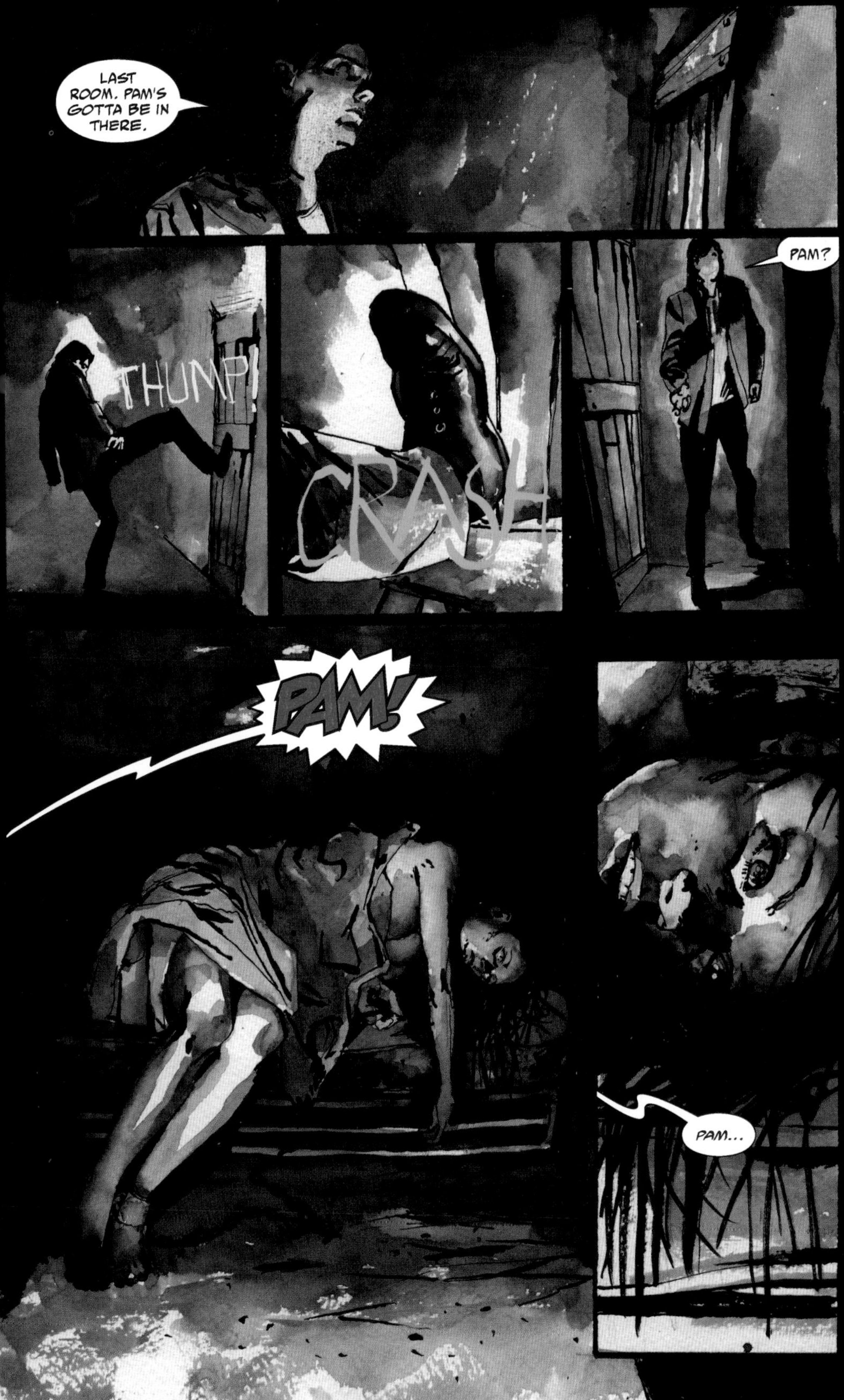
LAST ROOM. PAM'S GOTTA BE IN THERE.
THUMP!
CRASH
PAM?
PAM!
PAM...

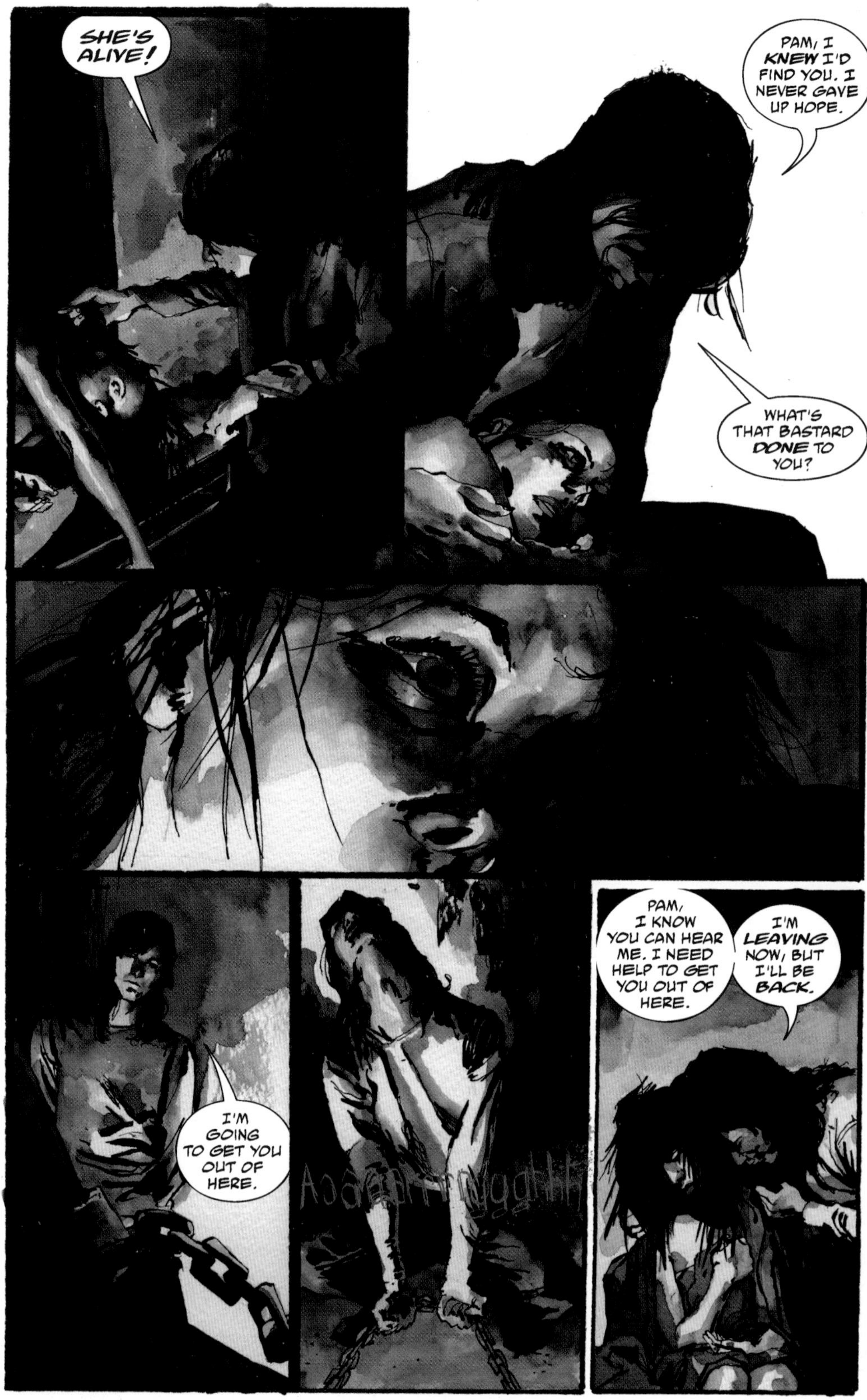
SHE'S ALIVE!
PAM, I KNEW I'D FIND YOU. I NEVER GAVE UP HOPE.
WHAT'S THAT BASTARD DONE TO YOU?
I'M GOING TO GET YOU OUT OF HERE.
PAM, I KNOW YOU CAN HEAR ME. I NEED HELP TO GET YOU OUT OF HERE.
I'M LEAVING NOW, BUT I'LL BE BACK.

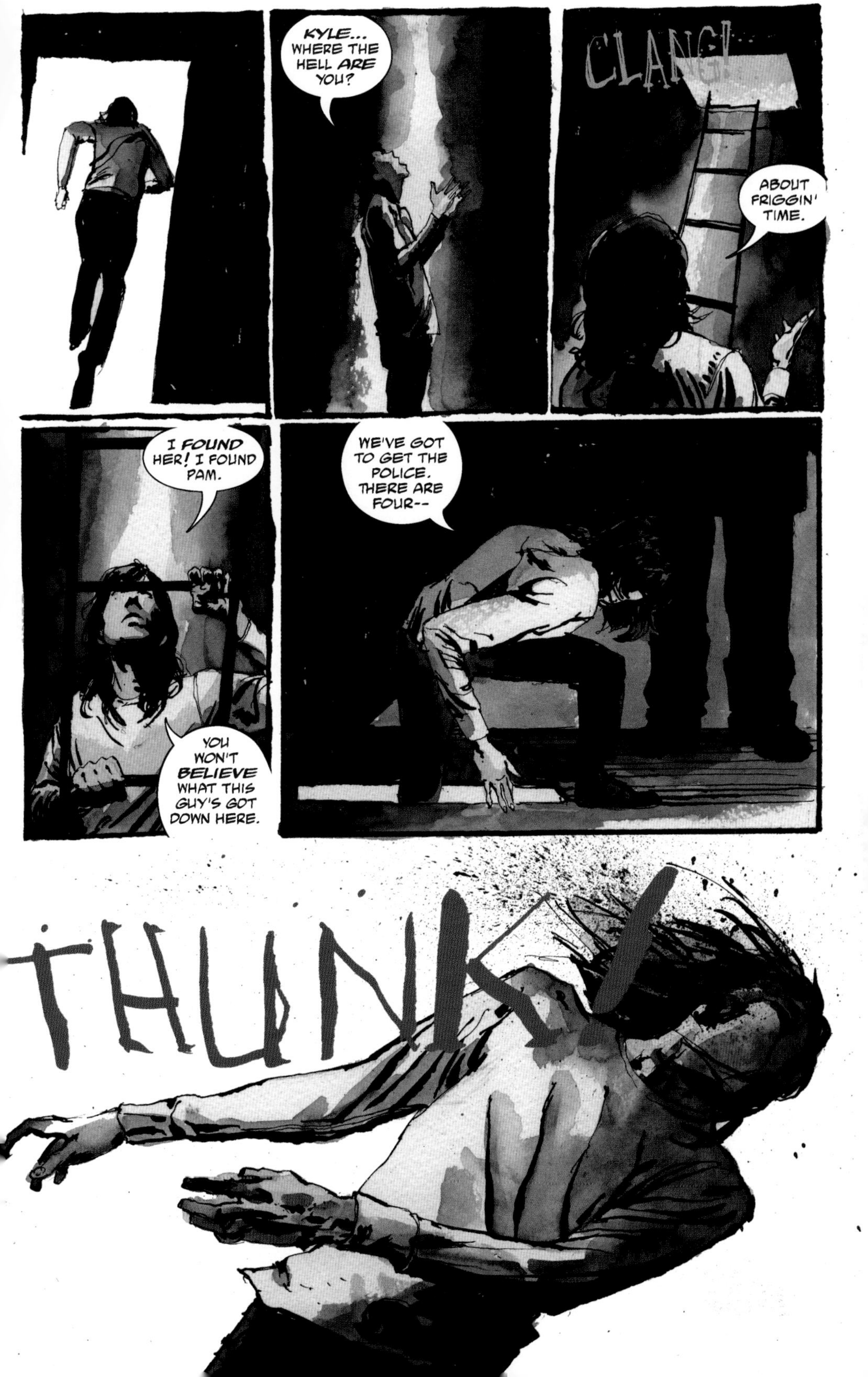
KYLE... WHERE THE HELL ARE YOU?
CLANG!
ABOUT FRIGGIN' TIME.
I FOUND HER! I FOUND PAM.
YOU WON'T BELIEVE WHAT THIS GUY'S GOT DOWN HERE.
WE'VE GOT TO GET THE POLICE. THERE ARE FOUR--
THUNK

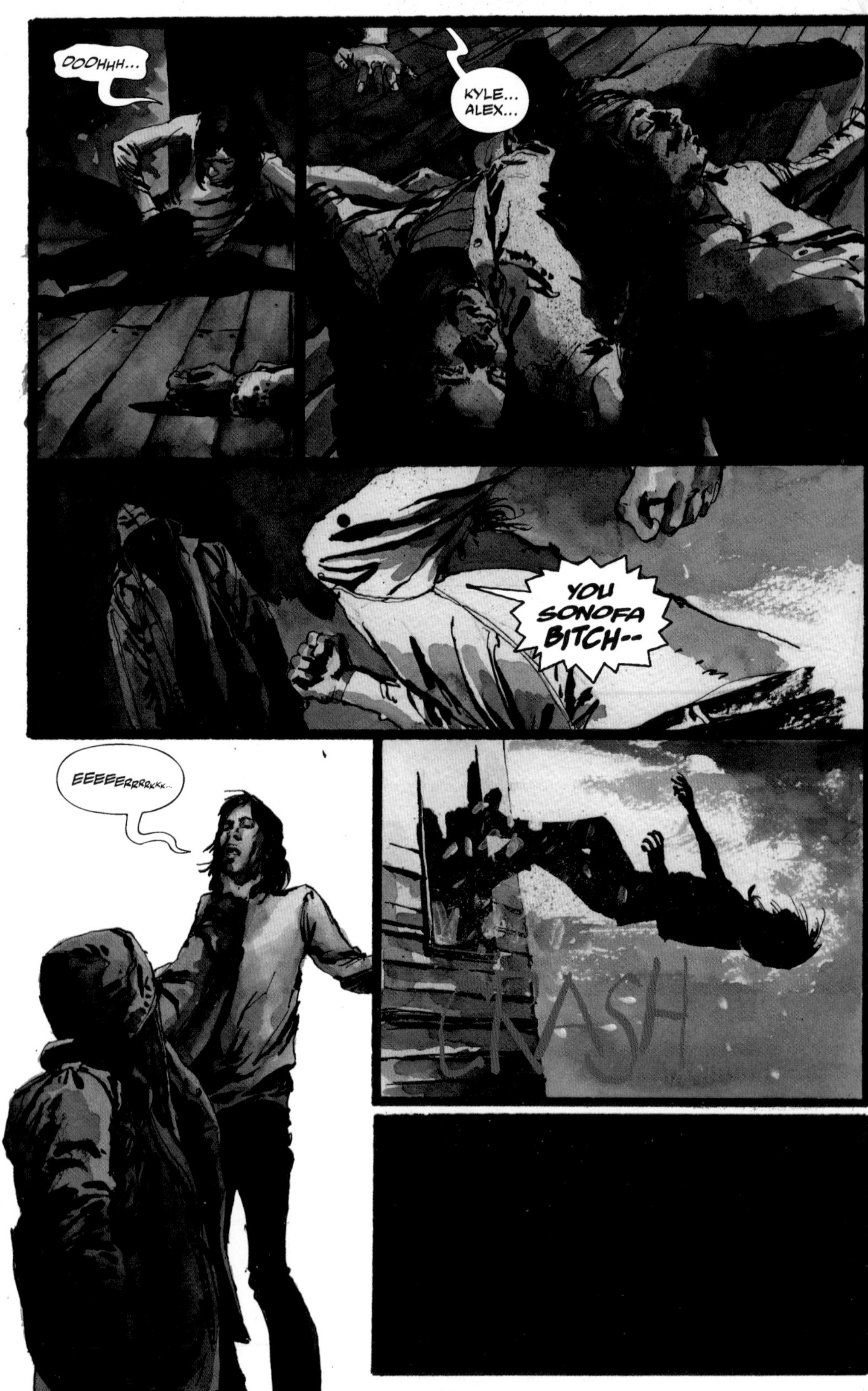
OOOHHH...
KYLE... ALEX...
YOU SONOFA BITCH--
EEEEERRRKKK...
CRASH

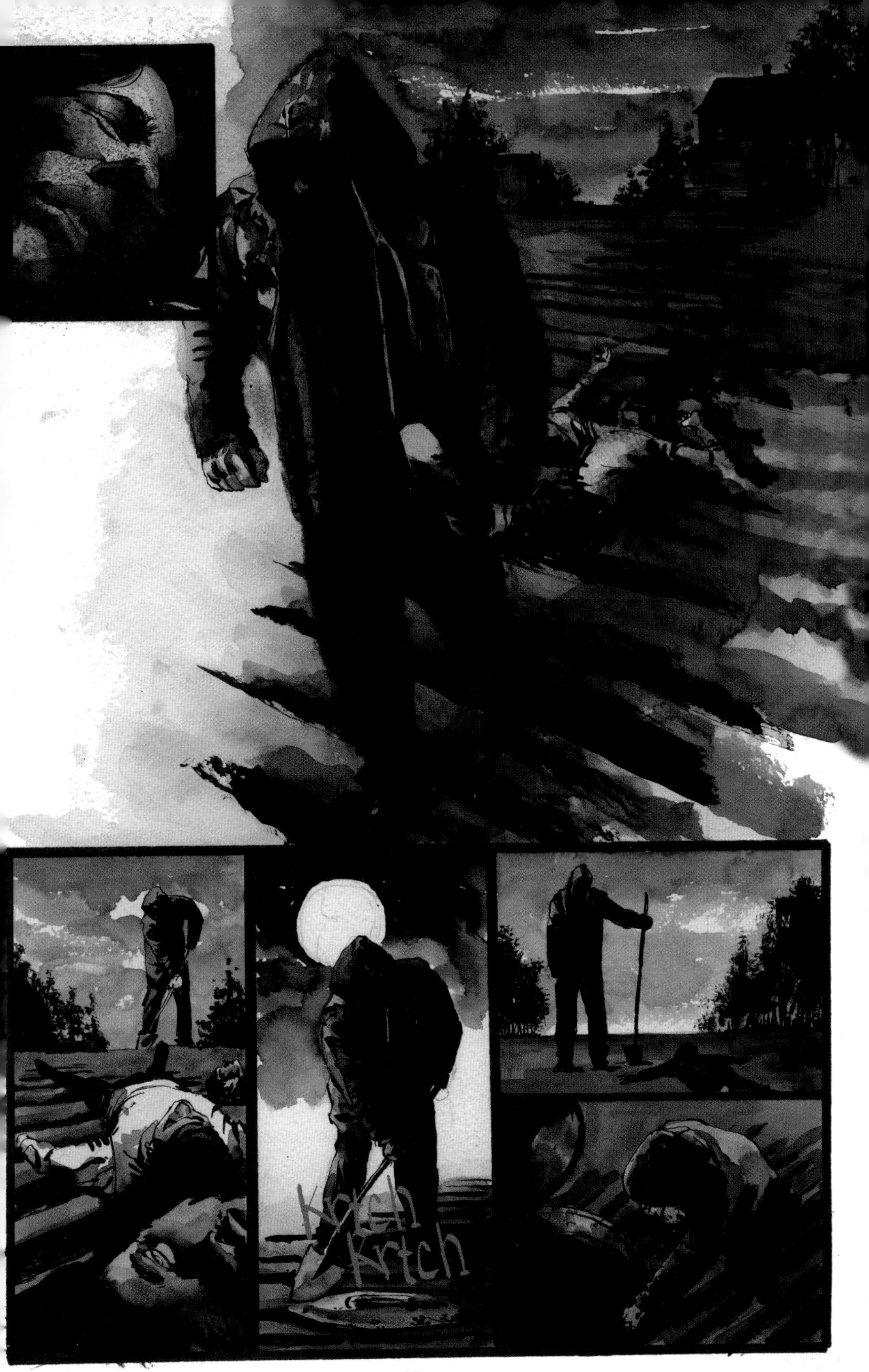
Krtch
Krtch

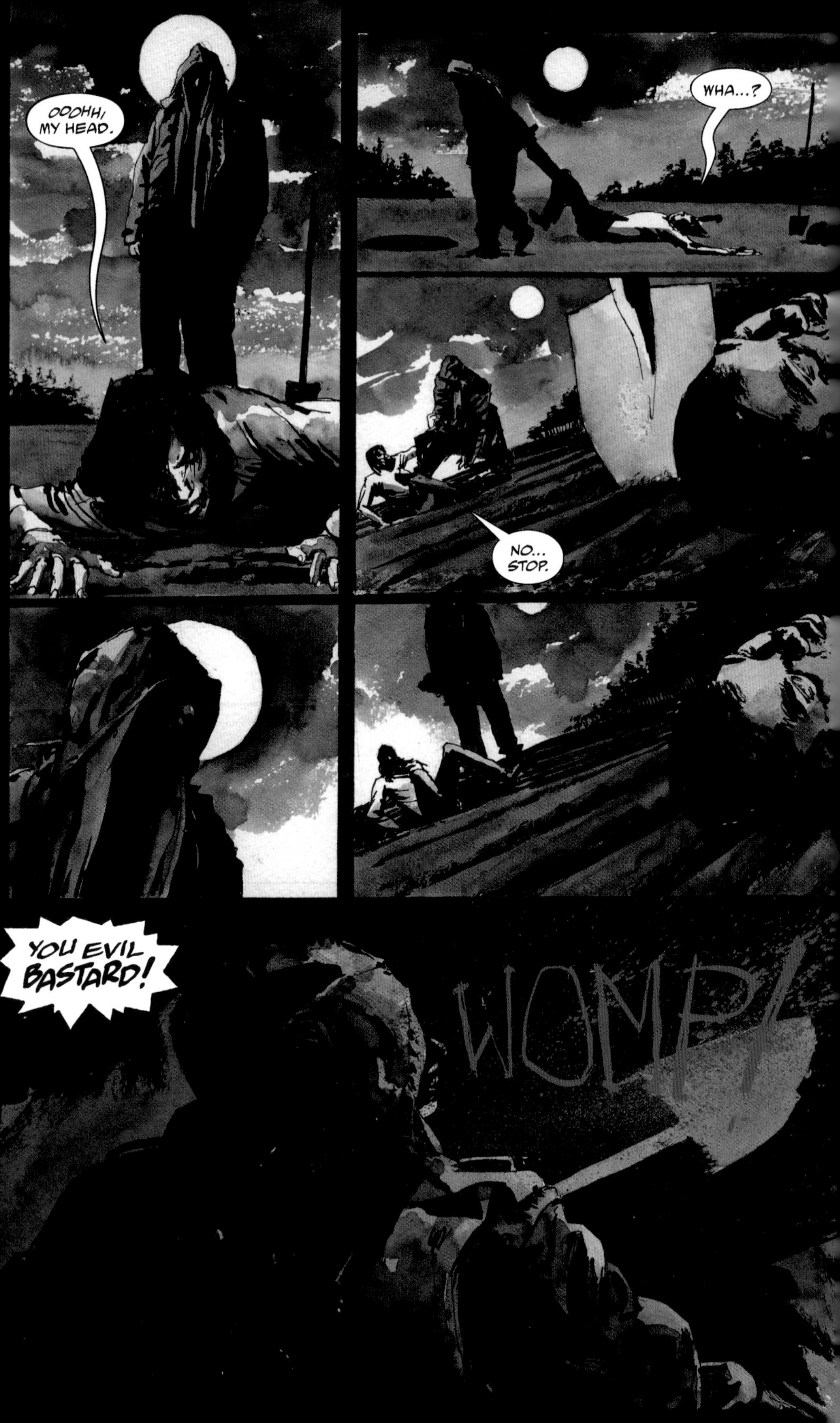
OOOHH, MY HEAD.
WHA...?
NO... STOP.
YOU EVIL BASTARD!
WOMP!

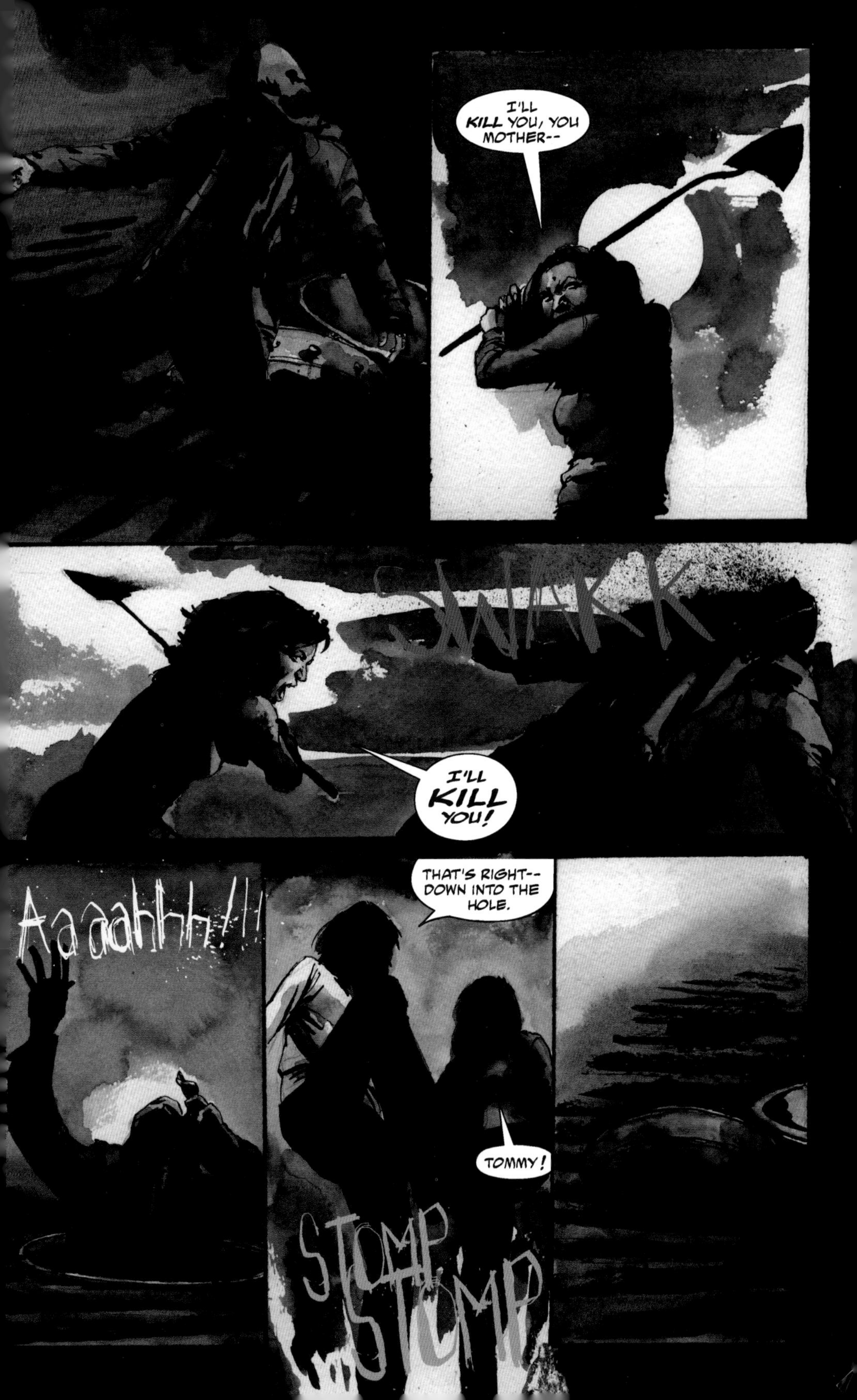
I'LL KILL YOU, YOU MOTHER--
SWAKK
I'LL KILL YOU!
Aaaahhh!!!
THAT'S RIGHT-- DOWN INTO THE HOLE.
TOMMY!
STOMP
STOMP

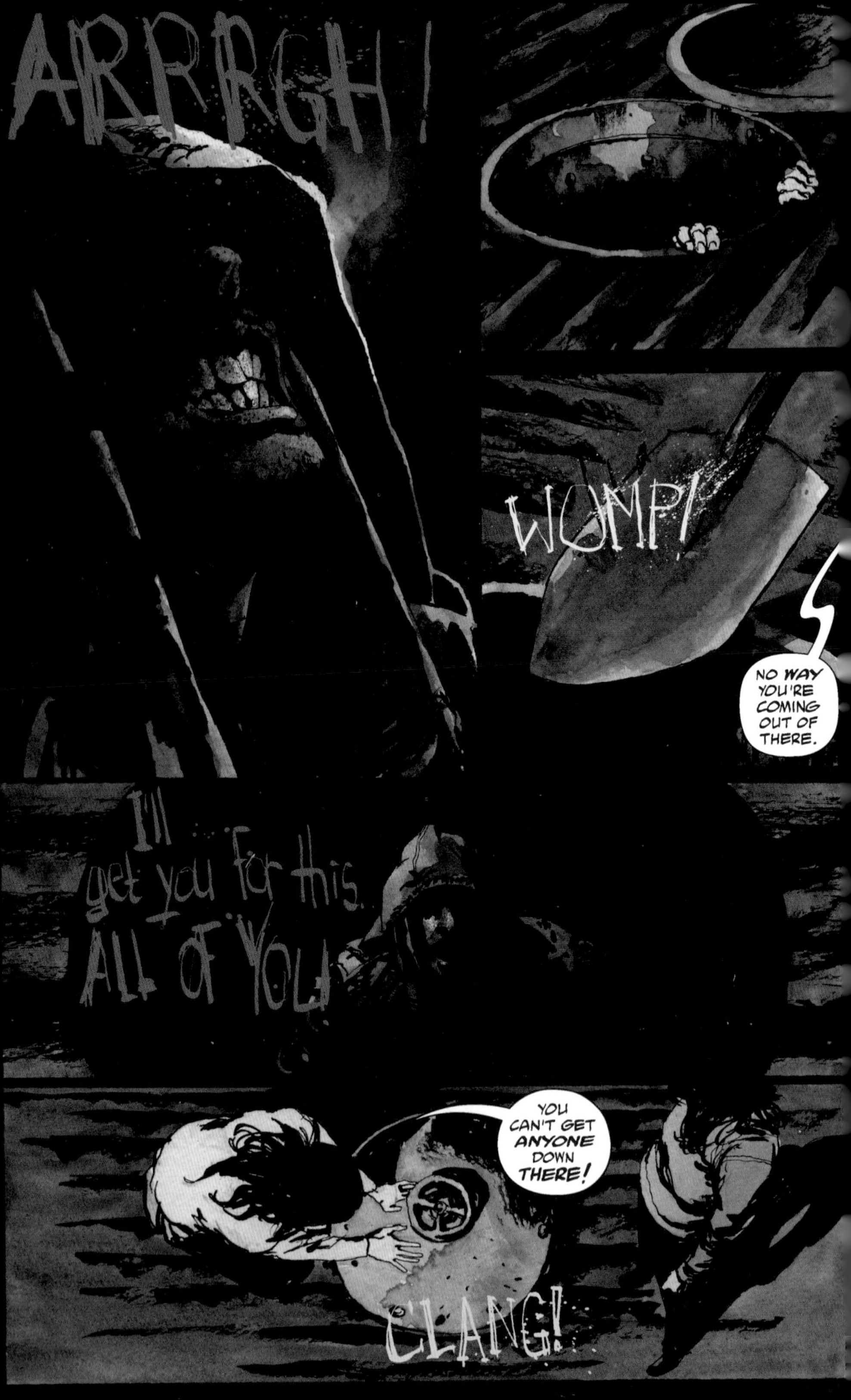
ARRRGH!
WOMP!
NO WAY YOU'RE COMING OUT OF THERE.
I'll ... get you for this. ALL OF YOU
YOU CAN'T GET ANYONE DOWN THERE!
CLANG!

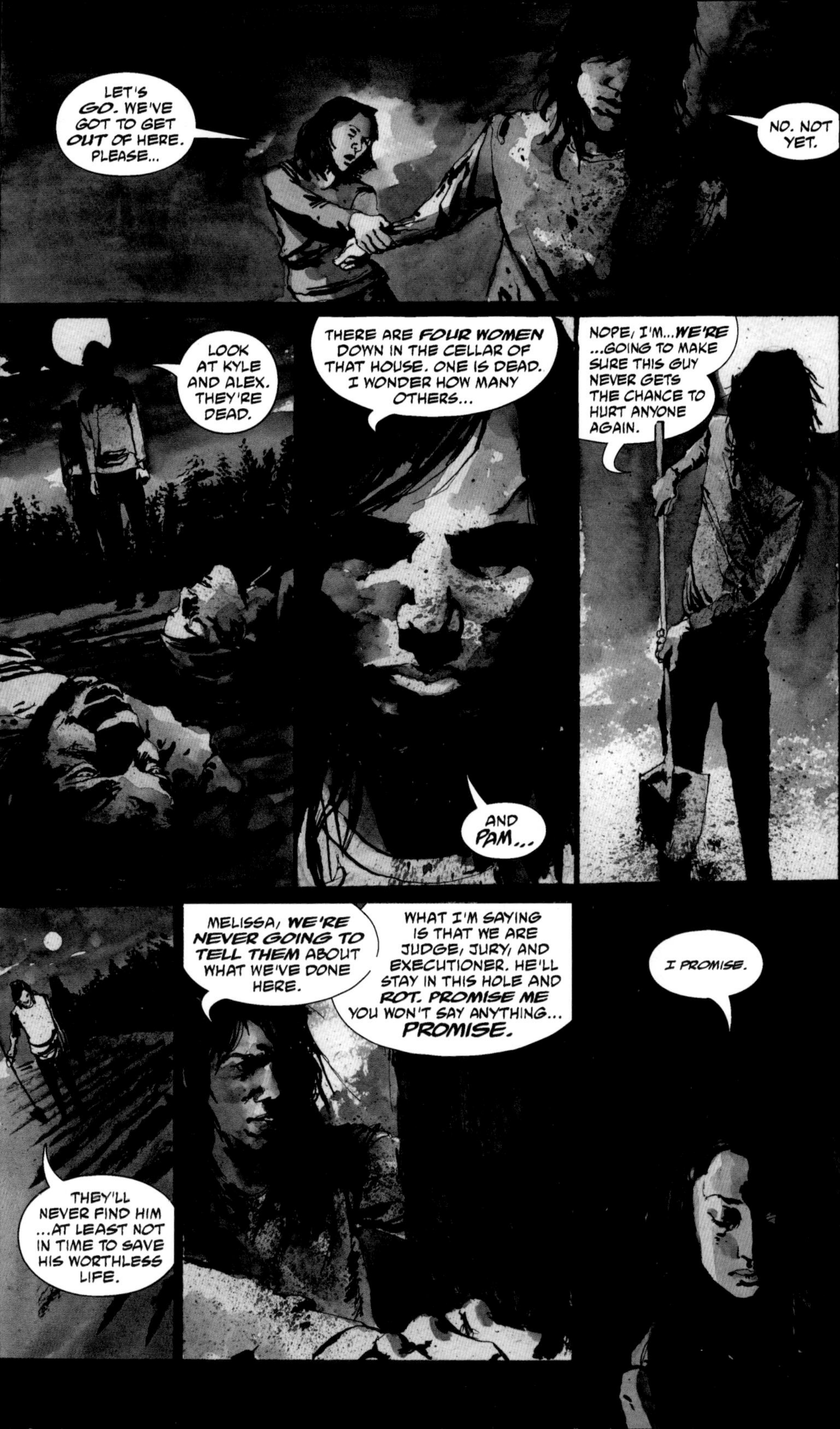
LET'S GO. WE'VE GOT TO GET OUT OF HERE. PLEASE...
NO. NOT YET.
LOOK AT KYLE AND ALEX. THEY'RE DEAD.
THERE ARE FOUR WOMEN DOWN IN THE CELLAR OF THAT HOUSE. ONE IS DEAD. I WONDER HOW MANY OTHERS...
AND PAM...
NOPE, I'M...WE'RE ...GOING TO MAKE SURE THIS GUY NEVER GETS THE CHANCE TO HURT ANYONE AGAIN.
THEY'LL NEVER FIND HIM ...AT LEAST NOT IN TIME TO SAVE HIS WORTHLESS LIFE.
MELISSA, WE'RE NEVER GOING TO TELL THEM ABOUT WHAT WE'VE DONE HERE.
WHAT I'M SAYING IS THAT WE ARE JUDGE, JURY, AND EXECUTIONER. HE'LL STAY IN THIS HOLE AND ROT. PROMISE ME YOU WON'T SAY ANYTHING... PROMISE.
I PROMISE.

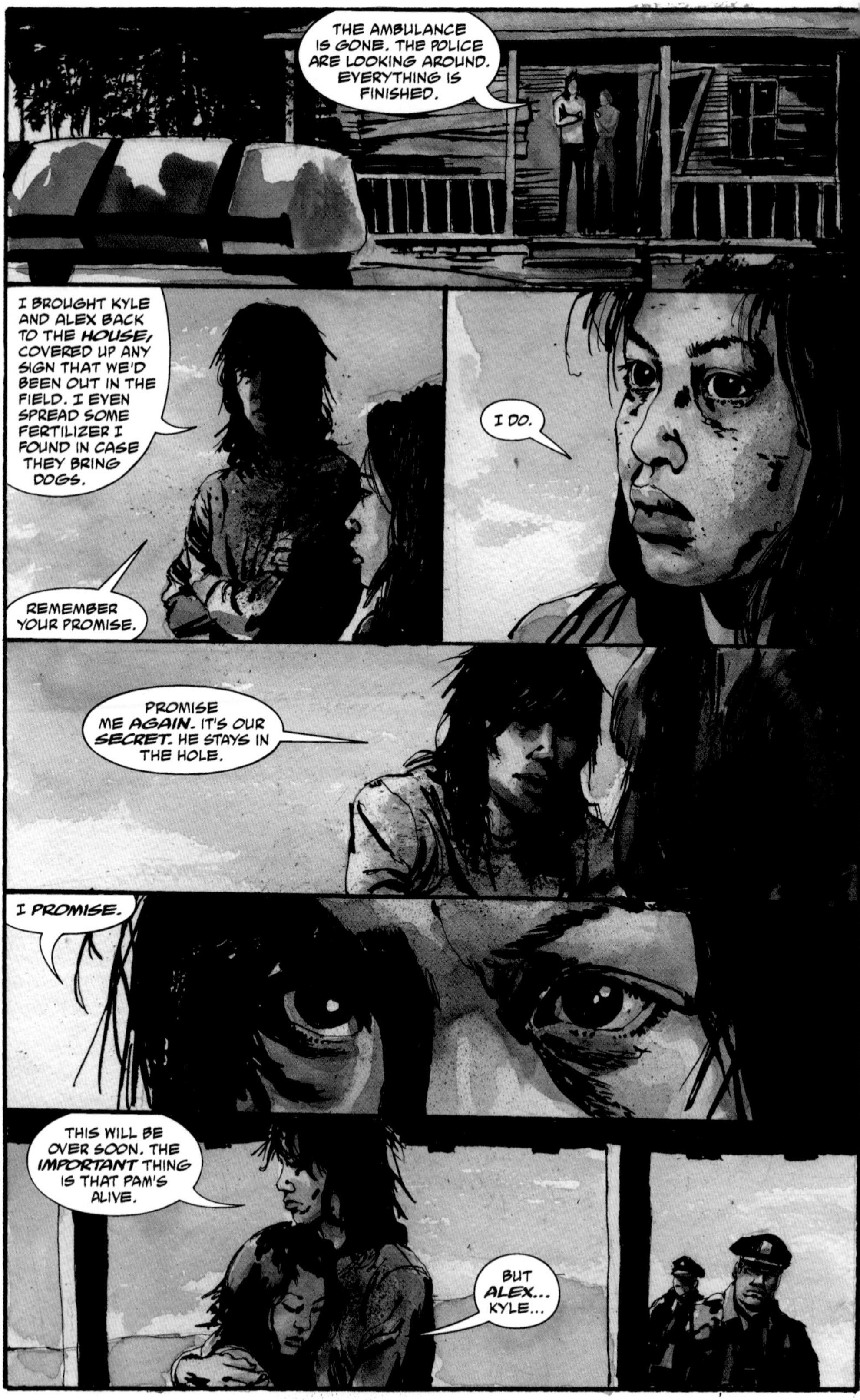
THE AMBULANCE IS GONE. THE POLICE ARE LOOKING AROUND. EVERYTHING IS FINISHED.
I BROUGHT KYLE AND ALEX BACK TO THE HOUSE, COVERED UP ANY SIGN THAT WE'D BEEN OUT IN THE FIELD. I EVEN SPREAD SOME FERTILIZER I FOUND IN CASE THEY BRING DOGS.
REMEMBER YOUR PROMISE.
I DO.
PROMISE ME AGAIN. IT'S OUR SECRET. HE STAYS IN THE HOLE.
I PROMISE.
THIS WILL BE OVER SOON. THE IMPORTANT THING IS THAT PAM'S ALIVE.
BUT ALEX... KYLE...

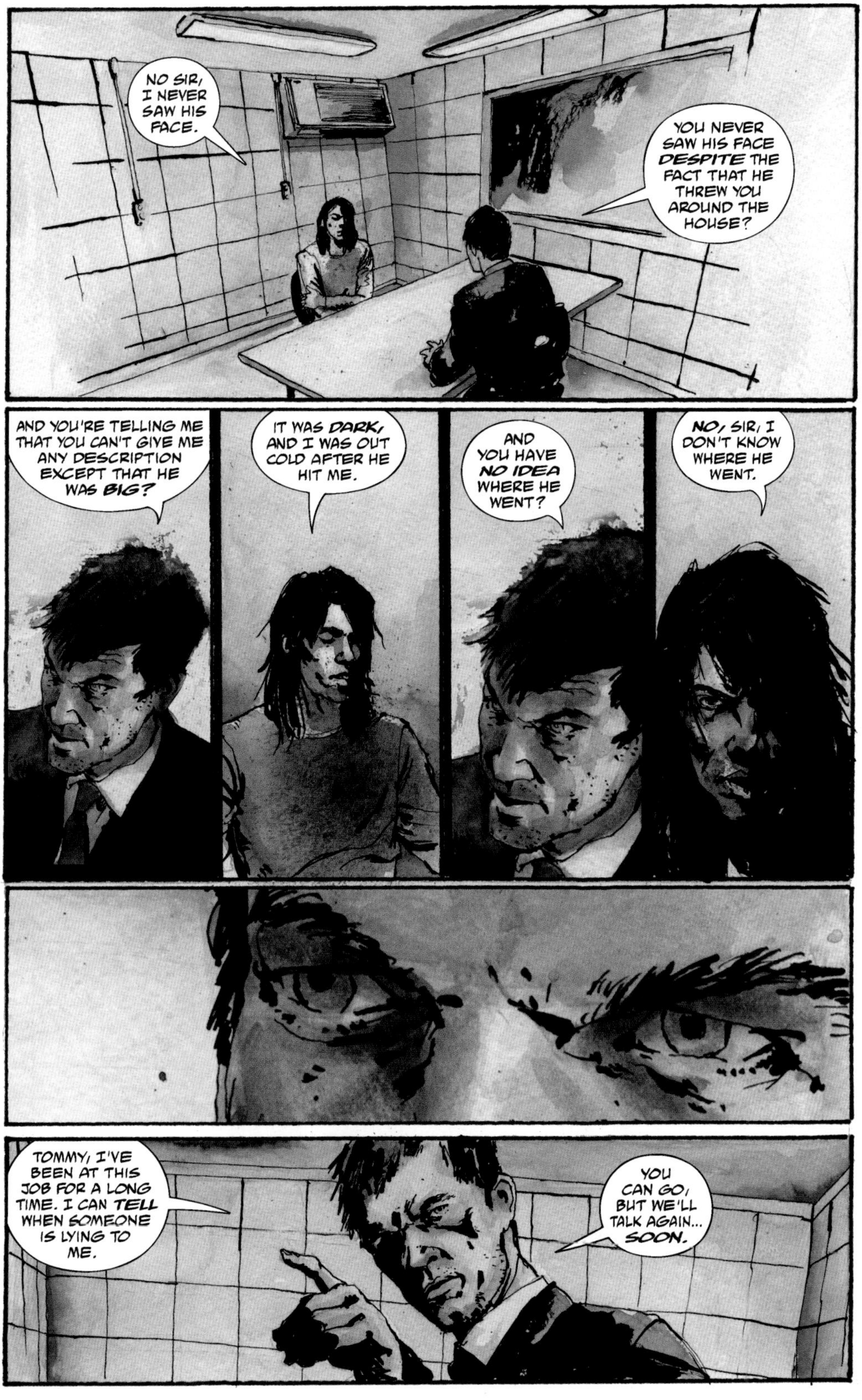
NO SIR, I NEVER SAW HIS FACE.
YOU NEVER SAW HIS FACE DESPITE THE FACT THAT HE THREW YOU AROUND THE HOUSE?
AND YOU'RE TELLING ME THAT YOU CAN'T GIVE ME ANY DESCRIPTION EXCEPT THAT HE WAS BIG?
IT WAS DARK, AND I WAS OUT COLD AFTER HE HIT ME.
AND YOU HAVE NO IDEA WHERE HE WENT?
NO, SIR, I DON'T KNOW WHERE HE WENT.
TOMMY, I'VE BEEN AT THIS JOB FOR A LONG TIME. I CAN TELL WHEN SOMEONE IS LYING TO ME.
YOU CAN GO, BUT WE'LL TALK AGAIN... SOON.

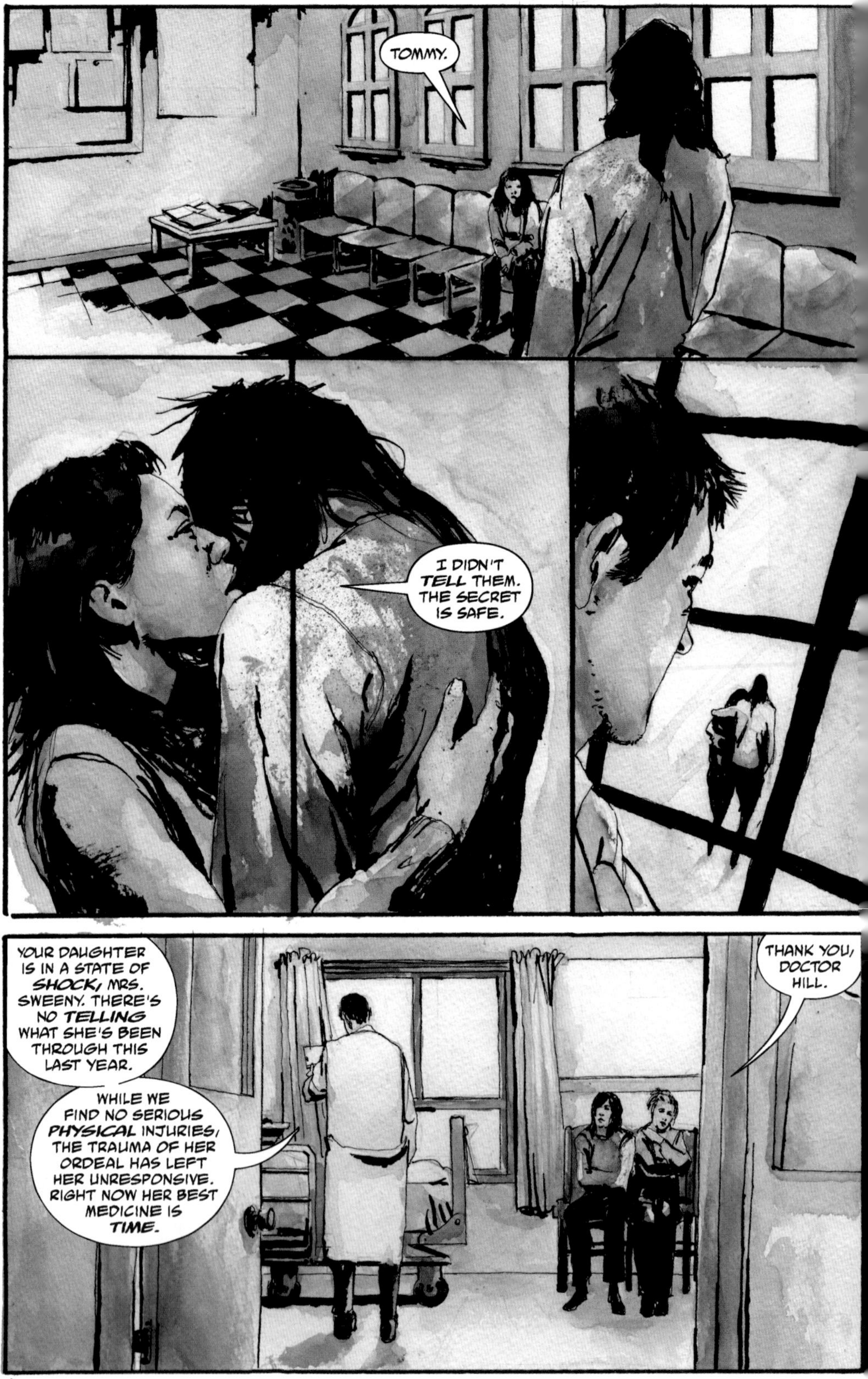
TOMMY.
I DIDN'T TELL THEM. THE SECRET IS SAFE.
YOUR DAUGHTER IS IN A STATE OF SHOCK, MRS. SWEENY. THERE'S NO TELLING WHAT SHE'S BEEN THROUGH THIS LAST YEAR.
WHILE WE FIND NO SERIOUS PHYSICAL INJURIES, THE TRAUMA OF HER ORDEAL HAS LEFT HER UNRESPONSIVE. RIGHT NOW HER BEST MEDICINE IS TIME.
THANK YOU, DOCTOR HILL.

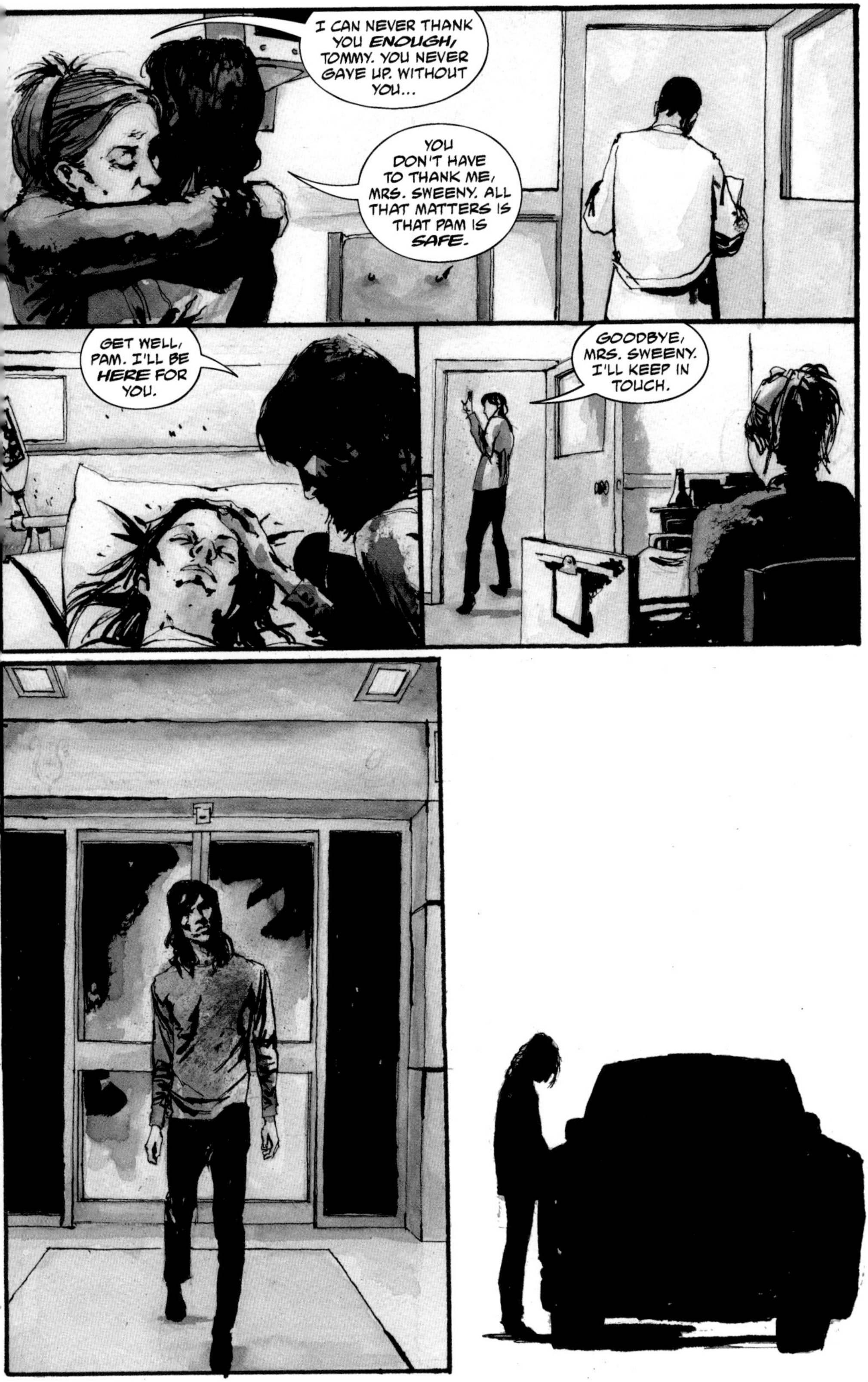
I CAN NEVER THANK YOU ENOUGH, TOMMY. YOU NEVER GAVE UP. WITHOUT YOU...
YOU DON'T HAVE TO THANK ME, MRS. SWEENY. ALL THAT MATTERS IS THAT PAM IS SAFE.
GET WELL, PAM. I'LL BE HERE FOR YOU.
GOODBYE, MRS. SWEENY. I'LL KEEP IN TOUCH.

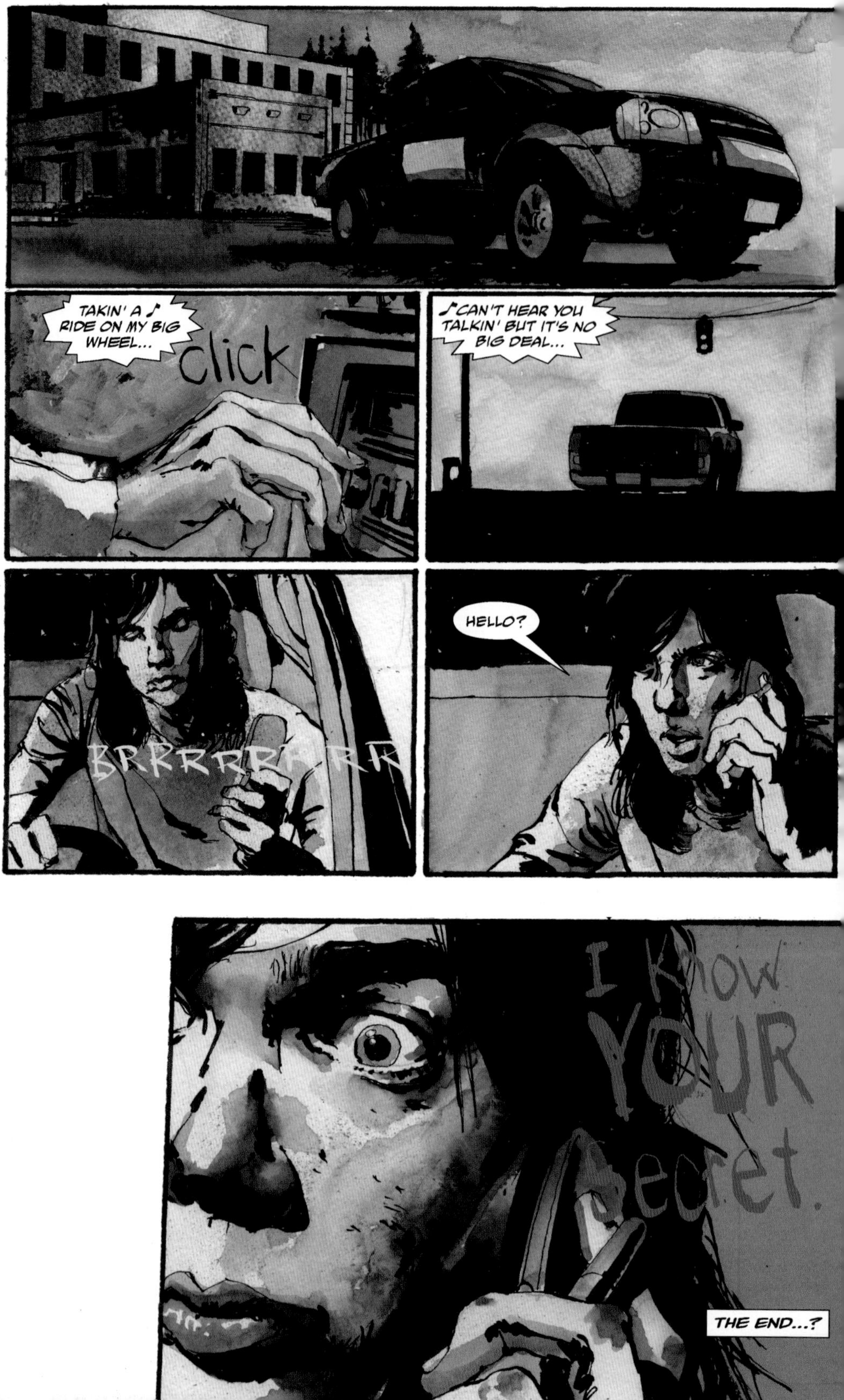
TAKIN' A ♪ RIDE ON MY BIG WHEEL...
click
♪CAN'T HEAR YOU TALKIN' BUT IT'S NO BIG DEAL...
BRRRRRRR
HELLO?
I know YOUR secret.
THE END...?

coVER GALLERy

All paintings by
JASON SHAWN ALEXANDER

Process
48x36 in.
Oil on canvas

Stranger II
36x24 in.
Oil on canvas

His Secret
36x24 in.
Oil on canvas

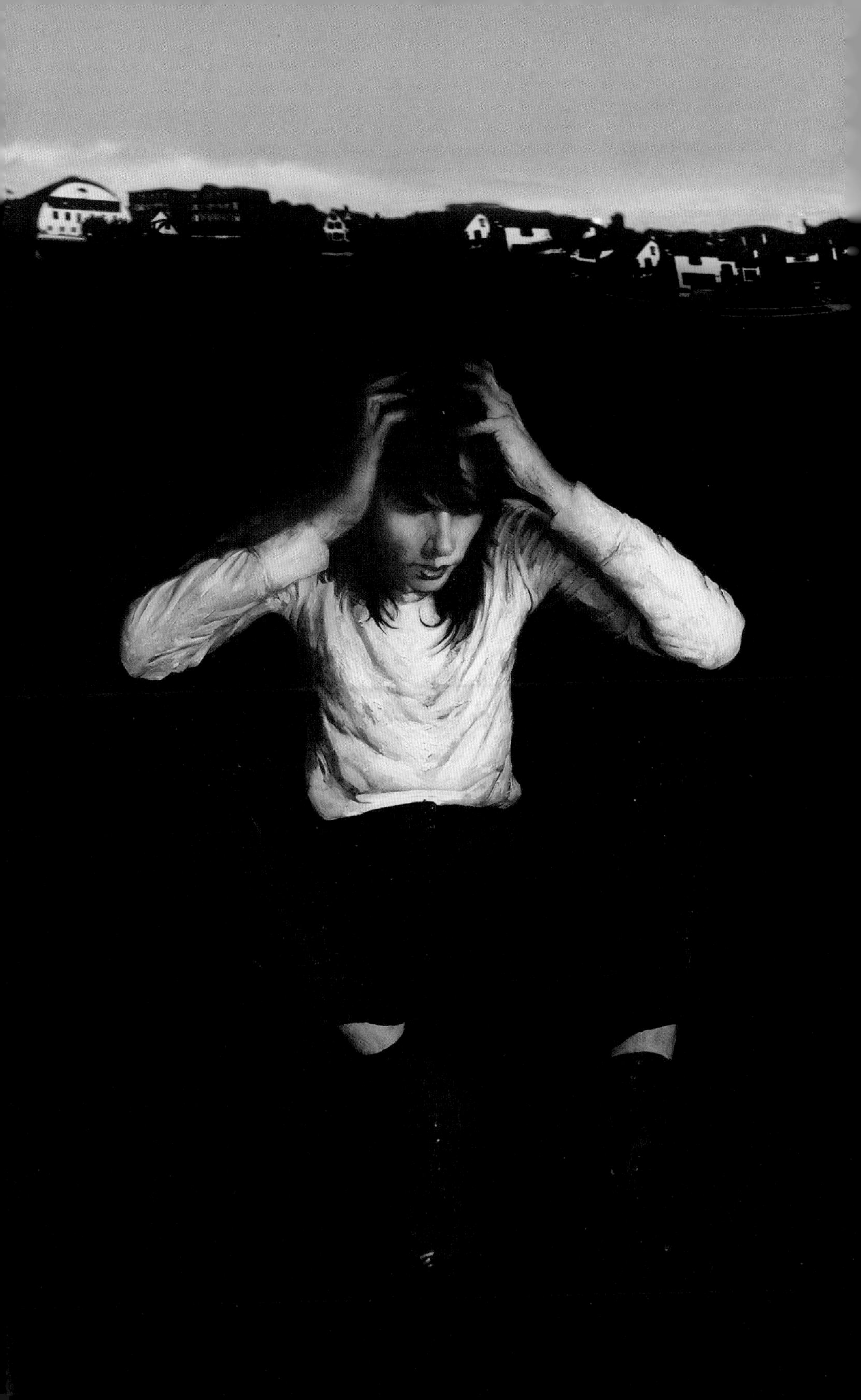

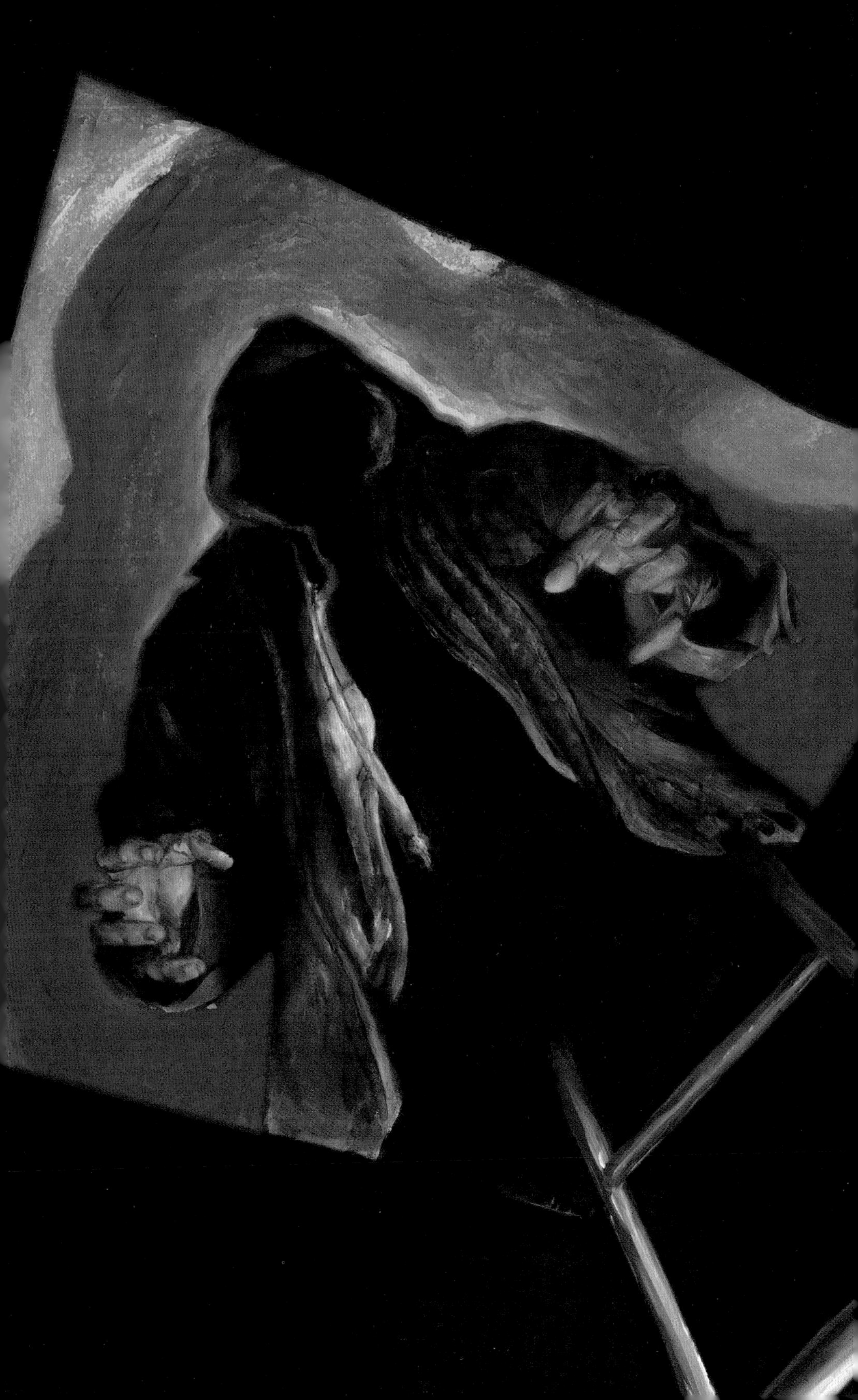

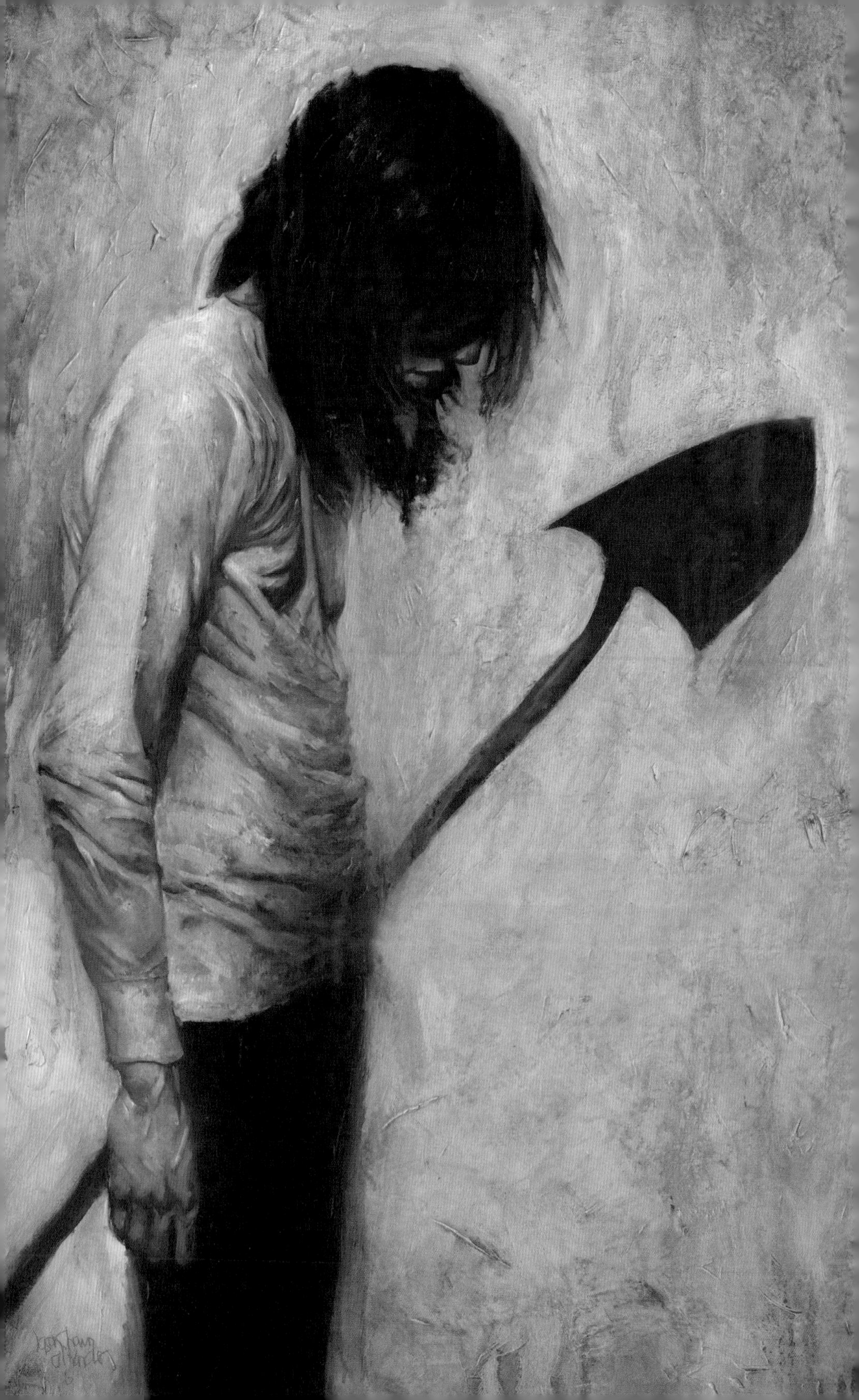

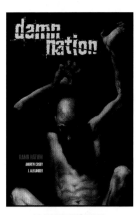

ALSO FROM DARK HORSE BOOKS

BOB FINGERMAN'S
RECESS PIECES

RECESS PIECES
Bob Fingerman

Bad things are brewing in the halls of The Ben Turpin School. When a science project goes wrong, only the prepubescent children are spared the fate of zombification . . . but can they escape being eaten alive? George Romero covered night, dawn, and day, but how about recess?

ISBN-10: 1-59307-450-6 / ISBN-13: 978-1-59307-450-0
$14.95

REX MUNDI
BOOK ONE
The Guardian of the Temple
ARVID NELSON • ERIC J
JEROMY COX

REX MUNDI VOLUME 1: THE GUARDIAN OF THE TEMPLE
Arvid Nelson, Eric J, Juan Ferreyra, and Jeromy Cox

A quest for the Holy Grail unlike any you've ever seen begins here—in a world where the American Civil War ended in a stalemate, the Catholic Church controls Europe, and sorcery determines political power!

ISBN-10: 1-59307-652-5 / ISBN-13: 978-1-59307-652-8
$16.95

Mike Mignola
Jill Thompson
Evan Dorkin
Kelley Jones
Eric Powell
Gary Gianni
and others
The Dark Horse
BOOK OF THE DEAD

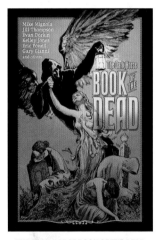

THE DARK HORSE BOOK OF THE DEAD
Guy Davis, Mike Mignola, Kelley Jones, Jill Thompson, Eric Powell, Gary Gianni, and others

Mike Mignola presents a Hellboy yarn combining Shakespeare and grave-robbing, Gary Gianni illustrates a rare story by Conan creator Robert E. Howard, and Jamie S. Rich and Guy Davis present a tale of horror and heartbreak set in feudal Japan. And that's just a taste of the tales inside this hardcover horror anthology featuring the finest talents in comics.

ISBN-10: 1-59307-281-3 / ISBN-13: 978-1-59307-281-0
$14.95

THE GOON
HEAPS OF RUINATION
by Eric Powell

THE GOON VOLUME 3: HEAPS OF RUINATION
Eric Powell

The Goon takes the fight to Lonely Street to save a mysterious gunslinger from the grips of the Zombie Priest, Modern Science triumphs over a marauding inter-dimensional lizard, and Franky and the Goon get a visit from a certain red-skinned paranormal investigator in the third volume of Eric Powell's Eisner Award-winning series.

ISBN-10: 1-59307-292-9 / ISBN-13: 978-1-59307-292-6
$12.95

AVAILABLE AT YOUR LOCAL COMICS SHOP OR BOOKSTORE! • To find a comics shop in your area, call 1-888-266-4226.
For more information or to order direct visit darkhorse.com or call 1-800-862-0052 Mon.-Fri. 9 A.M. to 5 P.M. Pacific Time. Prices and availability subject to change without notice.

DARK HORSE COMICS® *drawing on your nightmares*
darkhorse.com